Taste of Home Books

Taste of Home's CONTEST WINNING ANNUAL RECIPES 2005

Editor: Jean Steiner
Art Director: Lori Arndt
Senior Editor/Books: Heidi Reuter Lloyd
Associate Editor: Beth Wittlinger
Food Editor: Janaan Cunningham
Associate Food Editors: Coleen Martin, Diane Werner
Senior Recipe Editor: Sue A. Jurack
Recipe Editor: Janet Briggs
Editorial Assistant: Barb Czysz
Food Photography: Rob Hagen, Dan Roberts
Food Photography Artists: Julie Ferron, Sue Myers

Senior Vice President, Editor in Chief: Catherine Cassidy
President: Barbara Newton
Chairman and Founder: Roy Reiman

Taste of Home Books

5400 S. 60th St., Greendale WI 53129
International Standard Book Number:
0-89821-444-0
International Standard Serial Number:
1548-4157

Printed in U.S.A.

PICTURED ON FRONT COVER:
Orange Walnut Chicken (p. 84)
PICTURED ON BACK COVER:
Fruit-Pecan Pork Roast (p. 110) and Calgary Stampede Ribs (p. 113)

To order additional copies of this book, write to: *Taste of Home* Books, P.O. Box 908, Greendale WI 53129.
To order with a credit card, call toll-free 1-800/344-2560 or visit our Web site at ***www.reimanpub.com.***

Table of Contents

BLT Bites, p. 17

Parmesan Potato Soup, p. 52

Tangy Barbecue Sauce, p. 129

Scottish Shortbread, p. 163

Raspberry Marshmallow Delight, p. 210

A Year's Worth of Contest Winners in One Recipe-Packed Cookbook

THAT'S RIGHT! All 359 recipes in *Taste of Home's Contest Winning Annual Recipes 2005* are winners of our company's national recipe contests.

We think of this cookbook as the "cream of the crop" because it contains only prize-winning recipes. But the real winner is you, who gets a year's worth of winning entries from four of our publications all under one cover. That's *Taste of Home*—the No. 1 cooking magazine in North America—plus *Quick Cooking*, *Country Woman* and *Country* magazines.

The idea for this blue-ribbon recipe collection began last year, when readers sent letters asking for such a cookbook. We loved the notion, but soon discovered that all of the winners wouldn't fit into one book. So we decided to launch an annual cookbook series, starting with the 2004 edition.

The response to this first annual cookbook was amazing—in fact, thousands of people bought it and many wrote to tell us how much they enjoy the cookbook! We hope this beautiful 2005 edition will be just as successful.

So how exactly does a recipe become a prize-winner? It starts when home cooks from across the country read our call for contest entries and send in their family favorites. Our professional home economists then sort through the stacks of mail we receive and test the most-promising entries. Then they prepare the top contenders for our taste-test panel, which consists of experienced food editors, fellow home economists and magazine editors. After much sampling (a tough job, but somebody has to do it!), a grand-prize winner is announced as well as the runners-up.

Herb-Roasted Turkey, p. 93

Winners from Dozens of Contests

The contests featured in this cookbook serve up an appealing assortment of recipes—snacks and beverages, salads, soups and sandwiches, main dishes, side dishes and condiments, breads and rolls, brownies, bars and cookies, cakes and pies, just desserts and more! These are the chapters you'll find listed in the Table of Contents on page 3.

Here are the year's worth of contests and top prize-winner of each category:

- **Tempting Turkey.** Flavorful Herb-Roasted Turkey (p. 93) is the fairest of the fowl.
- **Savory Stir-Fry and Skillet Suppers.** Make Stovetop Pot Roast (p. 97) at home on your range.
- **Hearty Country Ham.** Sliced Ham with Roasted Vegetables (p. 74) satisfies country-style appetites.
- **Best-Ever Brownies.** Earn brownie points by whipping up a big batch of chocolaty Frosted Fudge Brownies (p. 178).
- **It's the Pits.** But Pretty Plum Parfaits (p. 213), the grand-prize winner of this pitted fruit contest, are anything but!

Summer Spinach Salad, p. 36

- **Scrumptious Squash.** Enjoy "vine" dining when you serve Baked Chicken and Acorn Squash (p. 118).
- **Slow-Simmered Recipes.** Folks will dig into Sweet 'n' Sour Ribs (p. 76) lickety-split.
- **Speedy Sandwiches.** Quickly have lunch or supper in hand with The Ultimate Grilled Cheese (p. 67).
- **Light 'n' Luscious.** Chicken with Spicy Fruit (p. 72) is doubly delicious—both light and tasty.
- **Splendid Salads.** Toss together pretty Summer Spinach Salad (p. 36) in no time for a pleasing meal-starter.
- **Bread Machine Recipes.** Multigrain Bread (p. 156) has from-scratch flavor and wholesome goodness without all the work.

- **Easy Chocolate Desserts.** Everyone will think you fussed over Chocolate and Fruit Trifle (p. 209).
- **Sunny Citrus.** Take a shine to the zesty taste of Orange Walnut Chicken (p. 84).
- **Sweetheart Treats.** Those dear to you will love heart-shaped Valentine Berries and Cream (p. 210).
- **Luscious Lasagna.** Traditional Lasagna (p. 111) is a tasty blend of melted cheese, seasoned meat, savory sauce and tender noodles.
- **Pork Parade.** Showcase Fruit-Pecan Pork Roast (p. 110) on your dinner table and you'll be showered with compliments.
- **Pear Pleasure.** Crowd-pleasing Pear Custard Bars (p. 182) have an appealing nature.
- **Thanksgiving Sides.** Family and friends will give thanks when you pass around Curried Pumpkin Soup (p. 60).

If that's not enough, every single recipe in this beautiful book is pictured in full color—so you can be sure these foods not only taste terrific but are eye-appealing as well.

It's no contest that you'll come out a winner with *Taste of Home's Contest Winning Annual Recipes 2005*! You be the judge of which fabulous recipe to try first!

Chocolate and Fruit Trifle, p. 209

Turkey Taco Dip, p. 12

Strawberry Lemonade, p. 11

Spinach Turnovers, p. 14

Snacks & Beverages

Half the fun of a party or casual gathering is the festive finger foods and refreshing beverages. The tasty tidbits featured here are an appetizing start to—or even a substitute for—a meal.

BLT Bites, p. 17

Sesame Chicken Strips, p. 8

Sesame Chicken Strips

(Pictured on page 7)

Teri Rasey, Cadillac, Michigan

These tasty chicken strips dipped in the lightly sweet sauce are a wonderful finger food. They go over really well at outdoor summer gatherings. This recipe puts a new twist on fried chicken—a staple at most picnics.

1 cup mayonnaise
2 teaspoons dried minced onion
2 teaspoons ground mustard
1 cup crushed butter-flavored crackers
1/2 cup sesame seeds
2 pounds boneless skinless chicken breasts

SAUCE:

1 cup mayonnaise
2 tablespoons honey

1. In a bowl, combine mayonnaise, onion and mustard. In another bowl, combine the crackers and sesame seeds. Cut chicken lengthwise into 1/4-in. strips. Dip strips into mayonnaise mixture, then into the sesame seed mixture.

2. Place in a single layer on a large greased baking sheet. Bake at 425° for 15-18 minutes or until juices run clear.

3. Combine sauce ingredients and serve with chicken strips. **Yield:** 10-12 servings.

Marinated Shrimp

Margaret DeLong, Gainesville, Florida

Seafood is a staple here in Florida. This recipe is quick and easy to make and can be prepared well in advance. I always seem to get a lot of requests for the recipe when I make it for a party or special occasion.

2 pounds cooked medium shrimp, peeled and deveined
1 medium red onion, cut into rings
2 medium lemons, cut into slices
1 cup pitted ripe olives
1/2 cup olive oil
1/3 cup minced fresh parsley
3 tablespoons red wine vinegar
3 tablespoons lemon juice
1 garlic clove, minced
1 bay leaf
1 tablespoon minced fresh basil *or* 1 teaspoon dried basil
1 teaspoon salt
1 teaspoon ground mustard
1/4 teaspoon pepper

1. In a 3-qt. glass serving bowl, combine the shrimp, onion, lemons and olives. In a jar with a tight-fitting lid, combine the remaining ingredients; shake well. Pour over shrimp mixture and stir gently to coat.

2. Cover and refrigerate for 24 hours, stirring occasionally. Discard bay leaf before serving. **Yield:** 14 servings.

Orange Sherbet Party Punch

Lannis Blunk, Mascoutah, Illinois

This punch is always a big hit with everyone. You can make the base for it several days ahead and chill. Before serving, add the sherbet and ginger ale.

4 cups water, *divided*
1 package (6 ounces) strawberry gelatin
1-1/2 cups sugar
1 can (46 ounces) pineapple juice
1 can (46 ounces) orange juice
1 cup lemon juice
1/2 gallon orange sherbet, softened
1 liter ginger ale, chilled

1. Heat 2 cups water to boiling; add gelatin and sugar, stirring until dissolved. Add 2 cups cold water and fruit juices. Chill until serving.

2. Just before serving, spoon in sherbet and add ginger ale. **Yield:** about 36 servings (6-1/2 quarts).

Almond Deviled Eggs

Martha Baechle, Nipomo, California

This recipe's one I've used many times for potlucks during the holidays as well as several times a month when entertaining. The eggs are scrumptious!

6 hard-cooked eggs
1/4 cup mayonnaise
1 teaspoon Dijon mustard
1/4 teaspoon garlic salt
3 tablespoons finely chopped roasted almonds
12 whole roasted almonds
Fresh parsley

1. Slice eggs in half lengthwise; remove yolks and set whites aside. In a small bowl, mash yolks, mayonnaise, mustard, garlic salt and chopped almonds.

2. Evenly fill the egg whites. Garnish with whole almonds and parsley. Chill until serving. **Yield:** 1 dozen.

Hot Macadamia Spread

Naomi Francis, Waukesha, Wisconsin

While my husband was in the Army, I'd get together with other wives for snacks and to exchange favorite recipes. I still enjoy serving this rich spread because most guests can't quite put their finger on the zippy ingredient—horseradish.

1 package (8 ounces) cream cheese, softened
2 tablespoons milk
1/2 cup sour cream
2 teaspoons prepared horseradish
1/4 cup finely chopped green pepper
1 green onion, chopped
1/2 teaspoon garlic salt
1/4 teaspoon pepper
1/2 cup chopped macadamia nuts *or* blanched almonds
2 teaspoons butter
Assorted crackers

1. In a mixing bowl, beat cream cheese and milk until smooth. Stir in sour cream, horseradish, green pepper, onion, garlic salt and pepper. Spoon into an ungreased shallow 2-cup baking dish; set aside.

2. In a skillet, saute the nuts in butter for 3-4 minutes or until lightly browned. Sprinkle over the cream cheese mixture.

3. Bake, uncovered, at 350° for 20 minutes. Serve with crackers. **Yield:** 6-8 servings.

Strawberry Lemonade

(Pictured on page 6)

Cindy DePue, Saylorsburg, Pennsylvania

Every summer for a number of years, I've entered this lemonade at a local fair, and it's taken first in canned juices each time. An abundant strawberry crop was its inspiration. Now, we make sure to can enough to enjoy year-round.

4 quarts fresh strawberries, hulled
4 cups lemon juice (about 16 lemons)
3 quarts water
6 cups sugar
Lemon-lime soda *or* ginger ale

1. In a blender or food processor, puree the strawberries. Place in a large kettle; add lemon juice, water and sugar. Bring to 165° over medium heat, stirring occasionally (do not boil). Remove from the heat; skim off foam.

2. Pour hot into hot jars, leaving 1/4-in. headspace. Adjust caps. Process for 15 minutes in a boiling-water bath.

3. To serve, mix about one-third concentrate with two-thirds soda or ginger ale. **Yield:** about 6 quarts concentrate.

Savory Bread Strips

Mary Nichols, Dover, New Hampshire

For a friend's surprise party, I decided to try a new recipe and came up with this crispy bread topped with ham, olives and more. The savory ingredients in this irresistible appetizer blend so well that I'm always asked for the recipe.

1 package (1/4 ounce) active dry yeast
6-1/2 teaspoons sugar, *divided*
1/2 cup warm water (110° to 115°)
3 tablespoons olive oil
2 tablespoons dried minced onion
2 teaspoons dried basil
1 teaspoon dried oregano
1 teaspoon rubbed sage
1 teaspoon garlic powder
1/2 cup cold water
3 cups all-purpose flour

TOPPING:

1-1/2 cups chopped fully cooked ham
1 cup shredded Parmesan cheese
1/2 cup chopped ripe olives
1/2 cup chopped onion
1/2 cup minced fresh parsley
1/4 cup olive oil
2 garlic cloves, minced

1. Dissolve yeast and 1/2 teaspoon sugar in warm water; set aside. In a saucepan, combine oil, onion, basil, oregano, sage and garlic powder; cook over medium heat for 1 minute. Remove from the heat; stir in cold water. In a mixing bowl, combine flour and remaining sugar. Stir in oil and yeast mixtures.

2. Turn onto a lightly floured surface; knead for 3 minutes. Place dough on a greased 15-in. x 10-in. x 1-in. baking pan. Cover and let stand for 15 minutes. Pat dough evenly into pan. Combine topping ingredients; sprinkle over dough.

3. Bake at 375° for 25-30 minutes or until well browned. Cut into 2-in. x 1-in. strips. **Yield:** about 6 dozen.

Turkey Taco Dip

(Pictured on page 6)

Liz Adcock, Rayville, Louisiana

I created this zippy snack when I had a craving for tacos, but didn't want all the fat and calories that go along with them. It's quick to fix and uses ingredients I usually have on hand. I served this appetizer at a bridal shower, and the bride liked it so much she asked me to make it for her wedding reception!

✓ Uses less fat, sugar or salt. Includes Nutritional Analysis and Diabetic Exchanges.

1 pound ground turkey
1 envelope reduced-sodium taco seasoning
1 cup water
1 package (8 ounces) fat-free cream cheese, softened
1 cup (8 ounces) fat-free sour cream
3/4 cup picante sauce
1/2 cup shredded lettuce
1 cup chopped fresh tomato
1 cup (4 ounces) shredded fat-free cheddar cheese
Baked tortilla chips

1. In a skillet, cook turkey over medium heat until no longer pink; drain. Add taco seasoning and water; cover and simmer for 10 minutes. Spoon turkey onto a 12-in. serving plate or pizza pan.

2. In a mixing bowl, beat the cream cheese until smooth. Add sour cream; spread over the meat mixture. Spread with picante sauce. Top with lettuce, tomato and cheese. Serve with tortilla chips. **Yield:** 10 servings.

Nutritional Analysis: One serving (calculated without chips) equals 135 calories, 569 mg sodium, 18 mg cholesterol, 11 g carbohydrate, 19 g protein, 1 g fat, trace fiber. **Diabetic Exchanges:** 2 very lean meat, 1 vegetable, 1/2 starch.

Sausage-Stuffed Mushrooms

Beatrice Vetrano, Landenberg, Pennsylvania

Pennsylvania is often referred to as the "Mushroom Capital of the World". This recipe's a delicious appetizer and is always the hit of the party.

12 to 15 large fresh mushrooms
2 tablespoons butter, *divided*
2 tablespoons chopped onion
1 tablespoon lemon juice
1/4 teaspoon dried basil
Salt and pepper to taste
4 ounces bulk Italian sausage
1 tablespoon chopped fresh parsley
2 tablespoons dried bread crumbs
2 tablespoons grated Parmesan cheese

1. Remove stems from the mushrooms. Chop stems finely; reserve caps. Place stems in paper towel and squeeze to remove any liquid.

2. In a skillet, heat 1-1/2 tablespoons butter. Cook stems and onion until soft. Add lemon juice, basil, salt and pepper; cook until almost all the liquid has evaporated. Cool.

3. Combine mushroom mixture with sausage and parsley. Stuff into the mushroom caps. Combine crumbs and cheese; sprinkle over stuffed mushrooms. Dot each with remaining butter.

4. Place in a greased baking pan and bake at 400° for 20 minutes. Baste occasionally with pan juices. Serve hot. **Yield:** 12-15 servings.

Salmon Appetizers

Evelyn Gebhardt, Kasilof, Alaska

As a cook for a commercial salmon fishing crew, I found this recipe to be a wonderful variation in the use of salmon. I often rely on these pretty pinwheels when entertaining. They're easy to prepare, and they prove to be popular at parties and other get-togethers.

1 can (14-3/4 ounces) salmon, drained, bones and skin removed
1 package (8 ounces) cream cheese, softened
4 tablespoons salsa
2 tablespoons chopped fresh parsley
1 teaspoon dried cilantro
1/4 teaspoon ground cumin, optional
8 flour tortillas (8 inches)

1. In a small bowl, combine the salmon, cream cheese, salsa, parsley, cilantro and cumin if desired. Spread about 2 tablespoons of the salmon mixture over each tortilla.

2. Roll each tortilla up tightly and wrap individually with plastic wrap. Refrigerate 2-3 hours. Slice each tortilla into bite-size pieces. **Yield:** about 48 appetizers.

1 package (14 ounces) dried apricots
1/2 cup whole almonds
1 pound sliced bacon
1/4 cup plum *or* apple jelly
2 tablespoons soy sauce

1. Fold each apricot around an almond. Cut bacon strips into thirds; wrap a strip around each apricot and secure with a toothpick. Place on two ungreased 15-in. x 10-in. x 1-in. baking pans. Bake, uncovered, at 375° for 25 minutes or until bacon is crisp, turning once.

2. In a small saucepan, combine jelly and soy sauce; cook and stir over low heat for 5 minutes or until warmed and smooth.

3. Remove apricots to paper towels; drain. Serve with sauce for dipping. **Yield:** about 4-1/2 dozen.

Apricot Wraps

Jane Ashworth, Beavercreek, Ohio

I accumulated a large recipe collection from around the world while my husband served in the Air Force for 25 years. This mouth-watering appetizer is one of our favorites, and we enjoy sharing it with friends.

Spinach Turnovers

(Pictured on page 6)

Jean von Bereghy, Oconomowoc, Wisconsin

The flaky cream cheese pastry adds sensational texture to these hot appetizers—and just wait until you taste the wonderful filling. I usually fix a double batch and freeze some to have on hand in case unexpected guests drop by.

2 packages (8 ounces *each*) cream cheese, softened
3/4 cup butter, softened
2-1/2 cups all-purpose flour
1/2 teaspoon salt

FILLING:

5 bacon strips, diced
1/4 cup finely chopped onion
2 garlic cloves, minced
1 package (10 ounces) frozen chopped spinach, thawed and well drained
1 cup small-curd cottage cheese
1/4 teaspoon salt
1/4 teaspoon pepper
1/8 teaspoon ground nutmeg
1 egg, beaten

Salsa, optional

1. In a mixing bowl, beat cream cheese and butter until smooth. Combine flour and salt; gradually add to creamed mixture (dough will be stiff). Turn onto a floured surface; gently knead 10 times. Cover and refrigerate at least 2 hours.

2. In a skillet, cook bacon until crisp. Remove bacon; reserve 1 tablespoon drippings. Saute onion and garlic in drippings until tender. Remove from heat; stir in bacon, spinach, cottage cheese and seasonings. Cool.

3. On a lightly floured surface, roll dough to 1/8-in. thickness. Cut into 3-in. circles; brush edges with egg. Place 1 heaping teaspoon of filling on each circle. Fold over; seal edges. Prick tops with a fork. Brush with egg.

4. Bake at 400° for 10-12 minutes or until golden brown. Serve with salsa if desired. **Yield:** about 4 dozen.

Editor's Note: Baked turnovers may be frozen. Reheat unthawed turnovers at 400° for 10 minutes.

California Fresh Fruit Dip

Nancy Cutright, San Jose, California

I tried this dip at a potluck lunch and loved it. I think it represents my region because of the abundance of fresh fruit grown in California. My family especially enjoys it as a refreshing snack on hot summer afternoons.

 Uses less fat, sugar or salt. Includes Nutritional Analysis and Diabetic Exchanges.

1 cup plain reduced-fat yogurt
2 tablespoons honey
2 tablespoons lime juice
1 teaspoon grated lime peel
1/4 teaspoon ground ginger
Assorted fresh fruit

In a small bowl, combine the first five ingredients. Serve with fresh fruit. Cover and refrigerate leftovers. **Yield:** about 1 cup.

Nutritional Analysis: 2 tablespoons dip equals 33 calories, 22 mg sodium, 1 mg cholesterol, 7 g carbohydrate, 2 g protein, trace fat. **Diabetic Exchanges:** 1/4 fruit, 1/4 skim milk.

Hawaiian Egg Rolls

Terri Wheeler, Vadnais Heights, Minnesota

An avid cook, I am constantly trying to come up with recipes for leftovers. This one gives a whole new twist to extra ham. My two children think these egg rolls are great, and they freeze well. I thaw as many as needed and bake them.

10 fresh spinach leaves, julienned
1/2 teaspoon ground ginger
2 tablespoons olive oil
1/2 pound fully cooked ham, coarsely ground (2 cups)
4 water chestnuts, chopped
1/4 cup undrained crushed pineapple
2 tablespoons chopped green onions
1 tablespoon soy sauce
7 egg roll wrappers
Oil for frying
Sweet-sour sauce

1. In a saucepan, saute spinach and ginger in oil for 1-2 minutes. In a bowl, combine the ham, water chestnuts, pineapple, onions and soy sauce. Stir in the spinach mixture.

2. Place 3 tablespoons of ham mixture in the center of each egg roll wrapper. Fold bottom corner over filling; fold sides over filling toward center. Moisten remaining corner with water; roll up tightly to seal.

3. In an electric skillet, heat 1 in. of oil to 375°. Fry egg rolls for 2 minutes on each side or until golden brown. Drain on paper towels. Serve with sweet-sour sauce. **Yield:** 7 egg rolls.

Taco Joe Dip

Lang Secrest, Sierra Vista, Arizona

This recipe was given to us by our daughter. My husband and I love it. Because it's made in a slow cooker, it's great for parties or busy days.

1 can (16 ounces) kidney beans, rinsed and drained
1 can (15-1/4 ounces) whole kernel corn, drained
1 can (15 ounces) black beans, rinsed and drained
1 can (14-1/2 ounces) stewed tomatoes
1 can (8 ounces) tomato sauce
1 can (4 ounces) chopped green chilies, drained
1 envelope taco seasoning
1/2 cup chopped onion
Tortilla chips

In a slow cooker, combine the first eight ingredients. Cover and cook on low for 5-7 hours. Serve with tortilla chips. **Yield:** about 7 cups.

BLT Bites

(Pictured on page 7)

Kellie Remmen, Detroit Lakes, Minnesota

These quick hors d'oeuvres may be mini, but their bacon-and-tomato flavor is full-size. I serve them at parties, brunches and picnics, and they're always a hit. Even my kids love to snack on them.

- **16 to 20 cherry tomatoes**
- **1 pound bacon, cooked and crumbled**
- **1/2 cup mayonnaise**
- **1/3 cup chopped green onions**
- **3 tablespoons grated Parmesan cheese**
- **2 tablespoons snipped fresh parsley**

1. Cut a thin slice off of each tomato top. Scoop out and discard pulp. Invert the tomatoes on a paper towel to drain.

2. In a small bowl, combine all remaining ingredients; mix well. Spoon into tomatoes. Refrigerate for several hours. **Yield:** 16-20 servings.

Entertaining Ideas

Whether you're entertaining a small group of friends or bringing a snack to the family reunion, choosing an appetizer that fits the occasion is often a challenge.

For potluck suppers, it's best to select a cold appetizer that can be prepared ahead and taken in a covered container. Hot appetizers requiring last-minute preparation are best served from your own kitchen.

If you plan to offer several appetizers, make it interesting for your guests and easy on yourself by preparing one cold make-ahead appetizer and one hot appetizer.

When you entertain friends and family throughout the year, welcome them into your home with a homemade beverage. Refreshing punches are perfect when feeding a crowd, while blender smoothies and freshly squeezed lemonade refresh smaller groups. Remember, beverages made in a blender need to be served immediately.

Clam Fritters

Cecelia Wilson, Rockville, Connecticut

We had clam fritters every time we went to Rhode Island. I looked for a recipe and finally found this one. Now we have them whenever we want.

- **2/3 cup all-purpose flour**
- **1 teaspoon baking powder**
- **1/4 teaspoon salt**
- **1/8 teaspoon pepper**
- **1 can (6-1/2 ounces) minced clams**
- **1 egg**
- **3 tablespoons milk**
- **1/3 cup diced onion**
- **Oil for frying**
- **Tartar sauce *and/or* lemon wedges, optional**

1. In a bowl, combine flour, baking powder, salt and pepper; set aside. Drain clams, reserving 2 tablespoons juice; set clams aside. In a small bowl, beat egg, milk and reserved clam juice; stir into dry ingredients just until moistened. Add the clams and onion.

2. In an electric skillet or deep-fat fryer, heat oil to 375°. Drop batter by tablespoonfuls into oil. Fry for 2-3 minutes, turning occasionally, until golden brown. Drain on paper towels. Serve with tartar sauce and/or lemon if desired. **Yield:** 14-16 fritters.

Festive Appetizer Spread

Edith Howe, Woburn, Massachusetts

Our state is known for its cranberries, and there are many bogs in our area. I won first place with this recipe in a contest sponsored by our local newspaper.

1 cup water
1 cup sugar
1 package (12 ounces) fresh *or* frozen cranberries
1/2 cup apricot preserves
2 tablespoons lemon juice
1/3 cup slivered almonds, toasted
1 package (8 ounces) cream cheese
Assorted crackers

1. In a saucepan over medium heat, bring water and sugar to a boil without stirring; boil for 5 minutes. Add cranberries; cook until berries pop and sauce is thickened, about 10 minutes. Remove from the heat.

2. Cut apricots in the preserves into small pieces; add to cranberry mixture. Stir in lemon juice. Cool. Add almonds.

3. Spoon over cream cheese; serve with crackers. Store leftovers in the refrigerator. **Yield:** about 3 cups.

Chickaritos

Nancy Coates, Oro Valley, Arizona

This is a great way to use leftover chicken. Chickaritos are easy to make and can be shaped ahead. Just bake right before serving. Enjoy them plain or serve with salsa and guacamole.

3 cups finely chopped cooked chicken
1-1/2 cups (6 ounces) shredded sharp cheddar cheese
1 can (4 ounces) chopped green chilies
1/2 cup finely chopped green onions
1 teaspoon hot pepper sauce
1 teaspoon garlic salt
1/4 teaspoon pepper
1/4 teaspoon ground cumin
1/4 teaspoon paprika
1 package (17-1/4 ounces) frozen puff pastry sheet, thawed *or* pie pastry for double-crust pie (10 inches)
Guacamole
Salsa

1. In a bowl, combine chicken, cheese, chilies, onions and seasonings. Mix well; chill until ready to use.

2. Remove half of the pastry from refrigerator at a time. On a lightly floured surface, roll to a 12-in. x 9-in. rectangle. Cut into nine small rectangles. Place about 2 tablespoons of filling down the center of each rectangle. Wet edges of pastry with water and roll pastry around filling. Crimp ends with a fork to seal. Repeat with remaining pastry and filling. Place seam side down on a lightly greased baking sheet. Refrigerate until ready to heat.

3. Bake at 425° for 20-25 minutes or until golden brown. Serve warm with guacamole and salsa. **Yield:** 18 servings.

Sweet Potato Cheese Ball

Edwina Harper, Bastrop, Louisiana

My husband and I farm 300 acres of sweet potatoes. I promote our product at fairs, ag expos and school functions. I pass out recipes, and this is one of the favorites.

1 package (8 ounces) cream cheese, softened
2 cups cold mashed sweet potatoes
1/4 cup finely chopped onion
2 tablespoons finely chopped jalapeno pepper
1 teaspoon seasoned salt
1 teaspoon Worcestershire sauce
1 teaspoon Louisiana hot sauce
1/2 to 1 teaspoon hot pepper sauce
1/4 cup chopped pecans
Assorted crackers, breadsticks *or* raw vegetables

1. In a mixing bowl, beat cream cheese and sweet potatoes until smooth. Add next seven ingredients; mix well. Cover; refrigerate for 4 hours or until easy to handle.

2. Shape into a ball; cover and refrigerate for 4 hours or until firm. Serve with crackers, breadsticks or vegetables. **Yield:** about 3 cups.

Editor's Note: When cutting or seeding hot peppers, use rubber or plastic gloves to protect your hands. Avoid touching your face.

Country Cheese Snacks

Sandy Thorn, Sonora, California

This is one of my favorite appetizers for family and friends. They take just minutes to prepare.

1 cup mayonnaise
1 cup grated Parmesan cheese
1 package (8 ounces) cream cheese, softened
2 green onions, minced
18 slices snack rye bread
Parsley sprigs
Sliced stuffed olives

1. In a small bowl, combine the first four ingredients. Spread on bread; place on a baking sheet.

2. Broil 4 in. from the heat for 1-2 minutes or until golden and bubbly. Garnish with parsley and olives. Serve immediately. **Yield:** 1-1/2 dozen.

Fried Jalapenos

DeLea Lonadier, Montgomery, Louisiana

Here's an appetizer that will heat up any gathering. Family and friends often request that I make these jalapenos.

2 jars (12 ounces *each*) whole jalapeno peppers, drained
1 jar (5 ounces) olive-pimiento cheese spread
3/4 cup all-purpose flour, *divided*
6 tablespoons cornmeal, *divided*
1/4 teaspoon salt
1/4 teaspoon pepper
1 cup buttermilk
Oil for frying

1. Cut off stems and remove seeds from peppers. Stuff with cheese spread. Refrigerate for at least 2 hours.

2. In a small bowl, combine 1/4 cup of flour, 2 tablespoons cornmeal, salt, pepper and buttermilk until smooth; set aside. In another bowl, combine remaining flour and cornmeal. Dip stuffed peppers into buttermilk batter, then dredge in flour mixture.

3. In an electric skillet or deep-fat fryer, heat oil to 375°. Fry peppers, two or three at a time, until golden brown. Drain on paper towels. **Yield:** 2 dozen.

Editor's Note: When cutting and seeding hot peppers, use rubber or plastic gloves to protect your hands; avoid touching your face.

Tomato Vegetable Juice

Sue Wille, Alexandria, Minnesota

I've used this delicious recipe for many years, and it's always been a favorite. The tangy juice is refreshing on its own and also works great in any recipe calling for tomato juice. Because of all the vegetables, it's full of vitamins.

 Uses less fat, sugar or salt. Includes Nutritional Analysis and Diabetic Exchanges.

10 pounds tomatoes, peeled and chopped (about 8 quarts)
3 garlic cloves, minced
2 large onions, chopped
2 large carrots, cut into 1/2-inch slices
2 cups chopped celery
1/2 cup chopped green pepper
1/4 cup sugar
1 tablespoon salt, optional
1 teaspoon Worcestershire sauce
1/2 teaspoon pepper
Lemon juice

1. Combine tomatoes, garlic, onions, carrots, celery and green pepper in a large Dutch oven. Bring to a boil; reduce heat and simmer for 20 minutes or until vegetables are tender. Cool.

2. Press mixture through a food mill or fine sieve. Return juice to Dutch oven; add sugar, salt if desired, Worcestershire sauce and pepper. Bring to a boil.

3. Ladle hot juice into hot sterilized quart jars, leaving 1/4-in. headspace. Add 2 tablespoons lemon juice to each jar. Adjust caps. Process for 40 minutes in a boiling-water bath. **Yield:** 56 servings (7 quarts).

Nutritional Analysis: One 1/2-cup serving (prepared without salt) equals 46 calories, 15 mg sodium, 0 cholesterol, 10 g carbohydrate, 2 g protein, trace fat. **Diabetic Exchange:** 2 vegetable.

Popcorn Caramel Crunch

Lucille Hermsmeyer, Scotia, Nebraska

For munching or gift-giving, this popcorn snack is chock-full of goodies. Store in airtight containers to keep the popcorn crisp.

4 cups popped popcorn
1 cup dry roasted peanuts
1 cup chow mein noodles
1/2 cup raisins
1 cup sugar
3/4 cup butter
1/2 cup light corn syrup
2 tablespoons water
1 teaspoon ground cinnamon

1. In a large greased bowl, combine the first four ingredients; set aside.

2. In a large saucepan, combine sugar, butter, corn syrup and water. Cook over medium heat, stirring occasionally, until a candy thermometer reads 280°-290° (soft-crack stage). Remove from the heat and stir in cinnamon.

3. Pour over popcorn mixture; stir until evenly coated. Immediately pour onto a greased 15-in. x 10-in. x 1-in. pan.

4. When cool enough to handle, break into pieces. Store in airtight containers. **Yield:** about 8 cups.

Sugar 'n' Spice Nuts

Debbi Baker, Green Springs, Ohio

To tell the truth, I can't recall where this recipe came from. It's been a regular in my holiday baking, though, for many years. Between Thanksgiving and New Year's, I hand these out to almost everybody—even the mailman's been known to find a batch in the mailbox!

3 cups lightly salted mixed nuts
1 egg white
1 tablespoon orange juice
2/3 cup sugar
1 tablespoon grated orange peel
1 teaspoon ground cinnamon
1/2 teaspoon ground ginger
1/2 teaspoon ground allspice

1. Place nuts in a large bowl. In a small bowl, beat egg white and orange juice with a fork until foamy. Add sugar, orange peel, cinnamon, ginger and allspice; mix well. Pour over nuts and stir to coat.

2. Spread into an ungreased 15-in. x 10-in. x 1-in. baking pan. Bake at 275°, stirring every 15 minutes, for 45-50 minutes or until nuts are crisp and lightly browned.

3. Cool completely. Store in an airtight container. **Yield:** 4 cups.

Chocolate Chip Cheese Ball

Kelly Glascock, Syracuse, Missouri

Your guests are in for a sweet surprise when they try this unusual cheese ball...it tastes just like cookie dough! Rolled in chopped pecans, the chip-studded spread is wonderful on regular or chocolate graham crackers.

1 package (8 ounces) cream cheese, softened
1/2 cup butter, softened
1/4 teaspoon vanilla extract
3/4 cup confectioners' sugar
2 tablespoons brown sugar
3/4 cup miniature semisweet chocolate chips
3/4 cup finely chopped pecans
Graham crackers

1. In a mixing bowl, beat the cream cheese, butter and vanilla until fluffy. Gradually add sugars; beat just until combined. Stir in chocolate chips. Cover and refrigerate for 2 hours.

2. Place cream cheese mixture on a large piece of plastic wrap; shape into a ball. Refrigerate for at least 1 hour.

3. Just before serving, roll cheese ball in pecans. Serve with graham crackers. **Yield:** 1 cheese ball (about 2 cups).

Mocha Punch

Yvonne Hatfield, Norman, Oklahoma

I first tried this smooth, creamy punch at a friend's Christmas open house. It was so special and distinctive I didn't leave until I had the recipe. Having a frosty glass of this chocolate punch is like sipping a chocolate shake.

1-1/2 quarts water
1/2 cup instant chocolate drink mix
1/2 cup sugar
1/4 cup instant coffee granules
1/2 gallon vanilla ice cream
1/2 gallon chocolate ice cream
1 cup heavy whipping cream, whipped
Chocolate curls, optional

1. In a large saucepan, bring the water to a boil. Remove from the heat. Add drink mix, sugar and coffee; stir until dissolved. Cover and refrigerate for 4 hours or overnight.

2. About 30 minutes before serving, pour into a punch bowl. Add ice cream by scoopfuls; stir until partially melted. Garnish with dollops of whipped cream and chocolate curls if desired. **Yield:** 20-25 servings (about 5 quarts).

Sausage Quiche Squares

Linda Wheeler, Middleburg, Florida

Having done some catering, I especially appreciate interesting, appetizing finger foods. I'm constantly asked to make these popular squares to serve at parties. They're almost like a zippy quiche.

- **1 pound bulk pork sausage**
- **1 cup (4 ounces) shredded cheddar cheese**
- **1 cup (4 ounces) shredded Monterey Jack cheese**
- **1/2 cup finely chopped onion**
- **1 can (4 ounces) chopped green chilies**
- **1 tablespoon minced jalapeno pepper, optional**
- **10 eggs**
- **1 teaspoon chili powder**
- **1 teaspoon ground cumin**
- **1 teaspoon salt**
- **1/2 teaspoon garlic powder**
- **1/2 teaspoon pepper**

1. In a large skillet, cook sausage over medium heat until no longer pink; drain. Place in a greased 13-in. x 9-in. x 2-in. baking dish. Layer with cheeses, onion, chilies and jalapeno if desired. In a bowl, beat eggs and seasonings. Pour over cheese.

2. Bake, uncovered, at 375° for 18-22 minutes or until a knife inserted near the center comes out clean. Cool for 10 minutes; cut into 1-in. squares. **Yield:** about 8 dozen.

Editor's Note: When cutting or seeding hot peppers, use rubber or plastic gloves to protect your hands. Avoid touching your face.

Fluffy Hot Chocolate

Jo Ann Schimcek, Weimar, Texas

Melted marshmallows provide the frothy texture that you'll savor in this sweet and speedy warm beverage. They're also what makes this hot chocolate different from (and better than) the instant kind you make from a store-bought mix.

8 teaspoons sugar
4 teaspoons baking cocoa
4 cups milk
1-1/2 cups miniature marshmallows
1 teaspoon vanilla extract

1. In a saucepan, combine the first four ingredients. Cook and stir over medium heat until the marshmallows are melted, about 8 minutes.

2. Remove from the heat; stir in vanilla. Ladle into mugs. **Yield:** 4 servings.

Wontons with Sweet-Sour Sauce

Korrin Grigg, Neenah, Wisconsin

This super-simple finger food makes an awesome appetizer and is perfect for potlucks. I serve these crispy pork rolls with sweet-and-sour sauce, and they disappear in a hurry. Folks can't seem to get enough of them.

1 can (14 ounces) pineapple tidbits
1/2 cup packed brown sugar
1 tablespoon cornstarch
1/3 cup cider vinegar
1 tablespoon soy sauce
1/2 cup chopped green pepper
1/2 pound ground pork
2 cups finely shredded cabbage
3/4 cup finely chopped fresh bean sprouts
1 small onion, finely chopped
2 eggs, lightly beaten
1/2 teaspoon salt
1/4 teaspoon pepper
2 packages (12 ounces *each*) wonton wrappers
Oil for frying

1. Drain pineapple, reserving juice. Set pineapple aside. In a saucepan, combine brown sugar and cornstarch; gradually stir in pineapple juice, vinegar and soy sauce until smooth. Bring to a boil; cook and stir for 2 minutes or until thickened. Reduce heat; stir in green pepper and pineapple. Cover and simmer for 5 minutes; set aside and keep warm.

2. In a bowl, combine pork, cabbage, sprouts, onion, eggs, salt and pepper. Place about 1 tablespoonful in the center of each wrapper. Moisten edges with water; fold opposite corners together over filling and press to seal.

3. In an electric skillet, heat 1 in. of oil to 375°. Fry wontons for 2-1/2 minutes or until golden brown, turning once. Drain on paper towels. Serve with sauce. **Yield:** about 8-1/2 dozen (2-1/2 cups sauce).

Editor's Note: Fill wonton wrappers a few at a time, keeping others covered until ready to use.

Citrus Pineapple Coleslaw, p. 37

BLT Chicken Salad, p. 28

Honey-Dijon Potato Salad, p. 32

Salads

Versatile salads can be served as a refreshing side dish, a crowd-pleasing addition to potlucks, part of a soup and sandwich lunch, or as a hearty meal in themselves. So toss one together soon!

Shrimp Taco Salad, p. 31

Grilled Three-Pepper Salad, p. 35

BLT Chicken Salad

(Pictured on page 26)

Cindy Moore, Mooresville, North Carolina

I like this salad because I can prepare all the ingredients ahead of time and just throw it together at the last minute. Barbecue sauce in the dressing gives a different taste to this green salad that features the fun fixings for a BLT chicken sandwich. Even picky eaters love it.

1/2 cup mayonnaise
3 to 4 tablespoons barbecue sauce
2 tablespoons finely chopped onion
1 tablespoon lemon juice
1/4 teaspoon pepper
8 cups torn salad greens
2 large tomatoes, chopped
1-1/2 pounds boneless skinless chicken breasts, cooked and cubed
10 bacon strips, cooked and crumbled
2 hard-cooked eggs, sliced

1. In a small bowl, combine the first five ingredients; mix well. Cover and refrigerate until serving.

2. Place salad greens on a large serving platter. Sprinkle with tomatoes, chicken and bacon; garnish with eggs. Drizzle with dressing. **Yield:** 8 servings.

Pasta Salad with Steak

Julie DeRuwe, Oakville, Washington

While there are quite a few ingredients in this salad recipe, it doesn't take too long to make, and cleanup afterward's a snap.

3/4 cup olive oil
2 tablespoons lemon juice
2 teaspoons dried oregano
1 tablespoon Dijon mustard
2 teaspoons red wine vinegar
1 teaspoon sugar
1/2 teaspoon salt
1/2 teaspoon pepper
3 cups cooked small shell pasta
1 sirloin steak (1 pound)

RUB:
1 tablespoon olive oil
3 garlic cloves, minced
2 teaspoons dried oregano
2 teaspoons pepper
1 teaspoon sugar

SALAD:
2/3 cup diced cucumber
1/2 cup crumbled feta cheese
1/4 cup sliced ripe olives
1/4 cup chopped red onion
1/4 cup minced fresh parsley
1 jar (2 ounces) diced pimientos, drained
Iceberg *or* romaine lettuce

1. Combine the first eight ingredients; set half of the dressing aside. Place pasta in a bowl; add remaining dressing. Toss to coat; cover and refrigerate.

2. Pierce steak with a fork. Combine rub ingredients; rub over steak. Cover and refrigerate for at least 15 minutes. Grill steak, uncovered, over medium heat for 9-10 minutes on each side or until meat reaches desired doneness (for rare, a meat thermometer should read 140°; medium, 160°; well-done, 170°). Let stand for 10 minutes.

3. Meanwhile, add cucumber, cheese, olives, onion, parsley and pimientos to pasta; mix well. Spoon onto a lettuce-lined platter. Slice steak and arrange over salad. Serve with reserved dressing. **Yield:** 4 servings.

Almond-Raspberry Tossed Salad

Jennifer Long, St. Peters, Missouri

My husband and I helped prepare this summery salad for a weekend retreat. The recipe served 60 to 80 people, so I modified it to use at home. The sweet-tart dressing is wonderful over romaine with toasted almonds and fresh raspberries.

8 cups torn romaine
1 cup fresh raspberries
1/2 cup sliced almonds, toasted
1/2 cup seedless raspberry jam
1/4 cup white wine vinegar
1/4 cup honey
2 tablespoons plus 2 teaspoons vegetable oil

1. In a salad bowl, combine the romaine, raspberries and almonds.

2. In a blender, combine the remaining ingredients; cover and process until smooth. Serve with salad. **Yield:** 10 servings.

Old-Fashioned Potato Salad

Nancy Grove-Nichols, Dillsburg, Pennsylvania

We live at the edge of Pennsylvania Dutch Country, where there are lots of small farms. Country markets are plentiful here, so potatoes are a staple.

4 cups cubed peeled potatoes
3 hard-cooked eggs, chopped
2 celery ribs, thinly sliced
1/4 cup chopped green onions
1/2 cup sour cream
1/2 cup mayonnaise
2 tablespoons vinegar
2 tablespoons sugar
1 teaspoon prepared mustard
1/2 teaspoon salt
1/4 teaspoon pepper

1. Place potatoes in a saucepan and cover with water; bring to a boil. Reduce heat. Cook for 20-25 minutes or until tender; drain. Place in a large bowl; add eggs, celery and onions.

2. In a small bowl, combine all of the remaining ingredients. Pour over the potato mixture and toss to coat.

Cover and refrigerate for at least 1 hour. **Yield:** 6-8 servings.

Pecan-Pear Tossed Salad

Marjean Claassen, Sedgwick, Kansas

To save time, I prepare the ingredients and dressing the day before, then combine them just before serving. This salad has become a star at family gatherings. Once, when I forgot to bring it, dinner was postponed so I could go home and get it!

2 tablespoons fresh raspberries
3/4 cup olive oil
3 tablespoons cider vinegar
2 tablespoons plus 1 teaspoon sugar
1/4 to 1/2 teaspoon pepper
SALAD:
4 medium ripe pears, thinly sliced
2 teaspoons lemon juice
8 cups torn salad greens
2/3 cup pecan halves, toasted
1/2 cup fresh raspberries
1/3 cup (2 ounces) crumbled feta cheese

1. Press raspberries through a sieve, reserving juice. Discard seeds. In a jar with a tight-fitting lid, combine oil, vinegar, sugar, pepper and reserved raspberry juice; shake well.

2. Toss pear slices with lemon juice; drain. In a salad bowl, combine salad greens, pears, pecans and raspberries. Sprinkle with cheese. Drizzle with dressing. **Yield:** 8 servings.

Working with Salad Greens

Wash salad greens thoroughly in cool water. Pat them dry with a clean towel or paper towel to remove water. Store in a covered container or plastic bag, and refrigerate at least 1 hour before serving to crisp the greens. Place a piece of paper towel in the bottom of the container or bag to absorb excess moisture.

Just before serving, tear the salad greens into bite-size pieces. Cutting them with a knife will turn the edges brown. Allow greens to stand at room temperature no longer than 15 minutes before serving.

Shrimp Taco Salad

(Pictured on page 27)

Ellen Morrell, Hazleton, Pennsylvania

I created this main-dish salad to satisfy our family's love of shrimp. It has lots of contrasting textures, including firm taco-seasoned shrimp, crispy tortilla strips and hearty black beans. A convenient bag of salad greens cuts down on prep time, so I can have this meal ready in half an hour.

- **1 pound uncooked large shrimp, peeled and deveined**
- **1 envelope taco seasoning, *divided***
- **1/2 cup plus 3 tablespoons olive oil, *divided***
- **1 small onion, finely chopped**
- **3 tablespoons red wine vinegar**
- **2 tablespoons diced green *or* sweet red pepper**
- **6 garlic cloves, minced**
- **1/2 teaspoon ground coriander**
- **1/4 teaspoon sugar**
- **3 corn tortillas (6 inches), cut into 1/4-inch strips**
- **1 package (8 ounces) ready-to-serve salad greens**
- **1 medium tomato, chopped**
- **1 can (8 ounces) black beans, rinsed and drained**
- **2 cups (8 ounces) finely shredded Colby-Monterey Jack cheese**

1. Remove shrimp tails if desired. Place shrimp in a bowl; sprinkle with half of the taco seasoning. Set aside.

2. In another bowl, combine 1/2 cup oil, onion, vinegar, green pepper, garlic, coriander and sugar; set aside.

3. In a skillet, stir-fry tortilla strips in remaining oil; drain on paper towels. Sprinkle with remaining taco seasoning. In the same skillet, saute shrimp for 8-10 minutes or until pink.

4. In a large bowl, combine the greens, tomato, beans, shrimp and tortilla strips. Drizzle with dressing. Sprinkle with cheese; toss. **Yield:** 6-8 servings.

Creamy Chicken Salad

Kristi Abernathy, Kalispell, Montana

I modified the original recipe for this chicken salad to make it healthier. The ingredients are so flavorful that my changes didn't take away from the taste. This refreshing salad never lasts long at our house. Even if I double the recipe, my husband asks, "Why didn't you make more?"

✓ Uses less fat, sugar or salt. Includes Nutritional Analysis and Diabetic Exchanges.

- **2 cups cubed cooked chicken breast**
- **1 cup cooked small ring pasta**
- **1 cup halved seedless red grapes**
- **1 can (11 ounces) mandarin oranges, drained**
- **3 celery ribs, chopped**
- **1/2 cup sliced almonds**
- **1 tablespoon grated onion**
- **1 cup reduced-fat mayonnaise**
- **1 cup reduced-fat whipped topping**
- **1/4 teaspoon salt**
- **Lettuce leaves, optional**

1. In a bowl, combine the chicken, pasta, grapes, oranges, celery, almonds and onion.

2. In another bowl, combine the mayonnaise, whipped topping and salt. Add to the chicken mixture; stir to coat. Serve in a lettuce-lined bowl if desired. **Yield:** 6 servings.

Nutritional Analysis: One 1-cup serving equals 261 calories, 307 mg sodium, 38 mg cholesterol, 25 g carbohydrate, 11 g protein, 13 g fat, 2 g fiber. **Diabetic Exchanges:** 1-1/2 fat, 1 starch, 1 meat, 1/2 fruit.

Honey-Dijon Potato Salad

(Pictured on page 26)

Kristie Kline Jones, Douglas, Wyoming

No matter which recipe I tried, my potato salad always turned out bland. So I came up with this creamy version that has plenty of pizzazz. It's so tangy and flavorful, you wouldn't realize it calls for fat-free mayonnaise and fat-free honey-Dijon salad dressing. It's a favorite at picnics.

✓ Uses less fat, sugar or salt. Includes Nutritional Analysis and Diabetic Exchanges.

2-1/4 pounds red potatoes (about 14 small)
3 tablespoons vinegar
3/4 cup chopped green pepper
1/2 cup chopped onion
5 tablespoons chopped dill pickles
1 teaspoon salt-free seasoning blend
1/4 teaspoon pepper
1 cup fat-free mayonnaise
1/3 cup fat-free honey-Dijon salad dressing
2 tablespoons Dijon mustard
2 hard-cooked egg whites, chopped

1. Place potatoes in a saucepan; cover with water. Bring to a boil; cook until tender, 15-30 minutes. Drain and cool. Cube the potatoes and place in a large bowl.

2. Sprinkle with vinegar. Add green pepper, onion, pickles, seasoning blend and pepper. Fold in mayonnaise, salad dressing, mustard and egg whites. Cover and refrigerate for at least 1 hour. **Yield:** 8 servings.

Nutritional Analysis: One 3/4-cup serving equals 165 calories, 513 mg sodium, 0 cholesterol, 36 g carbohydrate, 4 g protein, 1 g fat, 3 g fiber. **Diabetic Exchanges:** 2 starch, 1 vegetable.

Festive Tossed Salad

Jauneen Hosking, Greenfield, Wisconsin

With its unique medley of fruits and festive look, this salad is a holiday tradition at our house. Our three grown daughters have come to expect it. One forkful reminds us of all the things we can be thankful for.

1/2 cup sugar
1/3 cup red wine vinegar
2 tablespoons lemon juice
2 tablespoons finely chopped onion
1/2 teaspoon salt
2/3 cup vegetable oil
2 to 3 teaspoons poppy seeds
10 cups torn romaine
1 cup (4 ounces) shredded Swiss cheese
1 medium apple, cored and cubed
1 medium pear, cored and cubed
1/4 cup dried cranberries
1/2 to 1 cup chopped cashews

1. In a blender or food processor, combine the sugar, vinegar, lemon juice, onion and salt. Cover and process until blended. With blender running, gradually add oil. Add poppy seeds and blend.

2. In a salad bowl, combine the romaine, Swiss cheese, apple, pear and cranberries. Drizzle with desired amount of dressing. Add cashews; toss to coat. Serve immediately. **Yield:** 8-10 servings.

Minted Melon Salad

Terry Saylor, Vermillion, South Dakota

People can't resist digging into a salad made with colorful summer fruits. The unique dressing is what makes this salad a crowd-pleaser. I get compliments whenever I serve it, especially when I put it on the table in a melon boat. It's a warm-weather treat.

1 cup water
3/4 cup sugar
3 tablespoons lime juice
1-1/2 teaspoons chopped fresh mint
3/4 teaspoon aniseed
Pinch salt
5 cups cubed watermelon (about 1/2 medium melon)
3 cups cubed cantaloupe (about 1 medium melon)
3 cups cubed honeydew (about 1 medium melon)
2 cups peach slices (about 2 peaches)
1 cup fresh blueberries

1. In a small saucepan, bring the first six ingredients to a boil. Boil for 2 minutes; remove from the heat. Cover and cool syrup completely.

2. Combine the fruit in a large bowl; add syrup and stir to coat. Cover and chill for at least 2 hours, stirring occasionally. Drain before serving. **Yield:** 12-14 servings.

Sweet Floret Salad

Kathi Lavier, Hillsboro, Oregon

Everywhere I take this crunchy, fresh-tasting salad with its sweet creamy dressing, people invariably want the recipe. It's perfect for a potluck—best made the night before you serve it and easy to transport.

1/2 cup mayonnaise
1/3 cup sugar
1/4 cup vegetable oil
1/4 cup vinegar
1 medium head cauliflower, broken into florets
1-3/4 pounds fresh broccoli, broken into florets
1 medium red onion, sliced
1 medium sweet yellow pepper, cut into 1-inch pieces, optional
1/2 pound sliced bacon, cooked and crumbled

1. In a small saucepan, combine the mayonnaise, sugar, oil and vinegar. Bring to a boil, whisking constantly. Cool to room temperature.

2. In a large bowl, combine the remaining ingredients. Add dressing and toss to coat. Cover and refrigerate for several hours or overnight, stirring occasionally. **Yield:** 10-12 servings.

Editor's Note: Reduced-fat or fat-free mayonnaise should not be substituted for regular mayonnaise in this recipe.

Hearty Eight-Layer Salad

Noreen Meyer, Madison, Wisconsin

I have been making this satisfying salad for years. It's my most requested recipe for family gatherings. It's simple to make ahead of time and looks lovely with all of its tasty layers. Dijon mustard gives a nice kick to the dressing.

1-1/2 cups uncooked small shell macaroni
1 tablespoon vegetable oil
3 cups shredded lettuce
3 hard-cooked eggs, sliced
1/4 teaspoon salt
1/8 teaspoon pepper
1 cup julienned fully cooked ham
1 cup julienned hard salami
1 package (10 ounces) frozen peas, thawed
1 cup mayonnaise
1/4 cup sour cream
1/4 cup chopped green onions
2 teaspoons Dijon mustard
1 cup (4 ounces) shredded Colby *or* Monterey Jack cheese
2 tablespoons minced fresh parsley

1. Cook macaroni according to package directions; drain and rinse with cold water. Drizzle with oil and toss to coat. Place the lettuce in a 2-1/2-qt. glass serving bowl; top with macaroni and eggs. Sprinkle with salt and pepper. Layer with ham, salami and peas.

2. Combine mayonnaise, sour cream, green onions and mustard. Spread over the top. Cover and refrigerate for several hours or overnight. Just before serving, sprinkle with cheese and parsley. **Yield:** 10 servings.

Crunchy Corn Medley

Meredith Cecil, Plattsburg, Missouri

This recipe came from my husband's aunt, who's an excellent cook, friend and mentor. It's crunchy, colorful and combined with a light tasty dressing. I've shared it with friends and relatives, who think it's a great addition to their recipe collections.

- **2 cups frozen peas, thawed**
- **1 can (15-1/4 ounces) whole kernel corn, drained**
- **1 can (15-1/4 ounces) white *or* shoepeg corn, drained**
- **1 can (8 ounces) water chestnuts, drained and chopped**
- **1 jar (4 ounces) diced pimientos, drained**
- **8 green onions, thinly sliced**
- **2 celery ribs, chopped**
- **1 medium green pepper, chopped**
- **1/2 cup vinegar**
- **1/2 cup sugar**
- **1/4 cup vegetable oil**
- **1 teaspoon salt**
- **1/4 teaspoon pepper**

1. In a large bowl, combine the first eight ingredients. In a small bowl, combine vinegar, sugar, oil, salt and pepper; whisk until sugar is dissolved. Pour over corn mixture; mix well.

2. Cover; refrigerate at least 3 hours. Stir just before serving; serve with a slotted spoon. **Yield:** 10 servings.

Grilled Three-Pepper Salad

(Pictured on page 27)

Ruth Wickard, York, Pennsylvania

I have been cooking since my mother taught me how at an early age. I enjoy it, and I'm always trying new recipes. This one's both flavorful and colorful.

- **2 *each* large green, sweet red and yellow peppers, cut into 1-inch pieces**
- **1 large red onion, halved and thinly sliced**
- **1 pound bulk mozzarella cheese, cut into bite-size cubes**
- **1 can (6 ounces) pitted ripe olives, drained and halved**

VINAIGRETTE:

- **2/3 cup olive oil**
- **1/3 cup red wine vinegar**
- **2 tablespoons lemon juice**
- **2 tablespoons Dijon mustard**
- **1 tablespoon minced fresh basil**
- **1/2 teaspoon cayenne pepper**
- **1/2 teaspoon garlic powder**

1. Thread peppers onto metal or soaked wooden skewers; grill or broil for 10-12 minutes or until edges are browned.

2. Remove from skewers and place in a large bowl. Add onion, mozzarella and olives; toss gently. Cover and refrigerate.

3. Combine the vinaigrette ingredients in a jar with tight-fitting lid; shake well. Pour over the pepper mixture just before serving; toss to coat. **Yield:** 10-12 servings.

A Handle on Homemade Dressing

If you plan on serving a vinegar and oil dressing right away, you can combine all of the ingredients in a jar with a tight-fitting lid and shake well. (The mixture will separate upon standing; simply shake before serving.)

To mix a vinegar and oil dressing that will stand for an hour or two without separating, combine all of the ingredients except for the oil in a small bowl. Slowly add the oil while mixing vigorously with a wire whisk.

Experiment with homemade salad dressings by adding your favorite herbs and flavored vinegar or oil to the recipe.

Summer Spinach Salad

Callie Berger, Diamond Springs, California

Guests always request the recipe for this fabulous spinach salad. Tossed with ripe banana chunks, fresh strawberries and toasted almonds, it looks and tastes special enough for company. The tangy poppy seed dressing is a snap to combine in a blender or food processor.

1/2 cup vegetable oil
1/4 cup chopped onion
2 tablespoons plus 2 teaspoons red wine vinegar
2 tablespoons plus 2 teaspoons sugar
1-1/2 teaspoons ground mustard
1/2 teaspoon salt
1-1/2 teaspoons poppy seeds
8 cups torn fresh spinach
3 green onions, sliced
2 pints fresh strawberries, sliced
3 large ripe bananas, cut into 1/2-inch slices
1/2 cup slivered almonds, toasted

1. Place the first six ingredients in a blender or food processor; cover and process until the sugar is dissolved. Add the poppy seeds; process just until blended.

2. In a salad bowl, combine the remaining ingredients. Drizzle with dressing; toss to coat. Serve immediately. **Yield:** 14 servings.

Citrus Pineapple Coleslaw

(Pictured on page 26)

Carol Ross, Anchorage, Alaska

A blue-ribbon recipe, this slaw was a winner in our state fair competition. Alaska is famous for its giant cabbages, but any garden-variety head will taste yummy dressed in citrusy pineapple and marshmallow bits.

- **1/3 cup sugar**
- **1/4 cup cornstarch**
- **1/4 teaspoon salt**
- **1 cup unsweetened pineapple juice**
- **1/4 cup orange juice**
- **3 tablespoons lemon juice**
- **2 eggs, lightly beaten**
- **2 packages (3 ounces *each*) cream cheese, cubed**
- **1 medium head cabbage, shredded**
- **2 large carrots, shredded**
- **1 can (8 ounces) crushed pineapple, drained**
- **1 cup miniature marshmallows**
- **Carrot curls, optional**

1. In a saucepan, combine the first six ingredients until smooth. Bring to a boil over medium heat; cook and stir for 2 minutes or until thickened.

2. Stir a small amount into the eggs. Return all to saucepan, stirring constantly. Cook and stir until mixture reaches 160°. Cool for 5 minutes. Stir in cream cheese until melted. Refrigerate.

3. In a large salad bowl, combine cabbage, carrots, pineapple and marshmallows. Add dressing; toss to coat. Garnish with carrot curls if desired. **Yield:** 8-12 servings.

Heads Up on Cabbage

To shred cabbage by hand, cut it into wedges. Place cut side down on a cutting board. With a large sharp knife, cut the cabbage into thin slices.

For maximum flavor, coleslaw needs to be prepared several hours before serving to allow the cabbage to blend with the dressing.

Fruit-Filled Raspberry Ring

Janice Steinmetz, Somers, Connecticut

People love this fruity gelatin ring that gets extra flavor from an ambrosia-like mixture in the center. I've been bringing it to potlucks, buffets and showers for 25 years.

- **2 packages (6 ounces *each*) raspberry gelatin**
- **4 cups boiling water**
- **1 quart raspberry sherbet**
- **1 can (14 ounces) pineapple tidbits, drained**
- **1 can (11 ounces) mandarin oranges, drained**
- **1 cup flaked coconut**
- **1 cup miniature marshmallows**
- **1 cup (8 ounces) sour cream**

1. In a bowl, dissolve gelatin in boiling water. Stir in sherbet until melted. Pour into an 8-cup ring mold coated with nonstick cooking spray. Chill overnight or until firm.

2. In a bowl, combine the pineapple, oranges, coconut, marshmallows and sour cream. Cover and chill.

3. To serve, unmold gelatin onto a serving plate. Spoon fruit mixture into center of ring. **Yield:** 12-16 servings.

Herbed Cherry Tomatoes

Dianne Bahn, Yankton, South Dakota

My recipe's good for when you want a little fancier salad dish but one that's still quick to fix. I find it's especially popular served with grilled steak, baked potatoes and fresh ears of corn on the cob.

1 pint cherry tomatoes, halved
1/4 cup vegetable oil
3 tablespoons vinegar
1/4 cup minced fresh parsley
1-1/2 teaspoons minced fresh basil *or* 1/2 teaspoon dried basil
1-1/2 teaspoons minced fresh oregano *or* 1/2 teaspoon dried oregano
1/2 teaspoon salt
1/2 teaspoon sugar
Leaf lettuce, optional

1. Place tomatoes in a medium bowl; set aside. In a small bowl, combine oil and vinegar. Add parsley, basil, oregano, salt and sugar and mix well. Pour over the tomatoes.

2. Cover and refrigerate for at least 3 hours. Drain; serve on lettuce if desired. **Yield:** 4-6 servings.

Grandma's Potato Salad

Susan Plocher, Oklahoma City, Oklahoma

I've never found a better potato salad recipe than this one handed down from my grandma. Like many grandmothers, mine cooked with a dash of this and a dash of that, so I estimated the measurements on this recipe. Feel free to change them according to taste, just like Grandma did!

6 to 7 medium red potatoes (about 2 pounds)
3/4 cup mayonnaise
1/2 cup sour cream
1/2 cup plain yogurt
1/3 cup thinly sliced green onions
2 to 3 dill pickle spears, chopped
4-1/2 teaspoons Dijon mustard
1 teaspoon prepared horseradish
2 garlic cloves, minced
1/2 teaspoon celery seed
1/2 teaspoon salt
1/4 teaspoon pepper
Dash onion salt
Dash garlic powder
4 hard-cooked eggs, coarsely chopped

1. Place potatoes in a saucepan and cover with water; bring to a boil. Cook for 20-30 minutes or until tender; drain and cool slightly. Slice potatoes into a large bowl.

2. In a small bowl, combine the mayonnaise, sour cream, yogurt, onions, pickles, mustard, horseradish, garlic and seasonings. Pour over potatoes and toss to coat. Gently stir in eggs. Cover and refrigerate for 2-3 hours. **Yield:** 8 servings.

Blue Cheese Pear Salad

Sherry Duval, Baltimore, Maryland

Guests at a barbecue we hosted one summer brought this cool, refreshing salad. Now it's a mainstay at most all our cookouts. The mingling of zesty tastes and textures instantly wakes up the taste buds.

10 cups torn salad greens
3 large ripe pears, peeled and cut into large pieces
1/2 cup thinly sliced green onions
4 ounces crumbled blue cheese
1/4 cup slivered almonds, toasted

MUSTARD VINAIGRETTE:
1/3 cup olive oil
3 tablespoons red wine vinegar
1-1/2 teaspoons sugar
1-1/2 teaspoons Dijon mustard
1 garlic clove, minced
1/2 teaspoon salt
Pepper to taste

1. In a large bowl, combine the salad greens, pears, onions, cheese and almonds.

2. In a jar with a tight-fitting lid, combine the vinaigrette ingredients; shake well. Pour over salad; toss to coat. Serve immediately. **Yield:** 8-10 servings.

Mandarin Avocado Toss

Colleen Weisberg, Minot, North Dakota

A perky blend of colors, shapes and textures makes this salad appealing to adults and children alike. My family requests it for its juicy oranges, smooth avocado slices and crunchy almonds and sunflower kernels. It's a breeze to prepare and an ideal luncheon item.

1/2 cup sunflower kernels
1/2 cup slivered almonds
2 tablespoons butter
1/2 cup vegetable oil
3 tablespoons red wine vinegar
1 tablespoon lemon juice
2 teaspoons sugar
1/2 teaspoon salt
1/2 teaspoon ground mustard
1 garlic clove, minced
4 cups torn leaf lettuce
1 can (11 ounces) mandarin oranges, drained
1 ripe avocado, peeled and cubed
1 to 2 green onions, chopped

1. In a small skillet, saute sunflower kernels and almonds in butter. Cool. Meanwhile, in a jar with a tight-fitting lid, combine the oil, vinegar, lemon juice, sugar, salt, mustard and garlic; shake well.

2. In a large salad bowl, toss the lettuce, oranges, avocado, onions and sunflower kernel mixture. Drizzle with dressing. Serve immediately. **Yield:** 6-8 servings.

Carrot Broccoli Salad

Heather Hibbs, Middleburg, Pennsylvania

I created this salad for summer's round of family reunions and picnics. My in-laws provide me with all the fresh vegetables from their garden.

6 medium carrots, shredded
1 small bunch broccoli (about 12 ounces), chopped
1 cup raisins
1 small onion, chopped
1 garlic clove, minced
2/3 to 1 cup mayonnaise
1/2 cup sugar
1 teaspoon ground mustard
1/2 pound sliced bacon, cooked and crumbled

1. In a large bowl, combine the first five ingredients. In another bowl, combine mayonnaise, sugar and mustard; mix well. Add to vegetable mixture and toss to coat.

2. Cover and refrigerate. Stir in bacon just before serving. **Yield:** 6 servings.

Sesame Cucumber Salad

Linda Hodge, Kannapolis, North Carolina

I learned to cook at an early age and have collected many recipes. Whenever I take this salad to a church supper, it's the first one to disappear!

8 cups thinly sliced cucumbers
1 tablespoon salt
2 green onions, sliced
1 garlic clove, minced
2 to 3 tablespoons soy sauce
2 tablespoons vinegar
1 tablespoon vegetable oil
1 tablespoon sesame seeds, toasted
1/8 teaspoon cayenne pepper

1. Place cucumbers in a colander. Set the colander on a plate; sprinkle cucumbers with salt and toss. Let stand for 30 minutes. Rinse and drain well.

2. In a bowl, combine the onions, garlic, soy sauce, vinegar, oil, sesame seeds and cayenne. Add cucumbers and toss to coat. Cover and refrigerate until serving. **Yield:** 8-10 servings.

Chicken Chopped Salad

Diane Halferty, Corpus Christi, Texas

Lime dressing gives lively flavor to this crunchy salad tossed with peaches, peppers and peanuts. The unusual combination is a great way to use up leftover chicken or turkey and packs well for lunches or picnics. It's also terrific with the addition of grapefruit sections or pineapple tidbits.

2 cups chopped *or* torn mixed salad greens
2 cups chopped cooked chicken
1 cup chopped celery
1 can (15-1/4 ounces) peaches, drained and chopped
1 cup chopped sweet red *or* yellow pepper
1/3 cup limeade concentrate
1/4 cup vegetable oil
2 tablespoons vinegar
2 to 3 tablespoons minced fresh cilantro
1-1/2 teaspoons minced fresh gingerroot
1/4 teaspoon salt
1/2 cup dry roasted peanuts

1. In a large salad bowl, combine salad greens, chicken, celery, peaches and red pepper.

2. In a jar with a tight-fitting lid, combine the limeade concentrate, oil, vinegar, cilantro, ginger and salt; shake well. Pour over salad and toss to coat. Sprinkle with peanuts. Serve immediately. **Yield:** 6 servings.

Fruity Green Salad

Helen Petisi, Palm Coast, Florida

My family enjoys this fast and refreshing salad. It's jazzed up with a beautiful blend of red apple, pear, dried cranberries, toasted pecans and Swiss cheese. No matter when I serve it, the light dressing and fruity flavor remind me of springtime.

2/3 cup vegetable oil
1/3 cup lemon juice
1/4 cup sugar
2 teaspoons chopped green onions
3/4 teaspoon salt
1 teaspoon poppy seeds
8 cups torn mixed salad greens
1 medium red apple, chopped
1 medium pear, chopped
1 cup chopped pecans, toasted
1 cup (4 ounces) shredded Swiss cheese
1/4 cup dried cranberries

1. In a jar with a tight-fitting lid, combine the first six ingredients; shake well.

2. In a large bowl, combine the remaining ingredients. Drizzle with dressing and toss to coat. Serve immediately. **Yield:** 16 servings.

Ham Salad Puff

Cheryl McGarva, Taber, Alberta

Rarely do I come home with leftovers when I take this appetizing salad to family gatherings and potlucks at work. It's hearty yet refreshing, and the edible "bowl" makes it fun to serve. Our two sons consider it a treat.

1 cup water
1/2 cup butter
1 cup all-purpose flour
1/4 teaspoon salt
4 eggs
1-1/2 cups cubed fully cooked ham
2 celery ribs, chopped
1/2 cup cooked small shrimp
1/2 cup chopped green pepper
1/2 cup sliced green onions
1/2 cup mayonnaise
1 teaspoon dill weed
Salt and pepper to taste
Lettuce leaves
Additional dill weed, optional

1. In a large saucepan, bring water and butter to a boil. Add flour and salt all at once, stirring until a smooth ball forms. Remove from the heat; let stand for 5 minutes. Add eggs, one at a time, beating well after each addition. Continue beating until mixture is smooth and shiny.

2. Spread dough onto the bottom and up the sides of a greased 9-in. pie plate. Bake at 400° for 30-35 minutes or until puffed and golden brown. Prick the puff with a fork. Cool on a wire rack.

3. In a bowl, combine the ham, celery, shrimp, green pepper, onions, mayonnaise, dill, salt and pepper. Line puff with lettuce; fill with ham mixture. Garnish with dill if desired. Refrigerate leftovers. **Yield:** 4 servings.

Nectarine Chicken Salad

Cathy Ross, Van Nuys, California

When guests are coming for lunch or dinner in the warm summer months, I like to serve this attractive, colorful salad. The dressing is refreshingly tart. A neighbor shared the recipe years ago and I've passed it on many times.

1/4 cup lime juice
1 tablespoon sugar
1 tablespoon minced fresh thyme *or* 1 teaspoon dried thyme
1 tablespoon olive oil
1 garlic clove, minced
6 cups torn mixed salad greens
1 pound boneless skinless chicken breasts, cooked and sliced
5 medium ripe nectarines, thinly sliced

1. In a jar with a tight-fitting lid, combine the lime juice, sugar, thyme, oil and garlic; shake well.

2. On a serving platter, arrange salad greens, chicken and nectarines. Drizzle with dressing. Serve immediately. **Yield:** 4 servings.

Tortellini Caesar Salad

Tammy Steenbock, Sembach Air Base, Germany

This salad was served at a dear friend's baby shower by a health-conscious friend, who suggested the dressing be prepared with reduced-fat or fat-free ingredients. Either way, the creamy dressing has plenty of garlic flavor and coats the pasta, romaine and croutons nicely.

✓ Uses less fat, sugar or salt. Includes Nutritional Analysis and Diabetic Exchanges.

1 package (9 ounces) frozen cheese tortellini
1/2 cup mayonnaise
1/4 cup milk
1/4 cup plus 1/3 cup shredded Parmesan cheese, *divided*
2 tablespoons lemon juice
2 garlic cloves, minced
8 cups torn romaine
1 cup seasoned croutons
Halved cherry tomatoes, optional

1. Cook tortellini according to package directions. Meanwhile, in a small bowl, combine the mayonnaise, milk, 1/4 cup Parmesan cheese, lemon juice and garlic; mix well.

2. Drain tortellini and rinse in cold water; place in a large bowl. Add the romaine and remaining Parmesan.

3. Just before serving, drizzle with dressing and toss to coat. Top with croutons and tomatoes if desired. **Yield:** 10 servings.

Nutritional Analysis: One serving (prepared with fat-free mayonnaise and fat-free milk and without tomatoes) equals 144 calories, 318 mg sodium, 14 mg cholesterol, 18 g carbohydrate, 8 g protein, 4 g fat, 1 g fiber. **Diabetic Exchanges:** 1 starch, 1 vegetable, 1 fat.

Nutty Broccoli Slaw

Dora Clapsaddle, Kensington, Ohio

My daughter gave me the recipe for this delightful salad. The sweet dressing nicely coats a crisp blend of broccoli slaw mix, carrots, onions, almonds and sunflower kernels. Crushed ramen noodles provide even more crunch. It's a smash hit wherever I take it.

1 package (3 ounces) chicken ramen noodles
1 package (16 ounces) broccoli slaw mix
2 cups sliced green onions (about 2 bunches)
1-1/2 cups broccoli florets
1 can (6 ounces) ripe olives, drained and halved
1 cup sunflower kernels, toasted
1/2 cup slivered almonds, toasted
1/2 cup sugar
1/2 cup cider vinegar
1/2 cup olive oil

1. Set aside the noodle seasoning packet; crush the noodles and place in a large bowl. Add the slaw mix, onions, broccoli, olives, sunflower kernels and almonds.

2. In a jar with a tight-fitting lid, combine the sugar, vinegar, oil and contents of seasoning packet; shake well. Drizzle over salad and toss to coat. Serve immediately. **Yield:** 16 servings.

Festive Fruit Salad

Faith Bowman, Selah, Washington

One year I was asked to bring a fruit salad to a family Christmas dinner. I found several recipes, but none seemed special for the holidays. I devised this recipe, and everyone loved it. After that, I became the "official fruit salad person."

✓ Uses less fat, sugar or salt. Includes Nutritional Analysis and Diabetic Exchanges.

1 can (15 ounces) mandarin oranges, drained
1-1/2 cups halved red seedless grapes
1-1/2 cups halved green grapes
1 jar (10 ounces) red maraschino cherries, halved, rinsed and drained
1 jar (10 ounces) green maraschino cherries, halved, rinsed and drained
1 can (8 ounces) unsweetened pineapple chunks, drained
2 cups miniature marshmallows
1 cup flaked coconut
1 cup (8 ounces) sour cream

In a large bowl, combine the first eight ingredients. Just before serving, add sour cream and toss to coat. **Yield:** 12-16 servings.

Nutritional Analysis: One 1/2-cup serving (prepared with fat-free sour cream) equals 149 calories, 18 mg sodium, 1 mg cholesterol, 33 g carbohydrate, 2 g protein, 3 g fat, 1 g fiber. **Diabetic Exchanges:** 2 fruit, 1/2 fat.

Turkey Dumpling Soup, p. 66

Layered Deli Loaf, p. 50

Fresh Veggie Pockets, p. 48

Soups & Sandwiches

A hot bowl of hearty soup and a plate stacked high with tasty sandwiches make a comforting combination. So pair up any of this chapter's selections for a filling lunch or supper.

Parmesan Potato Soup, p. 52

Bacon 'n' Egg Sandwiches, p. 59

Meaty Three-Bean Chili

Sandra Miller, Lees Summit, Missouri

Doubling this recipe is automatic for me—just about everyone wants more than one bowl!

3/4 pound Italian sausage links, cut into 1/2-inch chunks
3/4 pound ground beef
1 large onion, chopped
1 medium green pepper, chopped
1 jalapeno pepper, seeded and minced
2 garlic cloves, minced
1 cup beef broth
1/2 cup Worcestershire sauce
1-1/2 teaspoons chili powder
1 teaspoon pepper
1 teaspoon ground mustard
1/2 teaspoon celery seed
1/2 teaspoon salt
6 cups chopped fresh plum tomatoes (about 2 pounds)
6 bacon strips, cooked and crumbled
1 can (15-1/2 ounces) kidney beans, rinsed and drained
1 can (15 ounces) pinto beans, rinsed and drained
1 can (15 ounces) garbanzo beans, rinsed and drained
Additional chopped onion, optional

1. In a 4-qt. kettle or Dutch oven over medium heat, cook the sausage and beef until no longer pink. Drain; discard all but 1 tablespoon drippings. Set meat aside.

2. Saute onion, peppers and garlic in the drippings for 3 minutes. Add the broth, Worcestershire sauce and seasonings; bring to a boil over medium heat. Reduce heat; cover and simmer for 10 minutes. Add tomatoes, bacon, and browned sausage and beef; return to a boil. Reduce heat; cover and simmer for 30 minutes.

3. Add all of the beans. Simmer for 1 hour, stirring occasionally. Garnish with chopped onion if desired. **Yield:** 10-12 servings (3 quarts).

Editor's Note: When cutting or seeding hot peppers, use rubber or plastic gloves to protect your hands. Avoid touching your face.

Fresh Veggie Pockets

(Pictured on page 46)

Linda Reeves, Cloverdale, Indiana

One summer I worked at a health food store that sold sandwiches. We were close to a college campus, so I made lots of these fresh filled pitas for the students. Crunchy with crisp vegetables and nutty sunflower kernels, they're a fast-to-fix lunch when you're on the go.

✓ Uses less fat, sugar or salt. Includes Nutritional Analysis and Diabetic Exchanges.

1 carton (8 ounces) cream cheese spread
1/4 cup sunflower kernels
1 teaspoon seasoned salt *or* salt-free seasoning blend
4 wheat pita breads, halved
1 medium tomato, thinly sliced
1 medium cucumber, thinly sliced
1 cup sliced fresh mushrooms
1 ripe avocado, peeled and sliced

In a bowl, combine the cream cheese, sunflower kernels and seasoned salt; spread about 2 tablespoons on the inside of each pita half. Layer with tomato, cucumber, mushrooms and avocado. **Yield:** 4 servings.

Nutritional Analysis: One serving (prepared with fat-free cream cheese, unsalted sunflower kernels and salt-free seasoning blend) equals 378 calories, 660 mg sodium, 5 mg cholesterol, 48 g carbohydrate, 18 g protein, 15 g fat, 9 g fiber. **Diabetic Exchanges:** 3 starch, 2 fat, 1 vegetable, 1 meat.

Hot Italian Patties

Brenda Jackson, Garden City, Kansas

I've been making these spicy and satisfying sandwiches for more than a dozen years. On occasion, I substitute country sausage for the Italian sausage, and they taste just as good. Served with a zesty sauce for dipping, they're my family's favorite.

- **1 can (8 ounces) tomato sauce**
- **1/4 teaspoon dried basil**
- **1/4 teaspoon crushed red pepper flakes**
- **1/8 teaspoon garlic powder**
- **1 pound bulk Italian sausage**
- **1 medium onion, thinly sliced and separated into rings**
- **8 slices mozzarella cheese (about 6 ounces)**
- **8 slices French bread (3/4 inch thick)**
- **1/4 to 1/2 cup butter, softened**

1. In a saucepan, combine tomato sauce, basil, pepper flakes and garlic powder. Bring to a boil over medium heat. Reduce heat; simmer for 15 minutes.

2. Meanwhile, shape sausage into four thin oval patties. In a skillet, cook patties over medium heat until no longer pink; remove and keep warm. In the drippings, saute onion until tender. Place a slice of cheese on four slices of bread; top each with a sausage patty, onion and remaining cheese. Top with remaining bread. Butter the outsides of sandwiches.

3. Cook on a griddle or in a large skillet over medium heat until both sides are golden brown and cheese is melted. Serve with herbed tomato sauce for dipping. **Yield:** 4 servings.

Colorful Chicken Croissants

Sheila Lammers, Englewood, Colorado

A friend of mine invented this fruity chicken salad. I've made it many times, and guests are always surprised at the pleasant blend of tastes and textures.

✓ Uses less fat, sugar or salt. Includes Nutritional Analysis and Diabetic Exchanges.

- **2 cups cubed cooked chicken breast**
- **1/4 cup diced celery**
- **1/4 cup golden raisins**
- **1/4 cup dried cranberries**
- **1/4 cup sliced almonds**
- **3/4 cup mayonnaise**
- **2 tablespoons chopped red onion**
- **1/4 teaspoon salt, optional**
- **1/4 teaspoon pepper**
- **4 croissants, split**

In a bowl, combine the first nine ingredients. Spoon about 1/2 cup into each croissant. **Yield:** 4 servings.

Nutritional Analysis: One serving (prepared with fat-free mayonnaise and without salt; calculated without croissant) equals 184 calories, 331 mg sodium, 43 mg cholesterol, 20 g carbohydrate, 13 g protein, 5 g fat, 2 g fiber. **Diabetic Exchanges:** 2 lean meat, 1 fruit, 1 vegetable.

Layered Deli Loaf

(Pictured on page 46)

Sarah Kraemer, Rockford, Illinois

This recipe is special to me because it was handed down from my grandma. A tangy sauce, flavored with horseradish and Dijon mustard, sparks a hearty assortment of meats and cheeses. It feeds a crowd, so it's perfect for a party or potluck. My husband says it's the best sub sandwich he's ever had.

1/4 cup mayonnaise
2 tablespoons prepared horseradish, drained
1 tablespoon Dijon mustard
1 loaf (1 pound) unsliced round bread
2 tablespoons butter, softened
1/3 pound thinly sliced deli ham
1/3 pound sliced Monterey Jack *or* Muenster cheese
1/3 pound thinly sliced deli turkey
1/3 pound sliced cheddar *or* Colby cheese
1/3 pound thinly sliced deli roast beef
1 medium tomato, sliced
1 large dill pickle, sliced lengthwise
1 small red onion, thinly sliced
Lettuce leaves

1. In a small bowl, combine the mayonnaise, horseradish and mustard. Cut bread in half. Carefully hollow out bottom and top of loaf, leaving a 3/4-in. shell (discard removed bread or save for another use). Spread butter on cut sides of bread.

2. In the shell, layer ham, a third of the mayonnaise mixture, Monterey Jack cheese, turkey, a third of the mayonnaise mixture, cheddar cheese, roast beef, remaining mayonnaise mixture, tomato, pickle, onion and lettuce.

3. Replace top. Wrap tightly in plastic wrap; cover and refrigerate for at least 1 hour. **Yield:** 8 servings.

Cajun Burgers

Julie Culbertson, Bensalem, Pennsylvania

My family tends to like its food spicy. I found the original recipe for these burgers in a cookbook, then added and subtracted ingredients until they suited our tastes. Now, Cajun Burgers are always on the menu whenever we have company over for a backyard cookout.

CAJUN SEASONING BLEND:
3 tablespoons ground cumin
3 tablespoons dried oregano
1 tablespoon garlic powder
1 tablespoon paprika
2 teaspoons salt
1 teaspoon cayenne pepper
BURGERS:
1/4 cup finely chopped onion
1 teaspoon salt
1 teaspoon Cajun Seasoning Blend (recipe above)
1/2 to 1 teaspoon hot pepper sauce
1/2 teaspoon dried thyme
1/4 teaspoon dried basil
1 garlic clove, minced
1 pound ground beef
4 hamburger buns
Sauteed onions, optional

1. Combine all seasoning blend ingredients in a small bowl or resealable plastic bag; mix well.

2. In a bowl, combine the first seven burger ingredients; crumble beef over mixture and mix well. Shape into four patties. Cook in a skillet or grill over medium-hot heat for 4-5 minutes per side or until burgers reach desired doneness.

3. Serve on buns; top with sauteed onions if desired. Store remaining seasoning blend in an airtight container. **Yield:** 4 servings.

Editor's Note: Purchased Cajun seasoning may be substituted for the homemade blend.

Split Pea Sausage Soup

Donna Mae Young, Menomonie, Wisconsin

When my husband and I eat out and enjoy a dish, I go home and try to duplicate it. That's how I came up with this recipe. While it's good at any time, we like it full and hearty over the winter.

1 pound smoked kielbasa
1 pound dry split peas
6 cups water
1 cup chopped carrots
1 cup chopped onion
1 cup chopped celery
1 tablespoon minced fresh parsley
1 teaspoon salt
1/2 teaspoon coarse black pepper
2 bay leaves

1. Cut sausage in half lengthwise; cut into 1/4-in. pieces. Place in a Dutch oven or soup kettle; add remaining ingredients. Bring to a boil.

2. Reduce heat; cover and simmer for 1-1/4 to 1-1/2 hours or until peas are tender. Remove bay leaves. **Yield:** 8 servings (2 quarts).

Sausage Broccoli Chowder

Donald Roberts, Amherst, New Hampshire

In New England, we frequently have cool fall evenings that call for a dinner that warms you all over. This chowder does just that. I must admit I don't care too much for the taste of broccoli, but I really like this chowder.

1 pound bulk Italian sausage
1 medium onion, chopped
3 garlic cloves, minced
1/2 pound fresh mushrooms, sliced
2 tablespoons butter
2 cups broccoli florets
2 to 3 carrots, diced
2 cans (14-1/2 ounces *each*) chicken broth
1 can (10-3/4 ounces) condensed cream of mushroom soup, undiluted
1 package (9 ounces) refrigerated cheese tortellini, cooked and drained
1/2 teaspoon pepper
1/2 teaspoon dried thyme
2 quarts half-and-half cream
1/2 cup grated Romano cheese

1. In a skillet, cook sausage over medium heat until no longer pink. Remove to paper towels to drain; set aside. In the same skillet, saute onion, garlic and mushrooms in butter until tender; set aside.

2. In a Dutch oven, cook the broccoli and carrots in chicken broth until tender. Stir in sausage and the mushroom mixture. Add soup, tortellini, pepper, basil and thyme; heat through. Stir in half-and-half cream and Romano cheese; heat through. **Yield:** 12-16 servings (4 quarts).

Ground Beef Gyros

Ruth Stahl, Shepherd, Montana

If your family likes gyros as much as mine, they'll love this easy version that's made with ground beef instead of lamb. I found the recipe in a newspaper and adapted it to fit our tastes. They're very much like the ones served at a local restaurant. A cucumber yogurt sauce adds an authentic finishing touch.

☑ Uses less fat, sugar or salt. Includes Nutritional Analysis and Diabetic Exchanges.

1 carton (8 ounces) plain yogurt
1/3 cup chopped seeded cucumber
2 tablespoons finely chopped onion
1 garlic clove, minced
1 teaspoon sugar

FILLING:

1 pound ground beef
1-1/2 teaspoons dried oregano
1 teaspoon garlic powder
1 teaspoon onion powder
1 teaspoon salt, optional
3/4 teaspoon pepper
4 pita breads, halved, warmed
3 cups shredded lettuce
1 large tomato, chopped
1 small onion, sliced

1. In a bowl, combine the first five ingredients. Cover and refrigerate.

2. In a bowl, combine beef and seasonings; mix well. Shape into four patties. Grill, covered, over medium-hot heat for 10-12 minutes, turning once.

3. Cut patties into thin slices; stuff into pita halves. Add lettuce, tomato and onion. Serve with the yogurt sauce. **Yield:** 4 servings.

Nutritional Analysis: One serving (prepared with fat-free yogurt and lean ground beef and without salt) equals 422 calories, 453 mg sodium, 42 mg cholesterol, 45 g carbohydrate, 33 g protein, 11 g fat, 3 g fiber. **Diabetic Exchanges:** 3-1/2 meat, 3 starch.

Parmesan Potato Soup

(Pictured on page 47)

Tami Walters, Kingsport, Tennessee

Even my husband, who's not much of a soup eater, likes this. Our two boys do, too. With homemade bread and a salad, it's a satisfying meal.

4 medium baking potatoes (about 2 pounds)
3/4 cup chopped onion
1/2 cup butter
1/2 cup all-purpose flour
1/2 teaspoon dried basil
1/2 teaspoon seasoned salt
1/4 teaspoon celery salt
1/4 teaspoon garlic powder
1/4 teaspoon onion salt
1/4 teaspoon pepper
1/4 teaspoon rubbed sage
1/4 teaspoon dried thyme
4-1/2 cups chicken broth
6 cups milk
3/4 to 1 cup grated Parmesan cheese
10 bacon strips, cooked and crumbled

1. Pierce potatoes with a fork; bake in the oven or microwave until tender. Cool, peel and cube; set aside.

2. In a large Dutch oven or soup kettle over medium heat, saute onion in butter until tender. Stir in flour and seasonings. Gradually add broth, stirring constantly. Bring to a boil; cook and stir for 2 minutes.

3. Add potatoes; return to a boil. Reduce heat; cover and simmer for 10 minutes. Add milk and cheese; heat through. Stir in bacon. **Yield:** 10-12 servings.

Savory Cheese Soup

Dee Falk, Stromsburg, Nebraska

This delicious soup recipe was shared by a friend and instantly became a hit with my husband. Its big cheese flavor blends wonderfully with the flavor of the vegetables. I first served this creamy soup as part of a holiday meal, but now we enjoy it throughout the year.

1/4 cup chopped onion
3 tablespoons butter
1/4 cup all-purpose flour
1/4 teaspoon salt
1/8 teaspoon pepper
1/8 teaspoon garlic powder
2 cups milk
1 can (14-1/2 ounces) chicken broth
1/2 cup shredded carrots
1/2 cup finely chopped celery
1-1/2 cups (6 ounces) shredded cheddar cheese
3/4 cup shredded mozzarella cheese
Fresh *or* dried chives, optional

1. In a large saucepan, saute onion in butter until tender. Add flour, salt, pepper and garlic powder; stir until smooth. Gradually add milk; cook and stir over medium heat until thickened and bubbly.

2. Meanwhile, bring chicken broth to a boil in a small saucepan. Add carrots and celery; simmer for 5 minutes or until vegetables are tender. Add to milk mixture and stir until blended. Add cheeses. Cook and stir until melted (do not boil). Garnish with chives if desired. **Yield:** about 4 servings.

Barbecued Turkey Sandwiches

Pamela Siegrist, Fort Recovery, Ohio

I have an excellent source for turkey recipes, since many of our neighbors are poultry farmers! These satisfying sandwiches, with their mildly tangy sauce, are a great way to use up leftover turkey from the holidays.

2 celery ribs, chopped
1/2 cup chopped onion
1/4 cup chopped green pepper
1/3 cup butter
1/2 cup ketchup
1/4 cup packed brown sugar
3 tablespoons Worcestershire sauce
1-1/2 teaspoons chili powder
1 teaspoon salt
1/8 teaspoon pepper
1/8 teaspoon hot pepper sauce
4 cups shredded cooked turkey
8 hamburger buns, split, toasted and buttered

1. In a saucepan, saute the celery, onion and green pepper in butter until tender. Add the next seven ingredients.

2. Bring to a boil. Reduce heat; cover and simmer for 5 minutes. Add turkey; heat through. Serve on buns. **Yield:** 8 servings.

Spinach Cheese Swirls

Mary Nichols, Dover, New Hampshire

Even my children like dividing up this super-easy sandwich, which is brimming with great spinach and onion flavor. Refrigerated pizza dough shaves minutes off prep time and creates a golden brown crust. The cheesy slices taste terrific warm or cold, so they're great for lunches, picnics or trips.

1 package (10 ounces) frozen chopped spinach, thawed and drained
2 cups (8 ounces) shredded mozzarella cheese
1 cup finely chopped onion
1 garlic clove, minced
1 tube (10 ounces) refrigerated pizza crust

1. In a bowl, combine the first four ingredients and mix well.

2. On a greased baking sheet, roll pizza dough into a 14-in. x 10-in. rectangle; seal any holes. Spoon filling over crust to within 1 in. of edge. Roll up jelly-roll style, starting with a long side; seal the ends and place the seam side down.

3. Bake at 400° for 25-27 minutes or until golden brown. Cut into slices. **Yield:** 4 servings.

Sizzling Rice Soup

Mary Woodke, Gardiner, New York

My family enjoys food with flair like this unique soup. Whenever I serve it, it's such a hit that no one has much room for the main course. The children get a real kick out of watching the rice sizzle when it gets added to the soup.

1 cup uncooked long grain rice
8 cups chicken broth
2 cups cubed cooked chicken
2 cups sliced fresh mushrooms
1/4 cup chopped green onions
1 can (8 ounces) bamboo shoots, drained
1 can (8 ounces) sliced water chestnuts, drained
4 chicken bouillon cubes
1/2 teaspoon garlic powder
1 package (10 ounces) frozen peas
1/4 cup vegetable oil

1. Cook rice according to package directions. Spread on a greased 15-in. x 10-in. x 1-in. baking pan. Bake at 325° for 2 hours or until dried and browned, stirring occasionally; set aside.

2. In a large soup kettle or Dutch oven, combine the broth, chicken, mushrooms, onions, bamboo shoots, water chestnuts, bouillon and garlic powder. Cover and simmer for 1 hour. Add peas; cook for 15 minutes.

3. Just before serving, heat oil in a skillet. Fry rice in hot oil until it is slightly puffed. Ladle soup into serving bowls. Immediately spoon some hot rice into each bowl and it will sizzle. **Yield:** 10-12 servings (3 quarts).

Garden-Fresh Tomato Soup

Charlotte Goldbery, Honey Grove, Pennsylvania

You'll never buy canned tomato soup again once you taste this super from-scratch version.

1/2 cup butter
2 tablespoons olive oil
1 large onion, sliced
2 sprigs fresh thyme *or* 1/2 teaspoon dried thyme
4 fresh basil leaves *or* 1/2 teaspoon dried basil
1 teaspoon salt
1/4 teaspoon pepper
2-1/2 pounds diced fresh ripe tomatoes *or* 2 cans (16 ounces *each*) Italian-style tomatoes, undrained
3 tablespoons tomato paste
1/4 cup all-purpose flour
3-3/4 cups chicken broth, *divided*
1 teaspoon sugar
1 cup heavy whipping cream

CROUTONS:

1 garlic clove, sliced lengthwise
8 slices day-old French *or* Italian bread
2 tablespoons olive oil

1. In a large kettle, heat butter and oil over medium-high heat. Add onion and seasonings. Cook, stirring occasionally, until the onion is soft. Add the tomatoes and paste. Stir to blend. Simmer for 10 minutes.

2. Place the flour in a small mixing bowl and stir in 1/4 cup chicken broth. Stir into the tomato mixture. Add the remaining broth. Simmer for 30 minutes, stirring frequently.

3. Allow mixture to cool and run through a sieve, food mill or food processor. Return pureed mixture to the kettle. Add the sugar and cream. Heat through, stirring occasionally.

4. For croutons, rub garlic over both sides of the bread. Brush with oil and place on a baking sheet. Bake at 350° for 10-12 minutes or until toasted. Turn and toast the other side for 2-3 minutes. Just before serving, top each bowl with croutons. **Yield:** 8 servings.

Curried Leek Soup

Arnold Foss, Mercer, Maine

New England is known for its hearty soups. I like to experiment with recipes. Luckily I have a wife who lets me mess up her kitchen! I came up with this recipe the first year I grew leeks in my garden.

3 medium leeks (white portion only), thinly sliced
1 garlic clove, minced
2 tablespoons butter
1 can (14-1/2 ounces) chicken broth
3/4 cup water
1-1/2 cups thinly sliced carrots
2 celery ribs, thinly sliced
2 teaspoons chicken bouillon granules
1/2 teaspoon curry powder
1/8 teaspoon pepper
1 can (12 ounces) fat-free evaporated milk

1. In a 3-qt. saucepan, saute leeks and garlic in butter over medium heat until tender. Add the broth, water, carrots, celery, bouillon, curry powder and pepper. Bring to a boil. Reduce heat; cover and simmer for 20-25 minutes or until vegetables are tender. Cool slightly.

2. Place 1 cup soup in a blender or food processor; cover and process until smooth. Return to pan. Add milk; heat through (do not boil). **Yield:** 4 servings.

Harvest Turkey Soup

Linda Sand, Winsted, Connecticut

The recipe for this super soup evolved over the years. I've been diabetic since I was 12, so I've learned to use herbs and spices to make dishes like this taste terrific. It also has a colorful blend of vegetables.

✓ Uses less fat, sugar or salt. Includes Nutritional Analysis and Diabetic Exchanges.

- **1 turkey carcass (from a 12-pound turkey)**
- **5 quarts water**
- **2 large carrots, shredded**
- **1 cup chopped celery**
- **1 large onion, chopped**
- **4 chicken bouillon cubes**
- **1 can (28 ounces) stewed tomatoes**
- **3/4 cup fresh *or* frozen peas**
- **3/4 cup long grain rice**
- **1 package (10 ounces) frozen chopped spinach**
- **1 tablespoon salt, optional**
- **3/4 teaspoon pepper**
- **1/2 teaspoon dried marjoram**
- **1/2 teaspoon dried thyme**

1. Place the turkey carcass and water in a Dutch oven or soup kettle; bring to a boil. Reduce heat; cover and simmer for 1-1/2 hours. Remove carcass; allow to cool.

2. Remove turkey from bones and cut into bite-size pieces; set aside. Strain broth. Add carrots, celery, onion and bouillon; bring to a boil. Reduce heat; cover and simmer for 30 minutes.

3. Add the tomatoes, peas, rice, spinach, salt if desired, pepper, marjoram, thyme and reserved turkey. Return to a boil; cook, uncovered, for 20 minutes or until rice is tender. **Yield:** 22 servings (5-1/2 quarts).

Nutritional Analysis: One 1-cup serving (prepared with reduced-sodium bouillon and without salt) equals 289 calories, 218 mg sodium, 107 mg cholesterol, 11 g carbohydrate, 43 g protein, 7 g fat. **Diabetic Exchanges:** 4 very lean meat, 1 fat, 1 starch, 1 vegetable.

Crabby Bagels

Connie Faulkner, Moxee, Washington

When my husband and I get tired of the peanut butter and jelly our daughter favors, we make this "grown-up" sandwich shared by a dear lady at church.

- **1 can (6 ounces) crabmeat, drained, flaked and cartilage removed**
- **1/2 cup shredded cheddar cheese**
- **1/4 cup finely chopped celery**
- **1/4 cup sour cream**
- **3/4 teaspoon Worcestershire sauce**
- **1/4 teaspoon salt**
- **4 onion bagels, split**
- **1 package (3 ounces) cream cheese, softened**
- **4 lettuce leaves**

1. In a bowl, combine the first six ingredients. Toast bagels; spread with cream cheese.

2. On the bottom of each bagel, place a lettuce leaf and 1/4 cup of crab mixture. Replace tops. **Yield:** 4 servings.

Mexican Chicken Corn Chowder

Susan Garoutte, Georgetown, Texas

I like to make this smooth, creamy soup when company comes to visit. Its zippy flavor is full of Southwestern flair. My family enjoys dipping slices of homemade bread in this chowder to soak up every bite!

1-1/2 pounds boneless skinless chicken breasts
1/2 cup chopped onion
1 to 2 garlic cloves, minced
3 tablespoons butter
2 chicken bouillon cubes
1 cup hot water
1/2 to 1 teaspoon ground cumin
2 cups half-and-half cream
2 cups (8 ounces) shredded Monterey Jack cheese
1 can (16 ounces) cream-style corn
1 can (4 ounces) chopped green chilies, undrained
1/4 to 1 teaspoon hot pepper sauce
1 medium tomato, chopped
Fresh cilantro, optional

1. Cut chicken into bite-size pieces. In a Dutch oven, cook chicken, onion and garlic in butter until chicken is no longer pink.

2. Dissolve the bouillon in hot water. Add to pan along with cumin; bring to a boil. Reduce heat; cover and simmer for 5 minutes.

3. Add cream, cheese, corn, chilies and hot pepper sauce. Cook and stir over low heat until the cheese is melted. Stir in tomato. Serve immediately; garnish with cilantro if desired. **Yield:** 6-8 servings (2 quarts).

Chunky Beef Noodle Soup

Lil Morris, Emerald Park, Saskatchewan

My husband and I lived for 11 years in the Arctic, where there was very little fresh produce and I had to order nonperishable groceries for a year ahead of time. This hearty soup—a meal in itself served with warm rolls—became a staple in our diet because it requires ingredients I could easily find.

- **1 pound boneless round steak, cut into 1/2-inch cubes**
- **1 medium onion, chopped**
- **2 garlic cloves, minced**
- **1 tablespoon vegetable oil**
- **2 cups water**
- **1 can (14-1/2 ounces) diced tomatoes, undrained**
- **1 can (10-1/2 ounces) condensed beef consomme, undiluted**
- **1 to 2 teaspoons chili powder**
- **1 teaspoon salt**
- **1/2 teaspoon dried oregano**
- **1 cup uncooked spiral pasta**
- **1 medium green pepper, chopped**
- **1/4 cup minced fresh parsley**

1. In a large saucepan, cook round steak, onion and garlic in oil until the meat is browned and the onion is tender, about 5 minutes.

2. Stir in water, tomatoes, consomme and seasonings; bring to a boil. Reduce heat; cover and simmer until meat is tender, about 1-1/2 hours.

3. Stir in pasta and green pepper. Simmer, uncovered, until noodles are tender, about 8 minutes. Add parsley. **Yield:** 8 servings (2 quarts).

Mushroom Steak Hoagies

Jennifer Walker, Logan, Utah

My Aunt Diane perfected the recipe for these hearty hoagies. We often double or triple it for family gatherings since they're such a hit. I begin marinating the beef the night before so the sandwiches can be put together in less than 30 minutes on a hectic evening.

- **1 cup water**
- **1/3 cup soy sauce**
- **1-1/2 teaspoons garlic powder**
- **1-1/2 teaspoons pepper**
- **1 pound round steak, cut into 1/4-inch strips**
- **1 medium onion, chopped**
- **1 medium green pepper, julienned**
- **1 can (4 ounces) mushroom stems and pieces, drained**
- **2 cups (8 ounces) shredded mozzarella cheese**
- **6 hoagie buns, split and toasted**

Sliced tomatoes

1. In a large resealable plastic bag or shallow glass container, combine the water, soy sauce, garlic powder and pepper. Add steak and turn to coat. Seal or cover and refrigerate for 6-8 hours or overnight. Drain and discard marinade.

2. In a large skillet, brown steak over medium heat. Add the onion, green pepper and mushrooms; stir-fry until tender. Reduce heat. Sprinkle with cheese.

3. Remove from the heat; stir until cheese is melted and meat is coated. Spoon onto buns; top with tomatoes. **Yield:** 6 servings.

Pear Waldorf Pitas

Roxann Parker, Dover, Delaware

Here's a guaranteed table-brightener for a shower, luncheon or party. Just stand back and watch these sandwiches vanish. For an eye-catching presentation, I tuck each one into a colorful folded napkin.

☑ Uses less fat, sugar or salt. Includes Nutritional Analysis and Diabetic Exchanges.

2 medium ripe pears, diced
1/2 cup thinly sliced celery
1/2 cup halved seedless red grapes
2 tablespoons finely chopped walnuts
2 tablespoons lemon yogurt
2 tablespoons mayonnaise
1/8 teaspoon poppy seeds
10 miniature pita pockets, halved
Lettuce leaves

1. In a bowl, combine pears, celery, grapes and walnuts. In another bowl, combine yogurt, mayonnaise and poppy seeds; mix well. Add to pear mixture; toss to coat. Refrigerate for 1 hour or overnight.

2. To serve, line pita halves with lettuce and add 2 tablespoons pear mixture. **Yield:** 10 servings.

Nutritional Analysis: One serving (prepared with fat-free yogurt and reduced-fat mayonnaise) equals 117 calories, 165 mg sodium, 1 mg cholesterol, 23 g carbohydrate, 4 g protein, 2 g fat, 2 g fiber. **Diabetic Exchanges:** 1 starch, 1/2 fruit.

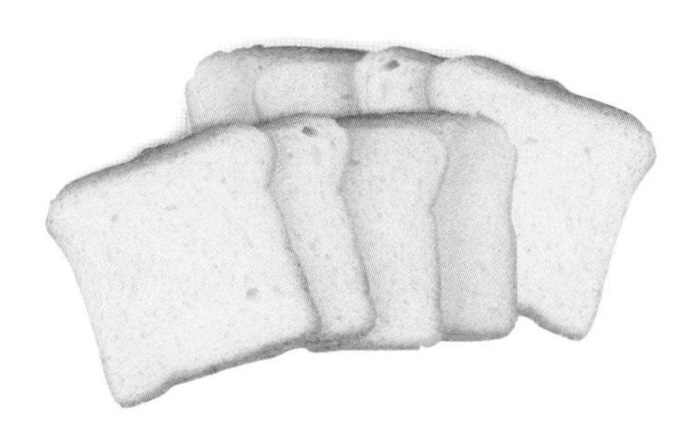

Bacon 'n' Egg Sandwiches

(Pictured on page 47)

Ann Fuemmeler, Glasgow, Missouri

I came across this unique grilled combo when I was digging in my mom's recipe box. The crisp bacon, hard-cooked eggs and crunchy green onions make these special sandwiches look impressive when company drops by for lunch. Best of all, they're a snap to assemble.

1/2 cup sour cream
8 slices bread
4 green onions, chopped
4 slices process American cheese
2 hard-cooked eggs, cut into 1/4-inch slices
8 bacon strips, cooked and drained
1/4 cup butter, softened

1. Spread sour cream on one side of four slices of bread. Top with onions, cheese, eggs and bacon. Top with the remaining bread.

2. Butter outsides of sandwiches; cook in a large skillet over medium heat until golden brown on both sides. **Yield:** 4 servings.

Curried Pumpkin Soup

Kimberly Knepper, Euless, Texas

I whipped up this satisfying soup one Thanksgiving for my family, and everyone was crazy about it! Even my brother, who is one of the pickiest eaters I know, asked for seconds.

1/2 pound fresh mushrooms, sliced
1/2 cup chopped onion
2 tablespoons butter
2 tablespoons all-purpose flour
1/2 to 1 teaspoon curry powder
3 cups vegetable broth
1 can (15 ounces) solid-pack pumpkin
1 can (12 ounces) evaporated milk
1 tablespoon honey
1/2 teaspoon salt
1/4 teaspoon pepper
1/4 teaspoon ground nutmeg
Fresh *or* frozen chives, optional

1. In a large saucepan, saute the mushrooms and onion in butter until tender. Stir in the flour and curry powder until blended. Gradually add the broth. Bring to a boil; cook and stir for 2 minutes or until thickened.

2. Add the pumpkin, milk, honey, salt, pepper and nutmeg; heat through. Garnish with chives if desired. **Yield:** 7 servings.

Cheesy Chicken Subs

Jane Hollar, Vilas, North Carolina

I've been part of the Food Services staff at Appalachian State University for over 30 years. One summer we created this flavorful sandwich which combines seasoned grilled chicken, Swiss cheese and sauteed mushrooms and onions. Thousands of students have enjoyed this wonderful sub since then.

12 ounces boneless skinless chicken breasts, cut into strips
1 envelope Parmesan Italian *or* Caesar salad dressing mix
1 cup sliced fresh mushrooms
1/2 cup sliced red onion
1/4 cup olive oil
4 submarine sandwich rolls, split and toasted
4 slices Swiss cheese

1. Place chicken in a bowl; sprinkle with salad dressing mix. In a skillet, saute mushrooms and onion in oil for 3 minutes. Add chicken; saute for 6 minutes or until chicken juices run clear.

2. Spoon mixture onto roll bottoms; top with cheese. Broil 4 in. from the heat for 4 minutes or until cheese is melted. Replace tops. **Yield:** 4 servings.

Beefy Wild Rice Soup

Marilyn Chesbrough, Wautoma, Wisconsin

Living in central Wisconsin, we experience many days of snow and cold temperatures. I like to prepare soup often, especially this one. My family loves it.

1 pound ground beef
1/2 teaspoon Italian seasoning
6 cups water, *divided*
2 large onions, chopped
3 celery ribs, chopped
1 cup uncooked wild rice
2 teaspoons beef bouillon granules
1/2 teaspoon pepper
1/4 teaspoon hot pepper sauce
3 cans (10-3/4 ounces *each*) condensed cream of mushroom soup, undiluted
1 can (4 ounces) mushroom stems and pieces, drained

1. In a Dutch oven or soup kettle, cook beef and Italian seasoning over medium heat until meat is no longer pink; drain. Add 2 cups water, onions, celery, rice, bouillon, pepper and hot pepper sauce; bring to a boil.

2. Reduce heat; cover and simmer for 45 minutes. Stir in the soup, mushrooms and remaining water. Cover and simmer for 30 minutes. **Yield:** 10-12 servings (3 quarts).

Apple Tuna Sandwiches

Ivy Eresmas, Dade City, Florida

My husband and his buddies love to pack these tasty sandwiches when they go on fishing trips. The tangy tuna salad gets fun flavor from sweet pickle relish and lots of crunch from apples, celery and walnuts. The satisfying sandwiches are a complete meal in themselves.

✓ Uses less fat, sugar or salt. Includes Nutritional Analysis and Diabetic Exchanges.

1 can (6 ounces) tuna in water, drained
1/2 cup chopped red apple
1/3 cup fat-free mayonnaise
1/4 cup finely chopped celery
1/4 cup finely chopped walnuts
2 tablespoons finely chopped onion
1 tablespoon sweet pickle relish
1 teaspoon sugar
1/4 teaspoon salt
6 slices reduced-calorie bread, toasted
6 lettuce leaves

In a bowl, combine the first nine ingredients. Spread 1/2 cup on three slices of bread. Top with lettuce and remaining bread. **Yield:** 3 servings.

Nutritional Analysis: One serving (calculated without bread) equals 262 calories, 817 mg sodium, 17 mg cholesterol, 31 g carbohydrate, 22 g protein, 7 g fat, 5 g fiber. **Diabetic Exchanges:** 2 starch, 2 lean meat.

Swedish Meatball Soup

Debora Taylor, Inkom, Idaho

To me, this is a very comforting, filling, homey soup. I especially like cooking it during winter months and serving it with hot rolls, bread or muffins.

- **1 egg**
- **2 cups half-and-half cream, *divided***
- **1 cup soft bread crumbs**
- **1 small onion, finely chopped**
- **1-3/4 teaspoons salt, *divided***
- **1-1/2 pounds ground beef**
- **1 tablespoon butter**
- **3 tablespoons all-purpose flour**
- **3/4 teaspoon beef bouillon granules**
- **1/2 teaspoon pepper**
- **1/8 to 1/4 teaspoon garlic salt**
- **3 cups water**
- **1 pound red potatoes, cubed**
- **1 package (10 ounces) frozen peas, thawed**

1. In a bowl, beat egg; add 1/3 cup cream, bread crumbs, onion and 1 teaspoon of salt. Add beef; mix well. Shape into 1/2-in. balls. In a Dutch oven or soup kettle, brown meatballs in butter, half at a time. Remove from the pan; set aside. Drain fat.

2. To pan, add flour, bouillon, pepper, garlic salt and remaining salt; stir until smooth. Gradually stir in water; bring to a boil, stirring often. Add the potatoes and meatballs.

3. Reduce heat; cover and simmer for 25 minutes or until the potatoes are tender. Stir in peas and remaining cream; heat through. **Yield:** 9 servings (about 2 quarts).

Cauliflower Ham Chowder

Arline Hofland, Deer Lodge, Montana

I came up with this recipe when I had a ham hock and wanted to make something other than the usual split pea soup. The resulting chowder was satisfying and good-tasting. Mashed potatoes help give it a rich, creamy texture.

- **1 meaty ham bone**
- **2 quarts water**
- **1 large onion, chopped**
- **1 medium green pepper, chopped**
- **1/2 cup butter**
- **3/4 cup all-purpose flour**
- **1-1/2 teaspoons salt**
- **1/4 teaspoon pepper**
- **4 cups milk**
- **4 cups cauliflowerets, cooked and drained**
- **2 cups mashed potatoes (prepared with milk and butter)**
- **Minced fresh parsley, optional**

1. In a Dutch oven or soup kettle, simmer ham bone in water for 1-1/2 hours. Remove ham bone; set cooking liquid aside. When cool enough to handle, remove meat from bone; discard bone. Return ham to cooking liquid; set aside.

2. In a saucepan, saute onion and green pepper in butter until tender. Stir in flour, salt and pepper until blended. Gradually add milk. Bring to a boil; cook and stir for 2 minutes or until thickened.

3. Add to ham and liquid. Add cauliflower and potatoes. Cook until heated through. Sprinkle with parsley if desired. **Yield:** 14 servings.

Apple-Walnut Turkey Sandwiches

Cathy Dobbins, Rio Rancho, New Mexico

When you live where temperatures easily climb to 100° or more in the summer, you look for recipes that get you in and out of the kitchen in minutes. This luscious sandwich, with its cool Waldorf salad filling, is a breeze to prepare.

3/4 cup mayonnaise
1/4 cup chopped celery
1/4 cup raisins
1/4 cup chopped walnuts, toasted
1 medium tart apple, chopped
3/4 pound sliced deli turkey
8 slices sourdough bread
Lettuce leaves

1. In a bowl, combine mayonnaise, celery, raisins and walnuts. Stir in apple; set aside.

2. Place turkey on four slices of bread. Top with the apple mixture, lettuce and remaining bread. **Yield:** 4 servings.

Rich French Onion Soup

Linda Adolph, Edmonton, Alberta

When entertaining guests, I bring out this savory soup while we're waiting for the main course. It's simple to make—just saute the onions early in the day and let the soup simmer until dinnertime. In winter, big bowls of it make a warming supper with a salad and biscuits.

6 large onions, chopped
1/2 cup butter
6 cans (10-1/2 ounces *each*) condensed beef broth, undiluted
1-1/2 teaspoons Worcestershire sauce
3 bay leaves
10 slices French bread, toasted
Shredded Parmesan and mozzarella cheeses

1. In a large skillet, saute onions in butter until crisp-tender. Transfer to an ungreased 5-qt. slow cooker. Add the broth, Worcestershire sauce and bay leaves.

2. Cover and cook on low for 5-7 hours or until the onions are tender. Discard bay leaves. Top each serving with French bread and cheeses. **Yield:** 10 servings.

Stock It in the Freezer

Before freezing homemade soup, refrigerate it until the fat rises to the surface; skim off the fat. Place resealable plastic freezer bags in individual soup bowls; fill with soup and freeze. When solid, remove the bag from the bowl. Seal and return to the freezer for up to 3 months.

Egg Salad Pitas

Ricquel Stinson, Mount Orab, Ohio

I came up with this recipe purely by accident. I was making egg salad and kept adding different seasonings. When my friend tried it, she raved about it.

2/3 cup mayonnaise
2 tablespoons sweet pickle relish
1 teaspoon prepared mustard
1/4 teaspoon pepper
1/4 teaspoon celery salt
1/4 teaspoon paprika
1/4 teaspoon dried basil
1/4 teaspoon salt
6 hard-cooked eggs, coarsely chopped
1/2 cup shredded cheddar cheese
1 small onion, finely chopped
1 large carrot, grated
2 bacon strips, cooked and crumbled
3 pita breads (6 inches), halved
Lettuce leaves and sliced tomatoes, optional

1. In a bowl, combine the first eight ingredients. Stir in the eggs, cheese, onion, carrot and bacon.

2. Spoon about 1/2 cup into each pita half. Add lettuce and tomatoes if desired. **Yield:** 3-6 servings.

Cheesy Sausage Stromboli

Vada McRoberts, Silver Lake, Kansas

I've had a hundred requests for this recipe over the years. Perfect for brunch or as an evening snack, this sausage-filled sandwich is not tricky to make...and I never have to worry about storing leftovers!

5 cups all-purpose flour
2 tablespoons sugar
2 teaspoons salt
2 packages (1/4 ounce *each*) active dry yeast
1-1/2 cups warm water (120° to 130°)
1/2 cup warm milk (120° to 130°)
2 tablespoons butter, melted
2 pounds bulk pork sausage
4 cups (16 ounces) shredded mozzarella cheese
3 eggs
1 teaspoon minced fresh basil *or* 1/4 teaspoon dried basil
2 tablespoons grated Parmesan cheese

1. In a mixing bowl, combine flour, sugar, salt and yeast. Add water, milk and butter; beat on low until well combined. Turn onto a well-floured surface; knead until smooth and elastic, 6-8 minutes. Place in a greased bowl, turning once to grease top. Cover and let rise in a warm place until doubled, about 1 hour.

2. Meanwhile, in a skillet, cook sausage over medium heat until no longer pink; drain and cool. Stir in mozzarella, 2 eggs and basil; set aside.

3. Punch dough down; divide in half. Roll one portion into a 15-in. x 10-in. rectangle on a greased baking sheet. Spoon half of the sausage mixture lengthwise down one side of rectangle to within 1 in. of edges. Fold dough over filling; pinch edges to seal. Cut four diagonal slits on top of stromboli. Repeat with remaining dough and filling.

4. Beat remaining egg; brush over loaves. Sprinkle with Parmesan. Cover and let rise until doubled, about 45 minutes. Bake at 375° for 20-25 minutes or until golden brown. Slice; serve warm. **Yield:** 2 loaves.

Fajita Pitas

Diana Jones, Springtown, Texas

I was late coming home one evening and forgot to pick up tortillas for the fajitas we planned for dinner. So we used pita bread that I had in the freezer instead. The warm chicken-filled pockets, garnished with a homemade sauce and other tasty toppings, are often requested when we're hungry for something in a hurry.

6 boneless skinless chicken breast halves
1 large onion, sliced
1 large green pepper, thinly sliced
1 tablespoon vegetable oil
2 cups (8 ounces) shredded Mexican cheese blend
8 pita breads, halved

SAUCE:

1 medium onion, finely chopped
1 medium tomato, finely chopped
1/2 jalapeno pepper, finely chopped
1 tablespoon minced fresh cilantro
1 tablespoon vegetable oil

Guacamole and sour cream, optional

1. Grill chicken, covered, over medium heat for 16-20 minutes or until juices run clear. Cut into strips.

2. In a skillet, saute onion and green pepper in oil. Add chicken and cheese. Stuff into pita halves; place on an ungreased baking sheet. Bake at 325° for 10 minutes or until cheese is melted.

3. Meanwhile, for sauce, combine the onion, tomato, jalapeno, cilantro and oil in a bowl; mix well. Serve sauce, guacamole and sour cream if desired with pitas. **Yield:** 8 servings.

Editor's Note: When cutting or seeding hot peppers, use rubber or plastic gloves to protect your hands. Avoid touching your face.

Turkey Dumpling Soup

(Pictured on page 46)

Debbie Wolf, Mission Viejo, California

Simmering up a big pot of this soup is one of my favorite holiday traditions. This is a variation on a recipe my mom made while I was growing up. My husband and children can't get enough of the tender dumplings.

1 meaty leftover turkey carcass (from an 11-pound turkey)
6 cups chicken broth
6 cups water
2 celery ribs, cut into 1-inch slices
1 medium carrot, cut into 1-inch slices
1 tablespoon poultry seasoning
1 bay leaf
1/2 teaspoon salt
1/2 teaspoon pepper

SOUP INGREDIENTS:

1 medium onion, chopped
2 celery ribs, chopped
2 medium carrots, sliced
1 cup fresh *or* frozen cut green beans
1 package (10 ounces) frozen corn
1 package (10 ounces) frozen peas
2 cups biscuit/baking mix
2/3 cup milk

1. In a large soup kettle or Dutch oven, combine the first nine ingredients. Bring to a boil. Reduce heat; cover and simmer for 3 hours.

2. Remove carcass and allow to cool. Remove meat and set aside 4 cups for soup (refrigerate any remaining meat for another use); discard bones. Strain broth, discarding vegetables and bay leaf.

3. Return broth to kettle; add onion, celery, carrots and beans. Bring to a boil. Reduce heat; cover and simmer for 10 minutes or until vegetables are tender. Add corn, peas and reserved turkey. Bring to a boil; reduce the heat.

4. Combine biscuit mix and milk. Drop by teaspoonfuls onto simmering broth. Cover and simmer for 10 minutes or until a toothpick inserted in a dumpling comes out clean (do not lift the cover while simmering). **Yield:** 16 servings (4 quarts).

The Ultimate Grilled Cheese

Kathy Norris, Streator, Illinois

These gooey grilled cheese sandwiches, subtly seasoned with garlic, taste great for lunch with sliced apples. And they're really fast to whip up, too. To save seconds, I soften the cream cheese in the microwave, then blend it with the rest of the ingredients in the same bowl. That makes cleanup a breeze.

1 package (3 ounces) cream cheese, softened
3/4 cup mayonnaise
1 cup (4 ounces) shredded cheddar cheese
1 cup (4 ounces) shredded mozzarella cheese
1/2 teaspoon garlic powder
1/8 teaspoon seasoned salt
10 slices Italian bread (1/2 inch thick)
2 tablespoons butter, softened

1. In a mixing bowl, beat cream cheese and mayonnaise until smooth. Stir in cheeses, garlic powder and seasoned salt. Spread five slices of bread with the cheese mixture, about 1/3 cup on each. Top with remaining bread.

2. Butter the outsides of sandwiches; cook in a large skillet over medium heat until golden brown on both sides. **Yield:** 5 servings.

New England Clam Chowder

Rachel Nydam, Uxbridge, Massachusetts

I wasn't satisfied with other recipes I came across for clam chowder, so I devised this one. Everyone who's tried it raves about it. The dish is great on a cold day.

4 medium potatoes, peeled and cubed
2 medium onions, chopped
1/2 cup butter
3/4 cup all-purpose flour
2 quarts milk
3 cans (6-1/2 ounces *each*) chopped clams, undrained
2 to 3 teaspoons salt
1 teaspoon rubbed sage
1 teaspoon ground thyme
1/2 teaspoon celery salt
1/2 teaspoon pepper
Minced fresh parsley

1. Place potatoes in a saucepan and cover with water; bring to a boil. Cover and cook until tender.

2. Meanwhile, in a Dutch oven, saute onions in butter until tender. Add flour; mix until smooth. Stir in milk. Cook over medium heat, stirring constantly, until thickened and bubbly.

3. Drain potatoes; add to Dutch oven. Add clams and remaining ingredients; heat through. **Yield:** 10-12 servings (3 quarts).

Navy Bean Squash Soup

Linda Eggers, Albany, California

On a chilly day, what could be more comforting than a pot of this homemade soup simmering on the stove? The mix of ham, beans and squash is such a hearty combination, you'll savor every steamy spoonful.

1 pound dry navy beans, sorted and rinsed
2 cans (14-1/2 ounces *each*) chicken broth
2 cups water
1 meaty ham bone
2 to 2-1/2 pounds butternut squash, peeled, seeded and cubed (about 5 cups)
1 large onion, chopped
1/2 teaspoon salt
1/2 teaspoon pepper

1. Place beans in a large saucepan or Dutch oven; add water to cover by 2 in. Bring to a boil; boil for 2 minutes. Remove from the heat; cover and let stand for 1 hour. Drain and discard liquid; return beans to pan.

2. Add the broth, water, ham bone, squash, onion, salt and pepper. Bring to a boil. Reduce heat; cover and simmer for 1-1/2 to 1-3/4 hours or until beans are tender. Remove ham bone. Mash the soup mixture, leaving some chunks if desired.

3. Remove ham from bone; cut into chunks. Discard bone and fat. Return meat to the soup; heat through.

Yield: 12-14 servings (about 3 quarts).

Red Pepper Soup

Barb Nelson, Victoria, British Columbia

While I don't have scientific proof of it, Red Pepper Soup works for me as a head cold remedy! It is a good gift to take when visiting a sick friend, too. For a pretty touch, top the soup with grated cheese and parsley. We enjoy it with jalapeno cheese buns. You can also serve it with warm garlic bread.

- **6 medium sweet red peppers, chopped**
- **2 medium carrots, chopped**
- **2 medium onions, chopped**
- **1 celery rib, chopped**
- **4 garlic cloves, minced**
- **1 tablespoon olive oil**
- **2 cans (one 49-1/2 ounces, one 14-1/2 ounces) chicken broth**
- **1/2 cup uncooked long grain rice**
- **2 tablespoons minced fresh thyme *or* 2 teaspoons dried thyme**
- **1-1/2 teaspoons salt**
- **1/4 teaspoon pepper**
- **1/8 to 1/4 teaspoon cayenne pepper**
- **1/8 to 1/4 teaspoon crushed red pepper flakes**

1. In a large Dutch oven or soup kettle, saute red peppers, carrots, onions, celery and garlic in oil until tender. Stir in the broth, rice, thyme, salt, pepper and cayenne; bring to a boil. Reduce heat; cover and simmer for 20-25 minutes or until vegetables and rice are tender.

2. Cool for 30 minutes. Puree in small batches in a blender; return to pan. Add red pepper flakes; heat through. **Yield:** 10-12 servings (about 3 quarts).

Beef Barbecue

Karen Walker, Sterling, Virginia

We like to keep our freezer stocked with plenty of beef roasts. When we're not in the mood for pot roast, I fix these satisfying sandwiches instead. The meat cooks in a tasty sauce while I'm at work. Then I just slice it thinly and serve it on rolls.

✓ Uses less fat, sugar or salt. Includes Nutritional Analysis and Diabetic Exchanges.

- **1 boneless chuck roast (3 pounds)**
- **1 cup barbecue sauce**
- **1/2 cup apricot preserves**
- **1/3 cup chopped green *or* sweet red pepper**
- **1 small onion, chopped**
- **1 tablespoon Dijon mustard**
- **2 teaspoons brown sugar**
- **12 sandwich rolls, split**

1. Cut the roast into quarters; place in a greased 5-qt. slow cooker. In a bowl, combine the next six ingredients; pour over roast. Cover and cook on low for 6-8 hours or until meat is tender.

2. Remove roast and thinly slice; return meat to slow cooker and stir gently. Cover and cook 20-30 minutes longer. Skim fat from sauce. Serve beef and sauce on rolls. **Yield:** 12 servings.

Nutritional Analysis: One serving (prepared with apricot spreadable fruit; calculated without roll) equals 218 calories, 253 mg sodium, 78 mg cholesterol, 11 g carbohydrate, 26 g protein, 7 g fat, 1 gm fiber. **Diabetic Exchanges:** 3 lean meat, 1 fruit.

Main Dishes

Whether your family is partial to pork, beef, poultry or fish, these hearty main dishes are sure to satisfy their taste buds—and yours, too!

Chicken with Spicy Fruit, p. 72

Very Veggie Lasagna, p. 80

Sweet 'n' Sour Ribs, p. 76

Tuna Mushroom Casserole, p. 83

Chicken with Spicy Fruit

(Pictured on page 70)

Kathy Rairigh, Milford, Indiana

This speedy stovetop entree is special enough to serve company, yet easy enough for everyday. The moist chicken gets wonderful flavor from a sweet sauce made with strawberry jam, dried cranberries and pineapple juice. I like to serve it with rice pilaf, peas, a garden salad and cloverleaf rolls.

✓ Uses less fat, sugar or salt. Includes Nutritional Analysis and Diabetic Exchanges.

1-1/4 cups unsweetened pineapple juice
1/4 cup dried cranberries
2 garlic cloves, minced
1/8 to 1/4 teaspoon crushed red pepper flakes
4 boneless skinless chicken breast halves (1 pound)
1/4 cup reduced-sugar strawberry fruit spread
1 teaspoon cornstarch
2 green onions, thinly sliced

1. In a large skillet, combine pineapple juice, cranberries, garlic and red pepper flakes; bring to a boil. Add chicken. Reduce heat; cover and simmer for 10 minutes or until chicken juices run clear.

2. Remove chicken to a platter and keep warm. Bring cooking liquid to a boil; cook for 5-7 minutes or until liquid is reduced to 3/4 cup.

3. Combine fruit spread and cornstarch until blended; add to the skillet. Boil and stir for 1 minute or until thickened. Spoon over chicken. Sprinkle with onions. **Yield:** 4 servings.

Nutritional Analysis: One serving equals 248 calories, 66 mg sodium, 73 mg cholesterol, 26 g carbohydrate, 27 g protein, 3 g fat, 1 g fiber. **Diabetic Exchanges:** 4 very lean meat, 1-1/2 fruit.

Pork Loin with Spinach Stuffing

Lois Kinneberg, Phoenix, Arizona

I can't say whether leftovers from this eye-catching roast are good, because we never have any! I've been making this flavorful main dish for years and have never been disappointed.

1 package (10 ounces) frozen chopped spinach, thawed and squeezed dry
1/2 cup chopped onion
1 garlic clove, minced
3 tablespoons butter
1 cup soft bread crumbs
1/2 teaspoon salt
1 boneless pork loin roast (3-1/2 pounds)
1/4 cup orange juice
2 tablespoons soy sauce
1 tablespoon ketchup
1 cup (8 ounces) sour cream
2 tablespoons prepared horseradish
1 teaspoon Dijon mustard
1/2 teaspoon seasoned salt
1/4 teaspoon dill weed

1. Set aside 1/2 cup spinach for sauce. In a skillet, saute onion, garlic and remaining spinach in butter until tender. Remove from the heat; stir in bread crumbs and salt.

2. Separate roast into two pieces; spoon spinach mixture onto one piece of meat. Top with the second piece; tie with kitchen string. Place in a shallow roasting pan.

3. Combine the orange juice, soy sauce and ketchup; pour half over roast. Bake, uncovered, at 350° for 1 hour. Baste with remaining orange juice mixture. Cover and bake 1 hour longer or until a meat thermometer reads 160°-170°. Let stand 10 minutes before slicing.

4. In a saucepan, combine the sour cream, horseradish, mustard, seasoned salt, dill and reserved spinach. Cook over medium heat just until heated through (do not boil). Serve warm with pork. **Yield:** 10-12 servings.

Bavarian Bratwurst Supper

Jill Cook, Perry, Iowa

My family enjoys the flavors of hot German potato salad and bratwurst, especially during the cooler months. This original skillet recipe is truly a one-dish meal, combining meat, potatoes, apple and sauerkraut. For a lower-fat version, try using turkey bratwurst and turkey bacon.

4 bacon strips, diced
4 fresh bratwurst, cut into 2-inch pieces
1 medium tart apple, chopped
1 medium onion, chopped
1/2 cup cider vinegar
3 tablespoons brown sugar
1 tablespoon spicy brown mustard
1/2 teaspoon salt
1/8 teaspoon pepper
4 cups frozen cubed hash brown potatoes, thawed
1 can (14 ounces) Bavarian-style sauerkraut, drained

1. In a skillet over medium heat, cook bacon until crisp. Remove with a slotted spoon to paper towels. In the drippings, cook and stir bratwurst for 10-12 minutes. Remove with a slotted spoon. Drain, reserving 2 tablespoons of drippings. Saute apple and onion in drippings until lightly browned.

2. Add vinegar, brown sugar, mustard, salt, pepper and bratwurst. Cover and cook for 12 minutes or until bratwurst are no longer pink and a meat thermometer reads 160°, stirring frequently.

3. Add potatoes and sauerkraut; cook and stir 12 minutes longer or until heated through. Sprinkle with bacon. **Yield:** 4 servings.

Corn-Stuffed Butterfly Chops

Marie Dragwa, Simpson, Pennsylvania

Corn stuffing is a delicious twist in this old family recipe from an aunt. I fix these chops for special meals with scalloped potatoes, coleslaw and pickled beets.

1-1/2 cups frozen corn, thawed
1-1/2 cups soft bread crumbs
1 tablespoon minced fresh parsley
1 tablespoon finely chopped onion
3/4 teaspoon rubbed sage
3/4 teaspoon salt
1/4 teaspoon pepper
1 egg
3 tablespoons milk
4 bone-in pork loin chops (1-1/2 inches thick)
2 tablespoons vegetable oil
1/4 cup water

1. In a bowl, combine the first seven ingredients. In another bowl, lightly beat egg and milk; stir into corn mixture. Cut a pocket in each chop almost to the bone. Stuff about 1/4 cup corn mixture into each chop; secure with toothpicks.

2. In a large skillet, cook chops in oil until browned on both sides. Transfer to a greased 13-in. x 9-in. x 2-in. baking dish; add water. Cover and bake at 350° for 1 hour or until a thermometer inserted into stuffing reads 160°-170°. Discard toothpicks. **Yield:** 4 servings.

Slow Cooker Lasagna

Lisa Micheletti, Collierville, Tennessee

Convenient no-cook lasagna noodles take the work out of this traditional favorite adapted for the slow cooker. Because it's so easy to assemble, it's great for workdays as well as weekends. We like it accompanied by garlic cheese toast.

1 pound ground beef
1 large onion, chopped
2 garlic cloves, minced
1 can (29 ounces) tomato sauce
1 cup water
1 can (6 ounces) tomato paste
1 teaspoon salt
1 teaspoon dried oregano
1 package (8 ounces) no-cook lasagna noodles
4 cups (16 ounces) shredded mozzarella cheese
1-1/2 cups (12 ounces) small-curd cottage cheese
1/2 cup grated Parmesan cheese

1. In a skillet, cook beef, onion and garlic over medium heat until meat is no longer pink; drain. Add the tomato sauce, water, tomato paste, salt and oregano. Mix well.

2. Spread a fourth of the meat sauce in an ungreased 5-qt. slow cooker. Arrange a third of the noodles over sauce (break the noodles if necessary). Combine the cheeses; spoon a third of the mixture over noodles. Repeat layers twice. Top with remaining meat sauce.

3. Cover and cook on low for 4-5 hours or until noodles are tender. **Yield:** 6-8 servings.

Sliced Ham with Roasted Vegetables

Margaret Pache, Mesa, Arizona

To prepare this colorful, zesty oven meal, I "shop" in my backyard for the fresh garden vegetables and oranges (we have our own tree!) that spark the ham's hearty flavor. It's my family's favorite main dish.

6 medium potatoes, peeled and cubed
5 medium carrots, julienned
1 medium turnip, peeled and cubed
1 large onion, cut into thin wedges
6 slices (4 to 6 ounces *each*) fully cooked ham, halved
1/4 cup orange juice concentrate
2 tablespoons brown sugar
1 teaspoon prepared horseradish
1 teaspoon grated orange peel

1. Line two 15-in. x 10-in. x 1-in. baking pans with foil and coat with nonstick cooking spray. Add potatoes, carrots, turnip and onion; generously coat with nonstick cooking spray. Bake, uncovered, at 425° for 25-30 minutes or until tender.

2. Arrange ham slices over the vegetables. In a bowl, combine remaining ingredients. Spoon over ham and vegetables. Cover and bake 10 minutes longer or until the ham is heated through. **Yield:** 6 servings.

Teriyaki Glazed Chicken

Kelly Brenneman, Kapolei, Hawaii

I love to experiment with food. For this recipe, I took advantage of the sweet onions grown on Maui. My whole family just loves this main dish.

- **4 boneless skinless chicken breast halves, cut into strips**
- **3 tablespoons vegetable oil, *divided***
- **4 medium carrots, julienned**
- **1 medium sweet onion, julienned**
- **1/2 cup soy sauce**
- **1/4 cup packed brown sugar**
- **Hot cooked rice**
- **Sesame seeds, toasted, optional**
- **Sliced green onions, optional**

1. In a large skillet or wok, stir-fry chicken in 2 tablespoons oil for 6-8 minutes or until juices run clear. Remove chicken and set aside. In the same skillet, stir-fry carrots in remaining oil for 2 minutes. Add onion; stir-fry about 2-4 minutes longer or until vegetables are tender.

2. Combine soy sauce and brown sugar; add to skillet. Bring to a boil. Return chicken to skillet. Boil for 5 minutes or until sauce is slightly thickened. Serve over rice. Sprinkle with sesame seeds and green onions if desired. **Yield:** 4 servings.

Steak with Citrus Salsa

Kathleen Smith, Pittsburgh, Pennsylvania

A lime juice marinade really perks up grilled steaks, and the snappy, light citrus salsa is a super change from the usual heavy steak sauce.

- **1/2 cup soy sauce**
- **1/4 cup chopped green onions**
- **3 tablespoons lime juice**
- **2 tablespoons brown sugar**
- **1/8 teaspoon hot pepper sauce**
- **1 garlic clove, minced**
- **1-1/2 pounds boneless sirloin steak (about 1 inch thick)**

SALSA:

- **2 navel oranges, peeled, sectioned and chopped**
- **1/4 cup chopped green onions**
- **2 tablespoons orange juice**
- **2 tablespoons red wine vinegar**
- **2 tablespoons chopped lemon**
- **1 tablespoon chopped lime**
- **1 tablespoon sugar**
- **1 tablespoon minced fresh cilantro**
- **1 teaspoon minced jalapeno pepper**
- **1/2 teaspoon grated lemon peel**
- **1/2 teaspoon grated lime peel**
- **1/8 teaspoon salt**

1. In a large resealable plastic bag, combine the first six ingredients; add beef. Seal and refrigerate for 2 hours or overnight, turning occasionally.

2. Drain and discard marinade. Broil or grill steak, uncovered, over medium heat for 4-6 minutes on each side or until meat reaches desired doneness (for rare, a meat thermometer should read 140°; medium, 160°; well-done, 170°).

3. Combine salsa ingredients in a bowl. Cut steak across the grain into thin slices. Serve with salsa. **Yield:** 4-6 servings.

Editor's Note: When cutting or seeding hot peppers, use rubber or plastic gloves to protect your hands. Avoid touching your face.

Sweet 'n' Sour Ribs

(Pictured on page 71)

Dorothy Voelz, Champaign, Illinois

If you're looking for a change from typical barbecue ribs, you'll enjoy this recipe my mom always prepared on birthdays and special occasions. The tender ribs have a slight sweet-and-sour taste that my family loves. I usually serve them with garlic mashed potatoes and a salad or coleslaw.

3 to 4 pounds boneless country-style pork ribs
1 can (20 ounces) pineapple tidbits, undrained
2 cans (8 ounces *each*) tomato sauce
1/2 cup thinly sliced onion
1/2 cup thinly sliced green pepper
1/2 cup packed brown sugar
1/4 cup cider vinegar
1/4 cup tomato paste
2 tablespoons Worcestershire sauce
1 garlic clove, minced
Salt and pepper to taste

1. Place ribs in an ungreased slow cooker. In a bowl, combine the remaining ingredients; pour over the ribs.

2. Cover and cook on low for 8-10 hours or until meat is tender. Thicken the sauce if desired. **Yield:** 8 servings.

Creamy Seafood Enchiladas

Evelyn Gebhardt, Kasilof, Alaska

Two types of seafood and a flavorful sauce make these enchiladas outstanding. I prepare them for an annual fund-raiser, where they're always in demand. Spice up the recipe to your taste by adding more green chilies and salsa.

1/4 cup butter
1/4 cup all-purpose flour
1 cup chicken broth
1 can (10-3/4 ounces) condensed cream of chicken soup, undiluted
1 cup (8 ounces) sour cream
1/2 cup salsa
1/8 teaspoon salt
1 cup (8 ounces) small-curd cottage cheese
1 pound small shrimp, cooked, peeled and deveined
1 cup cooked *or* canned crabmeat, drained, flaked and cartilage removed
1-1/2 cups (6 ounces) shredded Monterey Jack cheese
1 can (4 ounces) chopped green chilies
1 tablespoon dried cilantro
12 flour tortillas (7 inches)
Additional salsa

1. In a saucepan over low heat, melt butter; stir in flour until smooth. Gradually stir in broth and soup until blended. Bring to a boil; cook and stir for 2 minutes. Remove from the heat. Stir in sour cream, salsa and salt; set aside.

2. Place cottage cheese in a blender; cover and process until smooth. Transfer to a bowl; add the shrimp, crab, Monterey Jack cheese, chilies and cilantro.

3. Spread 3/4 cup sauce in a greased 13-in. x 9-in. x 2-in. baking dish. Place about 1/3 cup seafood mixture down the center of each tortilla. Roll up and place, seam side down, over sauce. Top with the remaining sauce.

4. Bake, uncovered, at 350° for 30-35 minutes or until heated through. Serve with additional salsa. **Yield:** 6 servings.

Ham 'n' Egg Pizza

Margaret Smith, Superior, Wisconsin

I like to fix this fun dish when we invite our children and grandchildren for brunch. There's never a slice left! The recipe is quick and easy to prepare, using refrigerated crescent rolls to form the crust. The ham makes it hearty.

1 tube (8 ounces) refrigerated crescent rolls
3 eggs
2 tablespoons milk
1/8 teaspoon pepper
2 cups finely chopped fully cooked ham
1 cup frozen shredded hash brown potatoes
1 cup (4 ounces) shredded cheddar cheese
1/2 cup shredded Parmesan cheese

1. Unroll crescent roll dough and place on an ungreased 12-in. pizza pan. Press onto the bottom and 1/4 in. up the sides, sealing seams and perforations. Bake at 375° for 5 minutes.

2. Meanwhile, in a bowl, beat eggs, milk and pepper. Sprinkle ham, hash browns and cheddar cheese over crust. Carefully pour egg mixture over cheese. Sprinkle with Parmesan. Bake for 25-30 minutes or until eggs are completely set. **Yield:** 6 servings.

Meaty Stuffed Onions

Lorraine Grasso, Allentown, Pennsylvania

I won a prize for this recipe in a contest sponsored by our local newspaper. I got it from my mother-in-law, who's originally from Italy.

4 large sweet onions
1 pound ground beef
1/2 pound bulk pork sausage
1 package (10 ounces) frozen chopped spinach, thawed and drained
5 slices day-old bread, crumbled
1/2 to 2/3 cup beef broth
1/2 cup grated Parmesan cheese
1 egg, beaten
1 tablespoon minced fresh parsley
1/2 teaspoon salt
1/4 teaspoon pepper
1/8 teaspoon ground nutmeg

1. Peel onions and cut 1/2 in. off tops and bottoms. Place onions in a large saucepan. Cover with boiling water. Cook until tender, about 20 minutes; drain.

2. Cool slightly. Carefully remove inside layers of onion, separating into eight individual shells (refrigerate remaining onion for another use). Drain on paper towels.

3. In a skillet, cook beef and sausage over medium heat until no longer pink; drain. Add spinach; cook and stir for 2 minutes. Remove from the heat; stir in the remaining ingredients. Spoon into the onion shells.

4. Place in a greased 13-in. x 9-in. x 2-in. baking pan. Bake, uncovered, at 350° for 15-20 minutes or until heated through and lightly browned. **Yield:** 8 servings.

Maple-Glazed Pork Chops

Cheryl Miller, Fort Collins, Colorado

Everyone cleaned their plates when my mother made these succulent pork chops when I was growing up. Now, I get the same results when I serve them to my family alongside applesauce and au gratin potatoes.

1/2 cup all-purpose flour
Salt and pepper to taste
4 bone-in pork loin chops (1 inch thick)
2 tablespoons butter
1/4 cup cider vinegar
1/3 cup maple syrup
1 tablespoon cornstarch
3 tablespoons water
2/3 cup packed brown sugar

1. In a large resealable plastic bag, combine flour, salt and pepper. Add pork chops and shake to coat. In a skillet, brown chops on both sides in butter. Place in an ungreased 13-in. x 9-in. x 2-in. baking pan. Bake, uncovered, at 450° for 20-25 minutes or until juices run clear.

2. Meanwhile, in a skillet, bring the vinegar to a boil. Reduce heat; add maple syrup. Cover and cook for 10 minutes. Combine cornstarch and water until smooth; add to the maple mixture. Bring to a boil; cook and stir for 2 minutes or until thickened.

3. Place chops on a broiler pan; sprinkle with brown sugar. Broil 4 in. from the heat for 2-3 minutes or until sugar is melted. Drizzle with maple glaze. **Yield:** 4 servings.

Turkey Scallopini

Karen Adams, Seymour, Indiana

Quick-cooking turkey breast slices make this recipe a winner when you have only a few minutes to fix a satisfying meal. I've also used flattened boneless skinless chicken breast halves in place of the turkey for this entree.

6 turkey breast slices (about 1-1/2 pounds)
1/4 cup all-purpose flour
1/8 teaspoon salt
1/8 teaspoon pepper
1 egg
2 tablespoons water
1 cup soft bread crumbs
1/2 cup grated Parmesan cheese
1/4 cup butter
Minced fresh parsley

1. Pound turkey to 1/4-in. thickness. In a shallow bowl, combine flour, salt and pepper. In another bowl, beat egg and water. On a plate, combine the bread crumbs and Parmesan cheese. Dredge turkey in flour mixture, then dip in egg mixture and coat with crumbs.

2. Melt butter in a skillet over medium-high heat; cook turkey for 2-3 minutes on each side or until meat juices run clear and coating is golden brown. Sprinkle with parsley. **Yield:** 6 servings.

Chicken Chili Lasagna

Cindee Rolston, St. Marys, West Virginia

This saucy lasagna is my adaptation of a chicken enchilada recipe. My husband and I enjoy the mild blend of seasonings, cheeses and tender chicken.

2 packages (3 ounces *each*) cream cheese, softened
1 medium onion, chopped
8 green onions, chopped
2 cups (8 ounces) shredded Mexican-cheese blend, *divided*
2 garlic cloves, minced
3/4 teaspoon ground cumin, *divided*
1/2 teaspoon minced fresh cilantro
3 cups cubed cooked chicken
1/4 cup butter
1/4 cup all-purpose flour
1-1/2 cups chicken broth
1 cup (4 ounces) shredded Monterey Jack cheese
1 cup (8 ounces) sour cream
1 can (4 ounces) chopped green chilies, drained
1/8 teaspoon dried thyme
1/8 teaspoon salt
1/8 teaspoon pepper
12 flour tortillas (6 inches), halved

1. In a mixing bowl, combine cream cheese, onions, 1-1/2 cups Mexican-cheese blend, garlic, 1/4 teaspoon cumin and cilantro. Stir in chicken; set aside.

2. In a saucepan, melt butter. Stir in flour until smooth; gradually add broth. Bring to a boil; cook and stir for 2 minutes or until thickened. Remove from the heat. Stir in Monterey Jack cheese, sour cream, chilies, thyme, salt, pepper and remaining cumin.

3. Spread 1/2 cup of the cheese sauce in a greased 13-in. x 9-in. x 2-in. baking dish. Top with six tortilla halves, a third of the chicken mixture and a fourth of the cheese sauce. Repeat tortilla, chicken and cheese sauce layers twice. Top with remaining tortillas, cheese sauce and Mexican cheese.

4. Cover and bake at 350° for 30 minutes. Uncover; bake 10 minutes longer or until heated through. Let stand 5 minutes before cutting. **Yield:** 12 servings.

Bell Pepper Enchiladas

Melissa Cowser, Greenville, Texas

Peppers are probably the vegetable that gets used most frequently in my kitchen. My freezer's constantly stocked in case I discover a new recipe or want to whip up an old favorite. These zesty enchiladas are a standby that I make often for supper throughout the year.

2 medium green peppers, chopped
1/2 cup shredded cheddar cheese
1/2 cup shredded Monterey Jack cheese
1/2 cup diced process cheese (Velveeta)
4 flour tortillas (8 inches)
1 small jalapeno pepper, minced, optional
1 cup salsa, *divided*
Additional shredded cheese, optional

1. Sprinkle the green peppers and cheeses down the center of tortillas; add jalapeno if desired. Roll up. Spread 1/2 cup salsa in a shallow baking dish. Place tortillas seam side down over salsa. Top with remaining salsa.

2. Bake at 350° for 20 minutes or until heated through. Sprinkle with additional cheese if desired. **Yield:** 4 enchiladas.

Editor's Note: When cutting or seeding hot peppers, use rubber or plastic gloves to protect your hands. Avoid touching your face.

Very Veggie Lasagna

(Pictured on page 70)

Berniece Baldwin, Glennie, Michigan

I concocted this quick and easy recipe to use up some of the abundant fresh produce from my garden. When I made a batch to share at a potluck, I received lots of compliments.

2 medium carrots, julienned
1 medium zucchini, cut into 1/4-inch slices
1 yellow summer squash, cut into 1/4-inch slices
1 medium onion, sliced
1 cup broccoli florets
1/2 cup sliced celery
1/2 cup julienned sweet red pepper
1/2 cup julienned green pepper
2 garlic cloves, minced
1 teaspoon salt
2 tablespoons vegetable oil
1 jar (28 ounces) spaghetti sauce
14 lasagna noodles, cooked and drained
4 cups (16 ounces) shredded mozzarella cheese

1. In a large skillet, stir-fry the vegetables, garlic and salt in oil until crisp-tender.

2. Spread 3/4 cup spaghetti sauce in a greased 13-in. x 9-in. x 2-in. baking dish. Arrange seven noodles over sauce, overlapping as needed. Layer with half of the vegetables, spaghetti sauce and cheese. Repeat layers.

3. Cover and bake at 350° for 60-65 minutes or until bubbly. Let stand for 15 minutes before cutting. **Yield:** 12 servings.

Sausage Bean Burritos

Eleanor Chlan, Ellicott City, Maryland

Like my mother and grandmother, I'm a frugal cook. I purchase meats in bulk, including sausage. This is one creative way I've found to use sausage in an evening entree. Our children often request these zippy burritos.

3/4 pound bulk pork sausage
1/2 cup chopped green pepper
1/3 cup chopped onion
1 can (15 ounces) black beans, rinsed and drained
1-1/2 cups cooked long grain rice
1-1/2 cups salsa, *divided*
10 flour tortillas (7 inches)
1 cup (4 ounces) shredded cheddar cheese, *divided*

1. In a large saucepan, cook sausage, green pepper and onion over medium heat until meat is no longer pink; drain. Stir in beans, rice and 1 cup salsa; mix well.

2. Spread about 1/2 cup sausage mixture down the center of each tortilla; sprinkle with 1 tablespoon cheese. Roll up and place, seam side down, in a greased 13-in. x 9-in. x 2-in. baking dish. Top with remaining salsa.

3. Cover and bake at 350° for 30 minutes. Uncover; sprinkle with remaining cheese. Bake 5-10 minutes longer or until cheese is melted. **Yield:** 10 burritos.

Hash Brown Ham Quiche

Sara Bowen, Upland, California

My family loves this cheesy ham quiche on Sunday morning after church. I'm a registered nurse, and I got this recipe from the mother of one of my patients. It's delicious for brunch and easy to prepare.

- **3 cups frozen shredded hash brown potatoes, thawed**
- **1/4 cup butter, melted, *divided***
- **1 cup (4 ounces) shredded pepper-Jack cheese**
- **1 cup (4 ounces) shredded Swiss cheese**
- **1 cup diced fully cooked ham**
- **2 eggs**
- **1/2 cup heavy whipping cream**
- **1/4 teaspoon seasoned salt**

1. Press hash browns between paper towels to remove excess moisture. Grease a 9-in. pie plate with 2 teaspoons butter. Press hash browns onto the bottom and up the sides of plate. Drizzle with remaining butter. Bake, uncovered, at 425° for 20-25 minutes or until edges are browned.

2. Combine cheeses and ham; spoon into the crust. In a bowl, beat the eggs, cream and seasoned salt; pour over ham.

3. Reduce heat to 350°. Bake, uncovered, for 20-25 minutes or until a knife inserted near the center comes out clean. Let stand 10 minutes before cutting. **Yield:** 6 servings.

Teriyaki Pork Roast

Roxanne Hulsey, Gainesville, Georgia

Since my husband works full time and attends school, I do a great deal around the house, including getting our three children where they need to go. I'm always looking for no-fuss recipes, so I was thrilled to find this one. The moist teriyaki-seasoned pork roast has become a family favorite.

✓ Uses less fat, sugar or salt. Includes Nutritional Analysis and Diabetic Exchanges.

- **3/4 cup unsweetened apple juice**
- **2 tablespoons sugar**
- **2 tablespoons soy sauce**
- **1 tablespoon vinegar**
- **1 teaspoon ground ginger**
- **1/4 teaspoon garlic powder**
- **1/8 teaspoon pepper**
- **1 boneless pork loin roast (about 3 pounds), halved**
- **7-1/2 teaspoons cornstarch**
- **3 tablespoons cold water**

1. Combine the first seven ingredients in a greased slow cooker. Add roast and turn to coat. Cover and cook on low for 7-8 hours or until a thermometer inserted into the roast reads 160°. Remove roast and keep warm.

2. In a saucepan, combine cornstarch and cold water until smooth; stir in cooking juices. Bring to a boil; cook and stir for 2 minutes or until thickened. Serve with the roast. **Yield:** 8 servings.

Nutritional Analysis: One serving (prepared with reduced-sodium soy sauce) equals 292 calories, 212 mg sodium, 101 mg cholesterol, 9 g carbohydrate, 36 g protein, 12 g fat, trace fiber. **Diabetic Exchanges:** 4-1/2 lean meat, 1/2 starch.

Pork and Pear Stir-Fry

Betty Phillips, French Creek, West Virginia

I've served this full-flavored stir-fry for years, always to rave reviews. Tender pork and ripe pears make a sweet combination, and a spicy sauce adds plenty of zip.

✓ Uses less fat, sugar or salt. Includes Nutritional Analysis and Diabetic Exchanges.

- **1/2 cup plum preserves**
- **3 tablespoons soy sauce**
- **2 tablespoons lemon juice**
- **1 tablespoon prepared horseradish**
- **2 teaspoons cornstarch**
- **1/4 teaspoon crushed red pepper flakes**
- **1 medium sweet yellow *or* green pepper, julienned**
- **1/2 to 1 teaspoon minced fresh gingerroot**
- **1 tablespoon vegetable oil**
- **3 medium ripe pears, peeled and sliced**
- **1 pound pork tenderloin, cut into 1/4-inch strips**
- **1 can (8 ounces) sliced water chestnuts, drained**
- **1-1/2 cups fresh *or* frozen snow peas**
- **1 tablespoon sliced almonds, toasted**
- **Hot cooked rice**

1. In a bowl, combine the first six ingredients; set aside. In a skillet or wok, stir-fry yellow pepper and ginger in oil for 2 minutes. Add pears; stir-fry for 1 minute or until pepper is crisp-tender. Remove and keep warm.

2. Stir-fry half of the pork at a time for 1-2 minutes or until meat is no longer pink. Return pear mixture and all of the pork to pan. Add water chestnuts and reserved sauce.

3. Bring to a boil; cook and stir for 2 minutes. Add peas; heat through. Sprinkle with almonds. Serve over rice. **Yield:** 4 servings.

Nutritional Analysis: One serving (prepared with reduced-sodium soy sauce and reduced-sugar apricot fruit spread instead of plum preserves; calculated without rice) equals 368 calories, 563 mg sodium, 67 mg cholesterol, 45 g carbohydrate, 28 g protein, 9 g fat, 8 g fiber. **Diabetic Exchanges:** 3 lean meat, 1-1/2 fruit, 1 starch, 1 vegetable.

Ham a la King

Jean Grubb, Austin, Texas

My mom and I used to have a catering business, and this recipe was a popular choice from our menu. It looks elegant on the plate and always gets rave reviews. Being able to make the sauce a day ahead is a big plus.

- **1 package (10 ounces) frozen puff pastry shells**
- **1/4 cup butter**
- **1/4 cup all-purpose flour**
- **1 teaspoon chicken bouillon granules**
- **1/2 cup hot water**
- **1-1/2 cups milk**
- **3 slices process American cheese**
- **1 teaspoon Worcestershire sauce**
- **1 teaspoon prepared mustard**
- **2 cups cubed fully cooked ham**
- **1/2 cup frozen peas, thawed, optional**
- **1 can (2-1/4 ounces) sliced ripe olives, drained**
- **2 tablespoons diced pimientos**
- **2 tablespoons minced fresh parsley**

1. Bake the pastry shells according to package directions. Meanwhile, in a saucepan, melt butter; stir in flour until smooth. Dissolve bouillon in water. Gradually add milk and bouillon to the saucepan. Bring to a boil; cook and stir for 2 minutes or until thickened.

2. Stir in cheese, Worcestershire and mustard until the cheese is melted. Add the ham, peas if desired, olives, pimientos and parsley; heat through. Serve in pastry shells. **Yield:** 6 servings.

Four-Cheese Spinach Lasagna

Kimberly Kneisly, Englewood, Ohio

This rich cheesy lasagna has become one of my specialties. It's packed with fresh-tasting vegetables like spinach, carrots, red pepper and broccoli. I'm never afraid to serve the colorful casserole to guests, since it's always a huge success.

2 cups chopped fresh broccoli
1-1/2 cups julienned carrots
1 cup sliced green onions
1/2 cup chopped sweet red pepper
3 garlic cloves, minced
2 teaspoons vegetable oil
1/2 cup all-purpose flour
3 cups milk
1/2 cup grated Parmesan cheese, *divided*
1/2 teaspoon salt
1/4 teaspoon pepper
1 package (10 ounces) frozen chopped spinach, thawed and well drained
1-1/2 cups small-curd cottage cheese
1 cup (4 ounces) shredded mozzarella cheese
1/2 cup shredded Swiss cheese
12 lasagna noodles, cooked and drained

1. In a skillet, saute the vegetables and garlic in oil until crisp-tender. Remove from the heat; set aside.

2. In a heavy saucepan, whisk flour and milk until smooth. Bring to a boil; cook and stir for 2 minutes. Reduce heat; add 1/4 cup Parmesan cheese, salt and pepper. Cook 1 minute longer or until cheese is melted. Remove from the heat; stir in spinach. Set 1 cup aside.

3. In a bowl, combine cottage cheese, mozzarella and Swiss. Spread 1/2 cup of spinach mixture in a greased 13-in. x 9-in. x 2-in. baking dish. Layer with four noodles, half of the cheese mixture and vegetables and 3/4 cup spinach mixture. Repeat layers. Top with remaining noodles, reserved spinach mixture and remaining Parmesan cheese.

4. Cover and bake at 375° for 35 minutes. Uncover; bake 15 minutes longer or until bubbly. Let stand 15 minutes before cutting. **Yield:** 12 servings.

Tuna Mushroom Casserole

(Pictured on page 71)

Jone Furlong, Santa Rosa, California

I love to serve this dressed-up version of a tuna casserole. The green beans add nice texture, color and flavor. The first time I made this dish, my uncle asked for seconds even though tuna casseroles are not usually his favorite.

1/2 cup water
1 teaspoon chicken bouillon granules
1 package (10 ounces) frozen green beans
1 cup chopped onion
1 cup sliced fresh mushrooms
1/4 cup chopped celery
1 garlic clove, minced
1/2 teaspoon dill weed
1/2 teaspoon salt
1/8 teaspoon pepper
4 teaspoons cornstarch
1-1/2 cups milk
1/2 cup shredded Swiss cheese
1/4 cup mayonnaise
2-1/2 cups medium noodles, cooked and drained
1 can (12-1/4 ounces) tuna, drained and flaked
1/3 cup dry bread crumbs
1 tablespoon butter

1. In a large saucepan, bring water and bouillon to a boil, stirring to dissolve. Add the next eight ingredients; bring to a boil. Reduce heat; cover and simmer 5 minutes or until vegetables are tender.

2. Dissolve cornstarch in milk; add to vegetable mixture, stirring constantly. Bring to a boil; boil 2 minutes or until thickened. Remove from the heat; stir in cheese and mayonnaise until cheese is melted. Fold in noodles and tuna.

3. Pour into a greased 2-1/2-qt. baking dish. Brown bread crumbs in butter; sprinkle on top of casserole. Bake, uncovered, at 350° for 25-30 minutes or until heated through. **Yield:** 4-6 servings.

Orange Walnut Chicken

(Pictured on front cover)

TerryAnn Moore, Haddon Township, New Jersey

For an impressive main dish that's not tricky to prepare, try this mouth-watering chicken. With orange juice concentrate, orange juice, lemon juice and marmalade, the pretty sauce has a zesty taste.

3 tablespoons orange juice concentrate
3 tablespoons vegetable oil, *divided*
1 tablespoon soy sauce
1 garlic clove, minced
4 boneless skinless chicken breast halves
1/2 cup coarsely chopped walnuts
1 tablespoon butter
4 green onions, thinly sliced, *divided*
1/2 cup orange marmalade
1/2 cup orange juice
1/4 cup lemon juice
2 tablespoons honey
1 to 2 tablespoons grated orange peel
2 to 3 teaspoons grated lemon peel
1/2 teaspoon salt
1/8 teaspoon pepper
Hot cooked rice

1. In a large resealable plastic bag, combine orange juice concentrate, 2 tablespoons oil, soy sauce and garlic. Add chicken; seal bag and turn to coat. Refrigerate for 2-3 hours.

2. Remove chicken; reserve marinade. In a skillet, cook chicken in remaining oil until juices run clear.

3. Meanwhile, in a saucepan, saute walnuts in butter until lightly browned; remove and set aside. Set aside 1/4 cup green onions for garnish. Add remaining onions to saucepan; saute until tender. Add reserved marinade and the next eight ingredients. Bring to a rolling boil; boil for 2 minutes.

4. Reduce heat; simmer, uncovered, for 5-10 minutes or until sauce reaches desired consistency. Serve chicken over rice; top with sauce and reserved walnuts and onions. **Yield:** 4 servings.

Pineapple Ham Loaf

Aleatha Smith, Billings, Montana

My cousin served this tender ham loaf at a family get-together, and I eagerly asked for the recipe. Since then, I've often taken it to church functions and served it when friends come to dinner. It's always well received.

2 eggs
1/2 cup milk
1 teaspoon Worcestershire sauce
3/4 cup dry bread crumbs
1-1/2 teaspoons ground mustard, *divided*
1/4 teaspoon salt
1/4 teaspoon pepper
1 pound fully cooked ham, ground (4 cups)
1 pound ground pork
1 can (20 ounces) sliced pineapple
1/2 cup packed brown sugar

1. In a bowl, combine eggs, milk, Worcestershire sauce, bread crumbs, 1 teaspoon mustard, salt and pepper. Add ham and pork; mix well. Shape into eight oval patties; set aside.

2. Drain pineapple, reserving 1/2 cup juice. Place a pineapple slice between each ham patty. (Refrigerate remaining pineapple and juice for another use.) Carefully place in an ungreased 9-in. x 5-in. x 3-in. loaf pan. Pat patties around pineapple to form a loaf.

3. Combine brown sugar, remaining mustard and reserved juice; pour a small amount over loaf. Bake, uncovered, at 350° for 1-1/4 hours or until lightly browned and a meat thermometer reads 160°, basting occasionally with remaining juice mixture. **Yield:** 8 servings.

Apricot-Filled Pork Tenderloin

Jo Ann Hettel, Bushnell, Florida

This flavorful main course is a great company offering. The tenderloin tastes wonderful and looks so pretty when it's sliced to reveal a golden apricot center. In the almost 20 years I've been using this recipe, it has never failed me.

2 pork tenderloins (1 pound *each*)
1 package (6 ounces) dried apricots

MARINADE:

1/3 cup sweet-and-sour salad dressing
1/4 cup packed brown sugar
3 tablespoons teriyaki sauce
2 tablespoons ketchup
1 teaspoon Dijon mustard
1 onion slice, separated into rings
1 garlic clove, minced
2 teaspoons minced fresh gingerroot
1/4 teaspoon pepper
1/8 teaspoon pumpkin pie spice

1. Make a lengthwise cut three-quarters of the way through each tenderloin; pound with a meat mallet to flatten evenly. Set aside three apricots for marinade. Stuff remaining apricots into tenderloins to within 1/2 in. of ends; secure with toothpicks or kitchen string. Place in a greased 11-in. x 7-in. x 2-in. baking dish.

2. In a blender, combine the marinade ingredients and reserved apricots. Cover and process until smooth; set aside 1/3 cup. Pour remaining marinade over tenderloins. Cover and refrigerate for at least 2 hours, turning meat often.

3. Drain and discard marinade from meat. Drizzle reserved marinade over meat. Bake, uncovered, at 400° for 30-35 minutes or until a meat thermometer reads 160°-170°. **Yield:** 6 servings.

Polish Kraut and Apples

Caren Markee, Cary, Illinois

My family loves this hearty, heartwarming meal on cold winter nights. The tender apples, brown sugar and smoked sausage give this dish fantastic flavor. I like making it because the prep time is very short.

1 can (14 ounces) sauerkraut, rinsed and well drained
1 pound fully cooked Polish sausage *or* kielbasa, cut into 2-inch pieces
3 medium tart apples, peeled and cut into eighths
1/2 cup packed brown sugar
1/2 teaspoon caraway seeds, optional
1/8 teaspoon pepper
3/4 cup apple juice

1. Place half of the sauerkraut in an ungreased slow cooker. Top with sausage, apples, brown sugar, caraway seeds if desired and pepper. Top with remaining sauerkraut. Pour apple juice over all.

2. Cover and cook on low for 4-5 hours or until apples are tender. **Yield:** 4 servings.

Cajun Pepper Steak

Martha Sue Kinnaird, Ruston, Louisiana

Cajun recipes have become popular across the country, but they've always been loved here. See if this recipe doesn't become a family favorite at your house.

1-1/2 pounds boneless round steak, cut into cubes
2 tablespoons vegetable oil
1 can (14-1/2 ounces) beef broth
1 can (14-1/2 ounces) diced tomatoes, undrained
1 cup chopped green pepper
1/2 cup chopped onion
3 garlic cloves, minced
2 teaspoons Worcestershire sauce
1 bay leaf
1/2 teaspoon dried basil
1/4 to 1/2 teaspoon Cajun seasoning
1/8 teaspoon salt
1/8 teaspoon pepper
2 tablespoons cornstarch
2 tablespoons cold water
Hot cooked rice *or* noodles

1. In a large skillet, cook beef in oil over medium heat until browned; drain. Stir in the broth, tomatoes, green pepper, onion, garlic, Worcestershire sauce and seasonings. Bring to a boil; reduce heat. Cover and simmer for 1 hour or until meat is tender.

2. Discard bay leaf. Combine cornstarch and water until smooth; stir into meat mixture. Bring to a boil; cook and stir for 2 minutes or until thickened. Serve over rice or noodles. **Yield:** 4-6 servings.

Herb-Crusted Chuck Roast

Rita Drewes, Craig, Missouri

This recipe turns an inexpensive cut of beef into a delicious main dish. I got the recipe from a family member several years ago and have made it often.

1/4 cup dry bread crumbs
2 tablespoons olive oil
1 garlic clove, minced
1 teaspoon ground mustard
1 teaspoon dried savory
1 teaspoon pepper
1/2 teaspoon dried rosemary, crushed
1 boneless chuck eye *or* top blade roast (about 3 pounds)

SAUCE:
1 cup (8 ounces) sour cream
3 tablespoons prepared horseradish
1 teaspoon lemon juice
1/4 teaspoon salt

1. In a bowl, combine the first seven ingredients. Rub over entire roast. Place on a rack in a shallow roasting pan. Bake, uncovered, at 325° for 1-1/2 to 2 hours or until meat is tender and reaches desired doneness (for medium-rare, a meat thermometer should read 145°; medium, 160°; well-done, 170°). Let stand 10 minutes before carving.

2. Meanwhile, in a bowl, combine the sauce ingredients. Serve with the roast. **Yield:** 8 servings.

Turkey Croquettes with Cranberry Salsa

Jacque Capurro, Anchorage, Alaska

This recipe is a fun and festive way to use up turkey after the holidays, though we enjoy the croquettes throughout the year. They're scrumptious served with the salsa.

1/3 cup chopped onion
2 tablespoons butter
1/4 cup all-purpose flour
1/4 cup milk
1/4 cup chicken broth
2 cups finely chopped cooked turkey
1/2 cup mashed sweet potato
1/2 teaspoon salt
1/4 teaspoon pepper
1/8 teaspoon cayenne pepper

SALSA:
3/4 cup chopped tart green apple
1 tablespoon lemon juice
1/2 cup chopped cranberries
2 green onions, chopped
2 jalapeno peppers, seeded and chopped
3 tablespoons golden raisins, chopped
1 tablespoon honey

CROQUETTES:
2 eggs
1 tablespoon water
1/2 cup all-purpose flour
1/2 cup dry bread crumbs
Oil for frying

1. In a saucepan, saute onion in butter until tender. Stir in flour until blended. Gradually add milk and broth. Bring to a boil; cook and stir for 2 minutes or until thickened. Remove from the heat; stir in turkey, sweet potato, salt, pepper and cayenne. Cover and refrigerate for 2 hours or until firm.

2. Meanwhile, toss apple with lemon juice in a bowl. Stir in remaining salsa ingredients. Cover and chill for at least 1 hour.

3. For croquettes, beat eggs and water in a shallow bowl. Place flour and bread crumbs in separate shallow bowls. Shape turkey mixture into 1-1/2-in. balls. Roll in flour; shake off excess. Roll in egg mixture, then in crumbs.

4. In an electric skillet or deep-fat fryer, heat 1-1/2 in. of oil to 375°. Fry croquettes, a few at a time, for 2 minutes or until golden brown. Drain on paper towels. Serve with salsa. **Yield:** 16 croquettes (2 cups salsa).

Editor's Note: When cutting or seeding hot peppers, use rubber or plastic gloves to protect your hands. Avoid touching your face.

Upside-Down Pizza

Debra Derstine, Mapleton, Pennsylvania

If you like pizza, I think you'll enjoy this recipe. I like making this better than regular pizza because I don't have to make a crust.

1 pound bulk Italian sausage
1 medium onion, chopped
1/4 cup chopped green pepper
2 tablespoons plus 1 cup all-purpose flour, *divided*
1/2 teaspoon dried basil
1/2 teaspoon fennel seed, crushed
1 can (15 ounces) tomato sauce
2 cups (8 ounces) shredded mozzarella cheese
2 eggs
1 cup milk
1 tablespoon vegetable oil
1/2 teaspoon salt
2 tablespoons grated Parmesan cheese, optional

1. In a saucepan, cook the sausage, onion and green pepper over medium heat until meat is no longer pink; drain. Stir in 2 tablespoons flour, basil and fennel; mix well. Add tomato sauce. Bring to a boil; cook and stir for 2 minutes.

2. Transfer to an ungreased 13-in. x 9-in. x 2-in. baking dish. Sprinkle with mozzarella cheese. Place the remaining flour in a mixing bowl. Beat in the eggs, milk, oil and salt until smooth; stir in Parmesan cheese if desired. Pour over casserole.

3. Bake, uncovered, at 425° for 25-30 minutes or until browned. **Yield:** 8 servings.

Pork and Onion Kabobs

Mary Lou Wayman, Salt Lake City, Utah

A sweet and savory marinade brings out the best in pork, as these grilled kabobs prove. They're a super summer supper, easy to prepare and fun to serve to company. The pork is so tasty grilled with onion wedges.

1/2 cup soy sauce
1/4 cup chili sauce
1/4 cup honey
2 tablespoons olive oil
2 teaspoons curry powder
2 tablespoons finely chopped onion
2 pounds boneless pork, cut into 1-inch cubes
3 medium onions, cut into 1-inch wedges

1. In a bowl, combine the first six ingredients. Remove half for basting; cover and refrigerate. Add pork to the remaining marinade; toss to coat. Cover and refrigerate for 3 hours or overnight.

2. Drain and discard the marinade. Alternately thread pork cubes and onion wedges on metal or soaked bamboo skewers.

3. Grill, uncovered, over medium heat for 5 minutes; turn. Baste with reserved marinade. Continue turning and basting for 15 minutes or until meat juices run clear. **Yield:** 6 servings.

Spinach Enchiladas

William Parman, Oxnard, California

We moved to Southern California many years ago from Minnesota. We especially like the Mexican food that's served here. These enchiladas have become a family favorite.

1 can (14-1/2 ounces) chicken broth
1 can (6 ounces) tomato paste
3 to 4 teaspoons chili powder
1 package (10 ounces) frozen chopped spinach, thawed and well drained
3 green onions, chopped
1/3 cup sour cream
1/4 cup small-curd cottage cheese, drained
1-1/2 cups (6 ounces) shredded Colby-Monterey Jack cheese, *divided*
6 to 8 corn tortillas (7 inches)

1. For the sauce, whisk the broth, tomato paste and chili powder in a saucepan. Simmer, uncovered, for 5 minutes.

2. Meanwhile, combine spinach, onions, sour cream and cottage cheese in a bowl; stir in 1 cup shredded cheese. Spoon 1/2 cup of the sauce into a greased 11-in. x 7-in. x 2-in. baking dish. Dip tortillas into the remaining sauce; spoon about 1/4 cup spinach mixture down the center of each tortilla.

3. Roll up and place, seam side down, in the baking dish. Top with the remaining sauce and cheese. Bake, uncovered, at 350° for 20 minutes or until bubbly. **Yield:** 6-8 servings.

Mother's Ham Casserole

Linda Childers, Murfreesboro, Tennessee

One of my mother's favorite dishes, this recipe always brings back fond memories of her when I prepare it. It's a terrific use of leftover ham from a holiday dinner.

2 cups cubed peeled potatoes
1 large carrot, sliced
2 celery ribs, chopped
3 cups water
2 cups cubed fully cooked ham
2 tablespoons chopped green pepper
2 teaspoons finely chopped onion
7 tablespoons butter, *divided*
3 tablespoons all-purpose flour
1-1/2 cups milk
3/4 teaspoon salt
1/8 teaspoon pepper
1 cup (4 ounces) shredded cheddar cheese
1/2 cup soft bread crumbs

1. In a saucepan, cook potatoes, carrot and celery in water until tender; drain. In a skillet, saute ham, green pepper and onion in 3 tablespoons butter until tender. Add to the potato mixture. Transfer to a greased 1-1/2-qt. baking dish.

2. In a saucepan, melt the remaining butter; stir in flour until smooth. Gradually add milk, salt and pepper. Bring to a boil; cook and stir for 2 minutes or until thickened. Stir in the cheese until melted; pour over the ham mixture. Sprinkle with bread crumbs.

3. Bake, uncovered, at 375° for 25-30 minutes or until heated through. **Yield:** 4-6 servings.

Barbecue Chicken Casserole

Gail Rector, Belle, Missouri

I am a minister's wife and have cooked for countless fellowships, funeral dinners and other church activities. This is a recipe I've used often for those occasions.

- **1 cup all-purpose flour**
- **1 broiler/fryer chicken (3 to 4 pounds), cut up**
- **2 tablespoons vegetable oil**
- **1 cup chopped onion**
- **1 cup chopped green pepper**
- **1 cup thinly sliced celery**
- **1 cup ketchup**
- **1/2 cup water**
- **3 tablespoons brown sugar**
- **3 tablespoons Worcestershire sauce**
- **1/2 teaspoon salt**
- **1/4 teaspoon pepper**
- **1 package (16 ounces) frozen corn, thawed**

1. Place flour in a large resealable plastic bag. Add chicken, a few pieces at a time, and shake to coat. In a large skillet, brown the chicken in oil; transfer to an ungreased 13-in. x 9-in. x 2-in. baking dish.

2. Drain skillet, reserving 2 tablespoons drippings. In the drippings, saute onion, green pepper and celery until tender. In a bowl, combine the ketchup, water, brown sugar, Worcestershire sauce, salt and pepper; add to vegetables. Bring to a boil. Pour over the chicken.

3. Cover and bake at 350° for 30 minutes. Sprinkle with corn. Bake 18-20 minutes longer or until chicken juices run clear and corn is tender. **Yield:** 4-6 servings.

Easter Brunch Lasagna

Sarah Larson, La Farge, Wisconsin

Ham, broccoli and hard-cooked eggs are terrific together in this unique brunch lasagna.

- **1/2 cup butter**
- **1/3 cup all-purpose flour**
- **1/4 teaspoon salt**
- **Dash white pepper**
- **3 cups milk**
- **1/4 cup finely chopped green onions**
- **1 teaspoon lemon juice**
- **1/4 teaspoon hot pepper sauce**
- **9 lasagna noodles, cooked and drained**
- **2 cups diced fully cooked ham**
- **1 package (10 ounces) frozen chopped broccoli, thawed**
- **1/2 cup grated Parmesan cheese**
- **3 cups (12 ounces) shredded cheddar cheese**
- **4 hard-cooked eggs, finely chopped**

1. In a heavy saucepan, melt butter over medium heat. Stir in flour, salt and pepper until smooth. Gradually add milk. Bring to a boil; cook and stir for 2 minutes or until thickened. Remove from the heat; stir in onions, lemon juice and hot pepper sauce.

2. Spread a fourth of the white sauce in a greased 13-in. x 9-in. x 2-in. baking dish. Top with three noodles, half of the ham and broccoli, 3 tablespoons Parmesan cheese, 1 cup cheddar cheese, half of the eggs and a fourth of the white sauce. Repeat layers. Top with the remaining noodles, white sauce and cheeses.

3. Bake, uncovered, at 350° for 40-45 minutes or until bubbly. Let stand 15 minutes before cutting. **Yield:** 12 servings.

Turkey Lime Kabobs

Shelly Johnston, Rochester, Minnesota

My husband loves to grill these deliciously different turkey kabobs, and everyone gets a kick out of the zingy taste from the limes and jalapenos. Its tongue-tingling combination of flavors makes this one company dish that draws compliments.

3 cans (6 ounces *each*) orange juice concentrate, thawed
1-1/4 cups lime juice
1 cup honey
4 to 5 jalapeno peppers, seeded and chopped
10 garlic cloves, minced
3 tablespoons ground cumin
2 tablespoons grated lime peel
1 teaspoon salt
2 pounds boneless turkey, chicken *or* pork, cut into 1-1/4-inch cubes
4 medium sweet red *or* green peppers, cut into 1-inch pieces
1 large red onion, cut into 1-inch pieces
3 small zucchini, cut into 3/4-inch slices
8 ounces fresh mushrooms
3 medium limes, cut into wedges

1. In a bowl, combine the first eight ingredients; mix well. Pour half of marinade into a large resealable plastic bag; add meat and turn to coat. Pour remaining marinade into another large resealable plastic bag. Add

vegetables and turn to coat. Seal and refrigerate for 8 hours or overnight, turning occasionally.

2. Drain meat, discarding marinade. Drain vegetables, reserving marinade for basting. On metal or soaked bamboo skewers, alternate meat, vegetables and lime wedges.

3. Grill, uncovered, over medium heat for 4-5 minutes on each side. Baste with reserved marinade. Continue turning and basting for 10-12 minutes or until meat juices run clear and vegetables are tender. **Yield:** 8 servings.

Editor's Note: When cutting or seeding hot peppers, use rubber or plastic gloves to protect your hands. Avoid touching your face.

Baked Cod

Ginny Morgan, Marblehead, Massachusetts

Fresh fish is a New England staple. This easy and delicious recipe has become a family favorite over the years.

1/4 cup butter, melted
1/4 cup lemon juice
1/4 cup chopped green onions
2 tablespoons water
1/2 teaspoon dill weed
1/2 teaspoon garlic salt
1 pound cod *or* haddock fillets, cut into serving-size pieces
Lemon-pepper seasoning
Lemon slices and dill sprigs, optional

1. In an ungreased 11-in. x 7-in. x 2-in. baking dish, combine the butter, lemon juice, onions, water, dill and garlic salt. Add fish fillets; turn to coat. Cover and refrigerate for 1 hour.

2. Loosely cover and bake at 350° for 25-30 minutes or until fish flakes easily with a fork. Sprinkle with lemon-pepper. Garnish with lemon and dill if desired. **Yield:** 3-4 servings.

🎗🎗🎗

Chicken Sausage Skillet

Connie Dowell, Orlando, Florida

My sister Mary, an excellent cook, shared this wonderful recipe—I've always loved its tantalizing blend of ingredients.

1 medium onion, thinly sliced
1 medium green pepper, thinly sliced
1 cup sliced fresh mushrooms
1 cup sliced zucchini
2 tablespoons olive oil
1/2 to 3/4 pound boneless skinless chicken breasts, thinly sliced
1/2 to 3/4 pound Italian sausage links, cut into 1/2-inch pieces
2 cans (14-1/2 ounces *each*) diced tomatoes, undrained
1 garlic clove, minced
3/4 teaspoon dried basil
3/4 teaspoon dried oregano
Hot cooked rice

1. In a large skillet, saute the onion, green pepper, mushrooms and zucchini in oil until tender. Remove vegetables with a slotted spoon; set aside.

2. Add chicken and sausage to skillet; cook until no longer pink. Drain. Stir in tomatoes, garlic, basil and oregano.

3. Return vegetables to pan. Bring to a boil. Reduce heat; cover and simmer for 10 minutes or until heated through. Serve over rice. **Yield:** 6-8 servings.

🎗🎗🎗

Gingered Pork Tenderloin

Rebecca Evanoff, Holden, Massachusetts

Ginger, onions and garlic pack a flavorful punch paired with pork tenderloin. These tasty medallions, smothered in golden caramelized onions, make a simple and satisfying main dish that your family is sure to love.

2 large onions, thinly sliced
4 teaspoons olive oil
1/4 cup water
4 teaspoons minced fresh gingerroot
2 garlic cloves, minced
1/2 cup apple jelly
1 pork tenderloin (1 pound)
1/4 teaspoon salt
Hot cooked rice pilaf *or* rice

1. In a skillet, saute onions in oil and water for 5-6 minutes. Stir in ginger and garlic. Cover and cook for 8-12 minutes or until onions are tender, stirring occasionally. Reduce heat; stir in apple jelly until melted.

2. Cut tenderloin into eight slices; flatten each to 1/2-in. thickness. Sprinkle with salt.

3. In a skillet coated with nonstick spray, saute pork for 4 minutes; turn. Top with reserved onions; cover and cook for 5-7 minutes or until the meat juices run clear. Serve with rice pilaf. **Yield:** 2-3 servings.

Herb-Roasted Turkey

Becky Goldsmith, Eden Prairie, Minnesota

Our guests always comment on how moist and flavorful this elegant entree is. Rubbed with garden-fresh herbs, this turkey has such a wonderful aroma when it's roasting that it lures everyone into the kitchen!

1 turkey (14 pounds)
1 tablespoon salt
1 teaspoon pepper
18 sprigs fresh thyme, *divided*
4 medium onions, sliced
4 celery ribs, sliced
2 medium carrots, sliced
3 bay leaves
1 tablespoon peppercorns
1/2 cup butter, melted
1 teaspoon minced fresh sage *or* 1/2 teaspoon rubbed sage
1 teaspoon minced fresh thyme *or* 1/2 teaspoon dried thyme
1 teaspoon minced chives

1. Rub the surface of the turkey and sprinkle cavity with salt and pepper. Place 12 sprigs of thyme in cavity. In a large heavy roasting pan, place onions, celery, carrots, bay leaves, peppercorns and remaining thyme sprigs. Place the turkey, breast side up, over vegetables. Drizzle butter over turkey and sprinkle with minced herbs.

2. Cover loosely with foil. Bake at 325° for 2-1/2 hours. Remove foil; bake 1-1/2 to 2 hours longer or until a meat thermometer reads 180°, basting every 20 minutes.

3. Cover and let stand for 20 minutes before carving. Discard bay leaves and peppercorns; thicken pan drippings for gravy if desired. **Yield:** 12-14 servings.

Pear-Stuffed Tenderloin

Aloma Hawkins, Bixby, Missouri

This succulent entree is a classic you'll be proud to serve your family. There's very little fuss to making this main dish, and the meat always turns out extremely tender.

1 cup chopped peeled ripe pears
1/4 cup chopped hazelnuts *or* almonds, toasted
1/4 cup soft bread crumbs
1/4 cup finely shredded carrot
2 tablespoons chopped onion
1/2 teaspoon minced fresh gingerroot
1/4 teaspoon salt
1/4 teaspoon pepper
1 pork tenderloin (3/4 to 1 pound)
Vegetable oil
2 tablespoons orange marmalade

1. In a bowl, combine the first eight ingredients; set aside. Make a lengthwise cut three-quarters of the way through the tenderloin; open and flatten to 1/4-in. thickness. Spread pear mixture over tenderloin. Roll up from a long side; tuck in ends and secure with toothpicks.

2. Place tenderloin on a rack in a shallow roasting pan. Brush lightly with oil. Bake, uncovered, at 425° for 20-25 minutes or until a meat thermometer inserted into pork reads 155°.

3. Brush with marmalade. Bake 5-10 minutes longer or until thermometer reads 160°-170°. Let stand for 5 minutes. Discard toothpicks and slice. **Yield:** 2-3 servings.

Skillet Enchiladas

Cathie Beard, Philomath, Oregon

This stovetop Mexican-style dish disappears fast when our two grown children and three grandchildren visit.

1 pound ground beef
1 medium onion, chopped
1 can (10-3/4 ounces) condensed cream of mushroom soup, undiluted
1 can (10 ounces) enchilada sauce
1/3 cup milk
1 to 2 tablespoons canned chopped green chilies
Vegetable oil
8 corn tortillas
2-1/2 cups (10 ounces) finely shredded cheddar cheese, *divided*
1/2 cup chopped ripe olives

1. In a large skillet, cook beef and onion over medium heat until meat is no longer pink; drain. Stir in the soup, enchilada sauce, milk and chilies. Bring to a boil. Reduce heat; cover and simmer for 20 minutes, stirring occasionally.

2. Meanwhile, in another skillet, heat 1/4 in. of oil. Dip each tortilla in hot oil for 3 seconds on each side or just until limp; drain on paper towels.

3. Top each tortilla with 1/4 cup cheese and 1 tablespoon olives. Roll up and place over beef mixture, spooning some of mixture over the enchiladas.

4. Cover and cook until heated through, about 5 minutes. Sprinkle with remaining cheese; cover and cook until cheese is melted. **Yield:** 8 enchiladas.

Almond Turkey Casserole

Jill Black, Troy, Ontario

A special cousin shared the recipe for this comforting casserole. The almonds and water chestnuts give it a fun crunch.

- **2 cans (10-3/4 ounces *each*) condensed cream of mushroom soup, undiluted**
- **1/2 cup mayonnaise**
- **1/2 cup sour cream**
- **2 tablespoons chopped onion**
- **2 tablespoons lemon juice**
- **1 teaspoon salt**
- **1/2 teaspoon white pepper**
- **5 cups cubed cooked turkey**
- **3 cups cooked rice**
- **4 celery ribs, chopped**
- **1 can (8 ounces) sliced water chestnuts, drained**
- **1 cup sliced almonds**

TOPPING:

- **1-1/2 cups crushed butter-flavored crackers (about 38 crackers)**
- **1/3 cup butter, melted**
- **1/4 cup sliced almonds**

1. In a large bowl, combine the soup, mayonnaise, sour cream, onion, lemon juice, salt and pepper. Stir in the turkey, rice, celery, water chestnuts and almonds. Transfer to a greased 13-in. x 9-in. x 2-in. baking dish.

2. Combine topping ingredients; sprinkle over turkey mixture. Bake, uncovered, at 350° for 35-40 minutes or until bubbly and golden brown. **Yield:** 8-10 servings.

Editor's Note: Reduced-fat or fat-free mayonnaise may not be substituted for regular mayonnaise in this recipe.

Ham 'n' Swiss Chicken

Dorothy Witmer, Ephrata, Pennsylvania

This saucy casserole allows you to enjoy all the rich flavor of traditional chicken cordon bleu with less effort. It's a snap to layer the ingredients and let them cook all afternoon. Just toss a salad to make this meal complete.

- **2 eggs**
- **2 cups milk, *divided***
- **1/2 cup butter, melted**
- **1/2 cup chopped celery**
- **1 teaspoon finely chopped onion**
- **8 slices bread, cubed**
- **12 thin slices deli ham, rolled up**
- **2 cups (8 ounces) shredded Swiss cheese**
- **2-1/2 cups cubed cooked chicken**
- **1 can (10-3/4 ounces) condensed cream of chicken soup, undiluted**

1. In a large bowl, beat the eggs and 1-1/2 cups milk. Add butter, celery and onion. Stir in bread cubes. Place half of the mixture in a greased slow cooker; top with half of the rolled-up ham, cheese and chicken.

2. Combine soup and remaining milk; pour half over the chicken. Repeat layers once.

3. Cover and cook on low for 4-5 hours or until a thermometer inserted into bread mixture reads 160°. **Yield:** 6 servings.

Pepperoni Lasagna

Barbara McIntosh, Midland, Texas

I've served this satisfying lasagna for years—when our children were small, they preferred it over a steak dinner! Now my grandchildren request that I bring a pan along when I visit...and, of course, I do.

1-1/2 pounds ground beef
1 small onion, chopped
2-1/2 cups water
1 can (8 ounces) tomato sauce
1 can (6 ounces) tomato paste
1 teaspoon beef bouillon granules
1 tablespoon dried parsley flakes
2 teaspoons Italian seasoning
1 teaspoon salt
1/4 teaspoon garlic salt
2 eggs
1 carton (12 ounces) small-curd cottage cheese
1/2 cup sour cream
8 lasagna noodles, cooked and drained
1 package (3-1/2 ounces) sliced pepperoni
2 cups (8 ounces) shredded mozzarella cheese
1/2 cup grated Parmesan cheese

1. In a skillet, cook beef and onion over medium heat until meat is no longer pink; drain. Add water, tomato sauce, tomato paste, bouillon and seasonings. Bring to a boil. Reduce heat; simmer, uncovered, for 30 minutes.

2. In a bowl, combine eggs, cottage cheese and sour cream. Spread 1/2 cup meat sauce into a greased 13-in. x 9-in. x 2-in. baking dish. Layer with four noodles, the cottage cheese mixture and pepperoni. Top with remaining noodles and meat sauce. Sprinkle with mozzarella and Parmesan cheeses.

3. Cover and bake at 350° for 35 minutes. Uncover; bake 10 minutes longer or until heated through. Let stand 15 minutes before cutting. **Yield:** 12 servings.

Horseradish Honey Ham

Beverly Loomis, Ithaca, Michigan

When my husband and I first tasted this delicious ham, we were surprised to learn that the sauce included horseradish. That secret ingredient definitely is the key to its tangy taste. I serve it for Easter and Christmas.

1 boneless fully cooked ham (5 to 7 pounds)
1/4 cup honey, warmed
1/8 teaspoon ground cloves
1 cup packed brown sugar
1/2 cup prepared horseradish
1/4 cup lemon juice

1. Cut ham into 1/4-in. slices and tie with kitchen string. Place ham on a rack in a shallow roasting pan. Combine honey and cloves; drizzle over ham. Bake, uncovered, at 325° for 1-1/2 to 2 hours or until a meat thermometer reads 140° and ham is heated through, basting often with drippings.

2. Meanwhile, combine the brown sugar, horseradish and lemon juice.

3. Increase oven temperature to 400°. Baste ham with brown sugar sauce so sauce penetrates between slices. Bake, uncovered, for 15-20 minutes. **Yield:** 15-18 servings.

Stovetop Pot Roast

Mary Lou Chernik, Taos, New Mexico

I make this hearty stovetop favorite at least twice a month. My husband, Jim, loves it!

1 boneless chuck roast (3 to 4 pounds)
2 to 3 garlic cloves, halved lengthwise
2 tablespoons olive oil
1 large onion, cut into 1/2-inch slices
3 celery ribs, cut into 1/2-inch slices
2 medium turnips, peeled and cut into chunks
4 cups water
2 beef bouillon cubes
4 medium potatoes, peeled and quartered
1 pound carrots, cut into chunks
1/2 pound fresh *or* frozen green beans, partially thawed
1/2 pound fresh mushrooms, sliced
3 tablespoons cornstarch
1/4 cup cold water
Salt and pepper to taste

1. Cut slits in roast; insert garlic slivers. In a large deep skillet, brown roast on all sides in oil. Remove roast. Add

onion, celery and turnips to skillet. Place roast over vegetables; add water and bouillon. Bring to a boil. Reduce heat; cover and simmer for 2 hours.

2. Add potatoes, carrots and beans; cover and cook for 45 minutes. Add mushrooms; cover and cook 15 minutes longer or until meat and vegetables are tender. Remove to a serving platter and keep warm.

3. Skim fat from pan juices. Combine cornstarch and cold water until smooth; stir into pan juices. Bring to a boil; cook and stir for 2 minutes. Season with salt and pepper. Slice roast; serve with vegetables and gravy. **Yield:** 8-10 servings.

Grilled Pork and Poblano Peppers

Donna Gay Harris, Springdale, Arkansas

My husband and I entertain a lot in summer, and this has quickly become our most-requested dish. I usually serve it with Mexican rice and a tossed salad.

4 large poblano peppers
2 cups (8 ounces) shredded Monterey Jack cheese
4-1/2 teaspoons chili powder
1-1/2 teaspoons onion powder
1-1/2 teaspoons ground cumin
1/2 teaspoon garlic powder
1/4 teaspoon salt
1/8 teaspoon aniseed, ground
1/8 teaspoon cayenne pepper
2 pork tenderloins (about 1 pound *each*)

1. Cut the top off each pepper and set tops aside. Remove seeds. Stuff peppers with cheese. Replace tops and secure with toothpicks; set aside.

2. Combine the seasonings; rub over pork. Grill, covered, over medium-hot heat for 18 minutes or until a meat thermometer reads 160°-170° and juices run clear.

3. Place peppers on sides of grill (not directly over coals); heat for 10 minutes or until browned. **Yield:** 6-8 servings.

Editor's Note: When cutting or seeding hot peppers, use rubber or plastic gloves to protect your hands. Avoid touching your face.

Shrimp Stir-Fry

Alberta Crowe, Staten Island, New York

When I need to fix a quick meal, I frequently turn to this well-loved dish that takes only a few minutes to cook. I've also used chicken instead of shrimp with delicious results.

1-1/2 cups broccoli florets
1 small sweet red pepper, julienned
1 small green pepper, julienned
1 to 2 tablespoons vegetable oil
1 pound uncooked shrimp, peeled and deveined
1 tablespoon cornstarch
2 teaspoons brown sugar
1 teaspoon ground ginger
1 cup orange juice
1/4 cup soy sauce
Hot cooked rice

1. In a skillet, stir-fry broccoli and peppers in oil until tender. Add shrimp; stir-fry for 3-5 minutes or until shrimp turn pink.

2. Combine the cornstarch, brown sugar, ginger, orange juice and soy sauce until smooth; add to skillet. Bring to a boil; cook and stir for 2 minutes or until thickened. Serve over rice. **Yield:** 3-4 servings.

Deluxe Ham Balls

Joan Settle, Oceanside, California

Whenever I serve these saucy baked ham balls to guests, they ask me for the recipe. It's one I've had for many years and is a great use for leftover ham. I love to entertain and know I can count on these ham balls to be a hit.

2 eggs
1/2 cup milk
3/4 cup dry bread crumbs
1/4 cup finely chopped onion
1 pound ground fully cooked ham
1/2 pound ground pork
1 can (8 ounces) crushed pineapple
1/2 cup packed brown sugar
1/3 cup vinegar
1/3 cup ketchup
2 tablespoons soy sauce
1 teaspoon ground ginger
Hot cooked rice

1. In a bowl, combine the eggs, milk, bread crumbs and onion. Crumble ham and pork over mixture; mix well. Shape into 1-1/4-in. balls. Place in a greased 13-in. x 9-in. x 2-in. baking dish.

2. In a saucepan, combine the pineapple, brown sugar, vinegar, ketchup, soy sauce and ginger. Cook and stir until sugar is dissolved. Pour over ham balls.

3. Bake, uncovered, at 350° for 40-45 minutes or until a meat thermometer reads 160°. Serve over rice. **Yield:** 6 servings.

Cranberry Pork Chops

Joan Dobbs, Evansville, Illinois

This meal is a proven winner to fix. I never have leftovers. I farm with my dad and brother, but in my spare time I love to cook delicious dishes like these pork chops.

1-1/2 cups sugar
1-3/4 cups water, *divided*
1 package (12 ounces) fresh *or* frozen cranberries
1/2 cup barbecue sauce
8 bone-in pork chops (1/2 to 3/4 inch thick)
Salt and pepper to taste
2 tablespoons vegetable oil
2 tablespoons cornstarch
1/4 cup cold water

1. In a saucepan, combine sugar and 1-1/2 cups water. Cook and stir over medium heat until the sugar is dissolved. Bring to a boil; boil, uncovered, for 5 minutes. Add cranberries; cook 5 minutes longer or until the berries pop. Skim off foam if necessary. Stir in barbecue sauce and remaining water. Mix well; set aside.

2. Season pork chops with salt and pepper. In a large skillet over medium heat, brown chops on both sides in oil; drain. Pour the cranberry sauce over chops. Cover and simmer for 35-40 minutes or until meat juices run clear.

3. Remove chops and keep warm. Combine cornstarch and cold water until smooth; add to skillet. Bring to a boil; cook and stir for 2 minutes or until thickened. Spoon over pork chops. **Yield:** 8 servings.

Bayou Country Seafood Casserole

Ethel Miller, Eunice, Louisiana

Since crabs and shrimp are so plentiful in our bayous and rivers, they're used in a variety of recipes like this one.

6 tablespoons butter
1 medium onion, chopped
1 medium green pepper, chopped
1 celery rib, chopped
1 garlic clove, minced
1 can (10-3/4 ounces) condensed cream of mushroom soup, undiluted
1 pound uncooked shrimp, peeled and deveined
1-1/2 cups cooked rice
2 cans (6 ounces *each*) crabmeat, drained and flaked with cartilage removed *or* 1-1/2 pounds cooked crabmeat
4 slices day-old bread, cubed
3/4 cup half-and-half cream *or* water
1/4 cup chopped green onion tops
1/2 teaspoon salt
1/4 teaspoon pepper
Dash cayenne pepper
TOPPING:
2 tablespoons butter, melted
1/3 cup dry bread crumbs
2 tablespoons snipped fresh parsley

1. In a skillet, melt butter over medium heat. Saute onion, green pepper, celery and garlic until tender. Add soup and shrimp. Cook and stir over medium heat 10 minutes or until shrimp turn pink. Stir in rice, crab, bread cubes, cream, onion tops and seasonings.

2. Spoon into a greased 2-qt. baking dish. Combine topping ingredients; sprinkle over casserole. Bake at 375° for 30 minutes or until heated through. **Yield:** 8 servings.

Potato Pork Pie

Michelle Ross, Stanwood, Washington

A true comfort food that's impossible to resist, this main dish is hearty and saucy with flavors that blend so nicely together. Many shepherd's pie recipes call for beef, so this pork version is a tasty change of pace.

- **2 pounds potatoes, peeled and cubed**
- **1/3 cup heavy whipping cream**
- **4 tablespoons butter, *divided***
- **3/4 teaspoon salt**
- **1/8 teaspoon pepper**
- **1 medium onion, chopped**
- **1 garlic clove, minced**
- **1/4 cup all-purpose flour**
- **1 can (14-1/2 ounces) beef broth**
- **1 tablespoon Dijon mustard**
- **1 teaspoon dried thyme**
- **4 tablespoons minced fresh parsley, *divided***
- **2-1/2 cups cubed cooked pork**

1. Place potatoes in a saucepan and cover with water; bring to a boil. Cover and cook for 20-25 minutes or until very tender. Drain well. Mash potatoes with cream, 2 tablespoons butter, salt and pepper. Spread 1-1/2 cups of mashed potatoes into a greased shallow 1-1/2-qt. baking dish.

2. In a skillet, saute onion and garlic in remaining butter until tender. Stir in flour until blended. Gradually stir in broth, mustard, thyme and 2 tablespoons parsley. Bring to a boil; cook and stir for 2 minutes or until thickened. Stir in pork; heat through. Pour over the potato crust. Pipe or spoon remaining mashed potatoes over top.

3. Bake, uncovered, at 375° for 35-40 minutes or until the potatoes are lightly browned. Sprinkle with remaining parsley. **Yield:** 6 servings.

Easy and Elegant Ham

Denise DiPace, Medford, New Jersey

I fix this moist, tender ham to serve my large family. It gets started quickly in the morning, frees up my oven, tastes outstanding and feeds a crowd. Covered with colorful pineapple slices, cherries and orange glaze, its showstopping appearance appeals to both children and adults.

- **2 cans (20 ounces *each*) sliced pineapple**
- **1 fully cooked boneless ham (about 6 pounds), halved**
- **1 jar (6 ounces) maraschino cherries, well drained**
- **1 jar (12 ounces) orange marmalade**

1. Drain pineapple, reserving juice; set juice aside. Place half of the pineapple in an ungreased 5-qt. slow cooker. Top with the ham. Add cherries, remaining pineapple and reserved pineapple juice. Spoon marmalade over ham.

2. Cover and cook on low for 6-7 hours or until heated through. Remove to a warm serving platter. Let stand for 10-15 minutes before slicing. Serve pineapple and cherries with sliced ham. **Yield:** 18-20 servings.

Stir-Fried Steak and Veggies

Inez Glover, Wainwright, Alberta

There's just enough ginger, chili powder and garlic powder in the sauce to spark the taste of this enjoyable steak specialty. For variety, you can substitute chicken or pork for the sirloin. If I'm in a hurry or don't have fresh vegetables on hand, I'll reach for two bags of frozen stir-fry vegetables instead.

1 tablespoon cornstarch
1 tablespoon brown sugar
3/4 teaspoon ground ginger
1/2 teaspoon chili powder
1/4 teaspoon garlic powder
1/4 teaspoon pepper
1/2 cup cold water
1/4 cup soy sauce
1 pound boneless sirloin steak, cut into thin strips
2 tablespoons vegetable oil
2 cups broccoli florets
2 cups cauliflowerets
1 large onion, chopped
1 cup sliced carrots
Hot cooked rice

1. In a small bowl, whisk together the first eight ingredients until smooth; set aside.

2. In a skillet or wok, stir-fry steak in oil for 3-5 minutes. Add broccoli, cauliflower, onion, carrots and soy sauce mixture; cover and cook for 8 minutes or until vegetables are crisp-tender, stirring occasionally. Serve over rice. **Yield:** 4 servings.

Herbed Chicken and Shrimp

Diana Knight, Reno, Nevada

Tender chicken and shrimp make a flavorful combination that's easy to prepare, yet elegant enough to serve at a dinner party. While I clean the house, this dish practically cooks itself. I serve it over hot cooked rice with crusty bread and a green salad.

1 teaspoon salt
1 teaspoon pepper
1 broiler/fryer chicken (3 to 4 pounds), cut up and skin removed
1/4 cup butter
1 large onion, chopped
1 can (8 ounces) tomato sauce
1/2 cup white wine *or* chicken broth
1 garlic clove, minced
1 teaspoon dried basil
1 pound uncooked medium shrimp, peeled and deveined

1. Combine salt and pepper; rub over the chicken pieces. In a skillet, brown chicken on all sides in butter. Transfer to an ungreased slow cooker.

2. In a bowl, combine the onion, tomato sauce, wine or broth, garlic and basil; pour over chicken. Cover and cook on low for 4-5 hours or until chicken juices run clear.

3. Add the shrimp and mix well. Cover and cook on high for 20-30 minutes or until shrimp turn pink. **Yield:** 4 servings.

Seafood Tortilla Lasagna

Sharon Sawicki, Carol Stream, Illinois

My husband and I enjoy lasagna, seafood and Mexican fare. One evening, I combined all three into this deliciously different entree. It certainly is a tempting, memorable change of pace from traditional Italian-style lasagnas.

1 jar (20 ounces) picante sauce
1-1/2 pounds uncooked medium shrimp, peeled and deveined
4 to 6 garlic cloves, minced
1/8 teaspoon cayenne pepper
1 tablespoon olive oil
1/3 cup butter
1/3 cup all-purpose flour
1 can (14-1/2 ounces) chicken broth
1/2 cup heavy whipping cream
15 corn tortillas (6 inches), warmed
1 package (16 ounces) imitation crabmeat, flaked
3 cups (12 ounces) shredded Colby-Monterey Jack cheese

1. Place the picante sauce in a blender or food processor; cover and process until smooth. Set aside.

2. In a skillet, cook shrimp, garlic and cayenne in oil until shrimp turn pink, about 3 minutes; remove and set aside. In the same skillet, melt the butter. Stir in flour until smooth. Gradually add broth. Bring to a boil; cook and stir for 2 minutes or until thickened. Reduce heat. Stir in cream and picante sauce; heat through.

3. Spread 1/2 cup of sauce in a greased 13-in. x 9-in. x 2-in. baking dish. Layer with six tortillas, half of the shrimp, crab and white sauce and 1-1/4 cups cheese. Repeat layers. Tear or cut remaining tortillas; arrange over cheese. Sprinkle with remaining cheese.

4. Bake, uncovered, at 375° for 30-35 minutes or until bubbly. Let stand 15 minutes before cutting. **Yield:** 12 servings.

Old-Fashioned Swiss Steak

Elaine DeWitt, Lake City, Minnesota

Our ladies' group held monthly dinners at our church to raise money, and this is one of the dishes we served. We never had to advertise these dinners—word about the good food got around quickly.

2 pounds round steak
1/2 cup all-purpose flour
1/2 teaspoon salt
1/2 teaspoon pepper, *divided*
2 tablespoons vegetable oil
1 cup chopped onion
1/2 cup chopped green pepper
1/4 cup soy sauce
1/2 teaspoon garlic salt
Hot cooked noodles, optional

1. Cut steak into serving-size pieces. Combine flour, salt and 1/4 teaspoon pepper; sprinkle over steak and pound into both sides. In a skillet over medium heat, brown steak on both sides in oil.

2. Transfer to a greased 13-in. x 9-in. x 2-in. baking dish; top with onion and green pepper. Drizzle with soy sauce; sprinkle with garlic salt and remaining pepper.

3. Cover and bake at 325° for 1-1/2 hours or until meat is tender. Serve over noodles if desired. **Yield:** 6-8 servings.

Pork Veggie Stir-Fry

Laurel Reisinger, Saskatoon, Saskatchewan

A colorful combination of vegetables, tender pork strips, seasonings and crunchy peanuts makes this an appealing main dish.

- **3 cups sliced cauliflower**
- **3 tablespoons vegetable oil, *divided***
- **2 medium carrots, julienned**
- **1 can (15 ounces) whole baby corn, rinsed and drained *or* 1-1/2 cups frozen corn, thawed**
- **1/2 cup frozen peas, thawed**
- **1 pound boneless pork, cut into thin strips**
- **2 green onions, thinly sliced**
- **2 garlic cloves, minced**
- **1 tablespoon minced fresh gingerroot**
- **1/2 to 1 teaspoon chili powder**
- **1 cup water**
- **1/4 cup soy sauce**
- **4 teaspoons honey**
- **2 teaspoons chicken bouillon granules**
- **4 teaspoons cornstarch**
- **2 tablespoons cold water**
- **1/4 cup salted peanuts**
- **Hot cooked rice**

1. In a skillet or wok, stir-fry cauliflower in 2 tablespoons oil for 3 minutes. Add carrots; stir-fry for 2 minutes. Add corn and peas; stir-fry until vegetables are crisp-tender. Remove; keep warm.

2. Stir-fry pork in remaining oil for 2 minutes. Add onions, garlic, ginger and chili powder; stir-fry until pork is no longer pink. Remove; keep warm.

3. Combine water, soy sauce, honey and bouillon in same pan. Combine cornstarch and cold water; gradually add to pan. Bring to a boil; cook and stir for 2 minutes or until thickened.

4. Return vegetables and pork mixture to pan; heat through. Stir in peanuts. Serve over rice. **Yield:** 6 servings.

Homemade Manicotti

SueAnn Bunt, Painted Post, New York

These tender manicotti are much easier to stuff than the purchased variety. People are amazed when I say I made my own noodles.

CREPE NOODLES:

- **1-1/2 cups all-purpose flour**
- **1 cup milk**
- **3 eggs**
- **1/2 teaspoon salt**

FILLING:

- **1-1/2 pounds ricotta cheese**
- **1/4 cup grated Romano cheese**
- **1 egg**
- **1 tablespoon minced fresh parsley *or* 1 teaspoon dried parsley flakes**
- **1 jar (28 ounces) spaghetti sauce**
- **Shredded Romano cheese, optional**

1. Place flour in a bowl; whisk in milk, eggs and salt until smooth. Pour about 2 tablespoons onto a hot greased 8-in. skillet; spread to a 5-in. circle. Cook over medium heat until set; do not brown or turn. Repeat with remaining batter, making 18 crepes. Stack crepes between waxed paper; set aside.

2. For filling, combine cheeses, egg and parsley. Spoon 3-4 tablespoons down the center of each crepe; roll up. Pour half of the spaghetti sauce into an ungreased 13-in. x 9-in. x 2-in. baking dish. Place crepes, seam side down, over the sauce; pour remaining sauce over top.

3. Cover and bake at 350° for 20 minutes. Uncover and bake 20 minutes longer or until heated through. Sprinkle with Romano cheese if desired. **Yield:** 6 servings.

Where's the Squash Lasagna

Norma Brinson, Greenville, North Carolina

I devised this recipe to hide zucchini from my unsuspecting grandchildren and any others who think they don't like it. It's always a hit at our house.

1 pound ground beef
2 large zucchini (about 1 pound), shredded
3/4 cup chopped onion
2 garlic cloves, minced
1 can (14-1/2 ounces) stewed tomatoes
2 cups water
1 can (12 ounces) tomato paste
1 tablespoon minced fresh parsley
1-1/2 teaspoons salt
1 teaspoon sugar
1/2 teaspoon dried oregano
1/2 teaspoon pepper
9 lasagna noodles, cooked, rinsed and drained
1 carton (15 ounces) ricotta cheese
2 cups (8 ounces) shredded mozzarella cheese
1 cup grated Parmesan cheese

1. In a skillet, cook beef, zucchini, onion and garlic over medium heat until meat is no longer pink; drain.

2. Place tomatoes in a food processor or blender; cover and process until smooth. Stir into beef mixture. Add the water, tomato paste, parsley and seasonings. Bring to a boil. Reduce heat; simmer, uncovered, for 30 minutes, stirring occasionally.

3. Spread 1 cup meat sauce in a greased 13-in. x 9-in. x 2-in. baking dish. Arrange three noodles over sauce. Spread with a third of the meat sauce; top with half of the ricotta. Sprinkle with a third of the mozzarella and Parmesan. Repeat. Top with remaining noodles, meat sauce and cheeses.

4. Cover and bake at 350° for 45 minutes. Uncover; bake 15 minutes longer or until bubbly. Let stand for 15 minutes before cutting. **Yield:** 12 servings.

Honey Walleye

Kitty McCue, St. Louis Park, Minnesota

Our state is known as the "Land of 10,000 Lakes", so fishing is a favorite recreation here. This recipe is a quick way to prepare all the fresh walleye that's hooked by the anglers in our family.

1 egg
2 teaspoons honey
2 cups crushed butter-flavored crackers (about 45 to 50 crackers)
1/2 teaspoon salt
4 to 6 walleye fillets (1-1/2 to 2 pounds)
1/3 to 1/2 cup vegetable oil
Lemon wedges, optional

1. In a shallow bowl, beat egg; add honey. In a plastic bag, combine crackers and salt. Dip fish in egg mixture, then shake in bag until coated.

2. In a skillet, cook fillets in oil for 3-5 minutes per side or until golden and fish flakes easily with a fork. Serve with lemon wedges if desired. **Yield:** 4-6 servings.

Sweet 'n' Sour Meatballs

Andrea Busch, Brackenridge, Pennsylvania

When I fixed this flavorful recipe for the first time, it was a welcome change from some of our regular ho-hum dinner menus. My husband, Eric, and our two sons are pretty picky—but there are no leftovers whenever I serve this dish!

1 egg
1/4 cup seasoned bread crumbs
1/2 teaspoon salt
1/4 teaspoon ground ginger
Dash pepper
1 pound ground beef
1 can (20 ounces) pineapple chunks
1/4 cup cider vinegar
1/4 cup packed brown sugar
2 tablespoons soy sauce
1 cup sliced carrots
1 medium green pepper, julienned
1 tablespoon cornstarch
2 tablespoons cold water
Hot cooked rice

1. In a bowl, combine the first five ingredients. Add beef; mix well. Shape into 1-in. balls. In a skillet over medium heat, cook meatballs until no longer pink; drain.

2. Drain pineapple, reserving juice; set pineapple aside. Add water to juice to measure 1 cup. Stir in vinegar, brown sugar and soy sauce; pour over meatballs. Add carrots. Bring to a boil. Reduce heat; cover and simmer for 5-8 minutes or until carrots are crisp-tender. Stir in green pepper and pineapple; cover and simmer 5 minutes longer or until pepper is crisp-tender.

3. Combine cornstarch and water until smooth; stir into meatball mixture. Bring to a boil; cook and stir for 2 minutes or until thickened. Serve over rice. **Yield:** 4-6 servings.

Potato Ham Bake

Arthur Heidorn, Hillside, Illinois

I like to make this casserole with the leftovers from a baked ham. It's a great meal all by itself.

3 medium potatoes, peeled and thinly sliced
2 cups cubed fully cooked ham
1 medium onion, sliced and separated into rings
8 slices process American cheese
1 can (10-3/4 ounces) condensed cream of mushroom soup, undiluted
1/2 cup frozen peas, thawed

1. In a greased 3-qt. baking dish, layer half of the potatoes, ham, onion, cheese and soup. Repeat layers. Cover and bake at 350° for 1-1/4 hours or until potatoes are almost tender.

2. Sprinkle with peas. Bake, uncovered, for 10 minutes or until heated through. **Yield:** 6 servings.

Turkey Potpie

Marie Basinger, Connellsville, Pennsylvania

My family raves over this comforting dish with its flaky homemade crust, saucy meat and veggie filling. Sometimes, I cook a bird specifically with this potpie in mind—when we just can't wait for leftovers to make it!

1 medium onion, chopped
1/3 cup butter
1/2 cup all-purpose flour
1 teaspoon salt
1/4 teaspoon pepper
1-3/4 cups chicken *or* turkey broth
2/3 cup milk
2 cups cubed cooked turkey
1 cup (4 ounces) shredded cheddar cheese
1 package (10 ounces) frozen peas and carrots, thawed

PASTRY:

2 cups all-purpose flour
2 teaspoons celery seed
1 teaspoon salt
2/3 cup plus 2 tablespoons shortening
4 to 5 tablespoons cold water
Milk, optional

1. In a saucepan, saute onion in butter. Stir in the flour, salt and pepper until blended. Gradually add broth and milk. Bring to a boil; cook and stir for 2 minutes or until thickened. Add the turkey, cheese and vegetables; cook until the cheese is melted. Set aside and keep warm.

2. For the crust, combine flour, celery seed and salt in a bowl. Cut in shortening until mixture resembles coarse crumbs. Add enough water until dough forms a ball.

3. Divide dough in half. Line a 9-in. pie plate with bottom pastry; trim even with edge of plate. Pour hot turkey filling into crust. Roll out remaining pastry to fit top of pie; place over the filling. Trim, seal and flute edges. Cut slits in pastry. Brush the top with milk if desired.

4. Bake at 375° for 40-45 minutes or until crust is golden brown. **Yield:** 6 servings.

Pork Chops Over Rice

Nancy Christenberry, Ortonville, Michigan

If you asked my husband to name his favorite foods, he'd mention these chops. I've also served this appealing skillet supper to company.

8 boneless pork chops (3/4 inch thick)
1 tablespoon vegetable oil
1 cup uncooked long grain rice
1 can (14-1/2 ounces) chicken broth
1/2 cup water
1 small onion, chopped
1 package (10 ounces) frozen peas
1/2 teaspoon salt
1/2 teaspoon dried thyme

1. In a large skillet over medium heat, brown pork chops in oil; remove. Drain. Add the remaining ingredients to skillet. Place pork chops over the rice mixture.

2. Bring to a boil. Reduce heat; cover and simmer for 20-25 minutes or until rice is tender. **Yield:** 8 servings.

Sausage Potato Lasagna

Melissa Pokorny, Abbotsford, British Columbia

I decided to pair up two of my favorites—lasagna and potatoes—in this scrumptious dish. Sliced potatoes take the place of noodles, and the comforting blend of flavors is sure to please anyone with a hearty appetite.

1/2 pound bulk Italian sausage
2 cups sliced fresh mushrooms
4 medium potatoes, peeled and thinly sliced
1 package (10 ounces) frozen chopped spinach, thawed and well drained
1-1/2 cups ricotta cheese
1/4 cup grated Parmesan cheese
1 egg, beaten
1 medium onion, chopped
2 garlic cloves, minced
2 tablespoons butter
2 tablespoons all-purpose flour
Salt and pepper to taste
1/4 teaspoon ground nutmeg
1-1/2 cups milk
1 cup (4 ounces) shredded mozzarella cheese, *divided*
Additional nutmeg, optional

1. In a skillet, cook sausage and mushrooms over medium heat until meat is no longer pink; drain and set aside.

2. Place potatoes in a saucepan; cover with water. Bring to a boil. Reduce heat; cover and cook for 5 minutes or until crisp-tender. Drain and set aside.

3. In a bowl, combine the spinach, ricotta, Parmesan and egg; set aside.

4. In a saucepan, saute onion and garlic in butter until tender. Stir in flour, salt, pepper and nutmeg until blended. Gradually add milk. Bring to a boil; cook and stir for 2 minutes. Remove from the heat.

5. Layer half of the potatoes in a greased 11-in. x 7-in. x 2-in. baking dish. Top with half of the spinach mixture, sausage mixture, white sauce and mozzarella. Layer with the remaining potatoes, spinach mixture, sausage mixture and white sauce.

6. Cover; bake at 350° for 30-35 minutes or until potatoes are tender. Sprinkle with remaining mozzarella. Bake, uncovered, 5 minutes or until cheese is melted. Let stand 15 minutes before cutting. **Yield:** 6-8 servings.

Turkey with Cherry Stuffing

Virginia Sacchetta, Leesburg, Florida

This moist stuffing, with its fruity blend of raisins and tart cherries, is a sweet twist on a traditional version. It's a tasty complement to tender poultry slices.

3/4 cup chopped celery
1/3 cup chopped onion
2 tablespoons butter
3/4 teaspoon dried thyme
1/4 teaspoon poultry seasoning
5 cups seasoned stuffing cubes
3/4 cup golden raisins
3/4 cup chicken broth
1 can (14-1/2 ounces) pitted tart cherries, drained
1 turkey (10 to 12 pounds)
2 tablespoons vegetable oil

1. In a saucepan, saute celery and onion in butter until tender. Stir in thyme and poultry seasoning. In a large bowl, combine stuffing, raisins and celery mixture. Add broth and cherries; toss to mix.

2. Loosely stuff turkey just before baking. Skewer openings; tie drumsticks together. Place the turkey, breast side up, on a rack in a roasting pan. Brush with oil.

3. Bake, uncovered, at 325° for 4 to 4-1/2 hours or until a meat thermometer reads 180° for the turkey and 165° for the stuffing. Baste occasionally with pan drippings. Cover loosely with foil if turkey browns too quickly.

4. Cover and let stand for 20 minutes before removing the stuffing and carving the turkey. If desired, thicken pan drippings for gravy. **Yield:** 10-12 servings (6 cups stuffing).

Editor's Note: The stuffing may be prepared as directed and baked separately in a greased 2-qt. baking dish. Cover and bake at 325° for 50-60 minutes. Uncover and bake 10 minutes longer or until lightly browned.

Grilled Chicken with Peach Sauce

Beverly Minton, Milan, Michigan

I've been cooking since I was a young girl growing up on a farm in Indiana. This recipe was adapted from a pie filling. I've served it many times to family and friends.

1 cup sugar
2 tablespoons cornstarch
1 cup water
2 tablespoons peach gelatin powder
1 medium fresh peach, peeled and finely chopped
4 boneless skinless chicken breast halves

1. In a saucepan, combine sugar, cornstarch and water until smooth. Bring to a boil over medium heat; cook and stir for 2 minutes. Remove from the heat. Stir in gelatin and peach; mix well. Set aside 1 cup for serving.

2. Grill chicken, uncovered, over medium heat for 3 minutes on each side. Baste with some of the remaining peach sauce. Continue grilling for 6-8 minutes or until meat juices run clear, basting and turning several times. Serve with the reserved peach sauce. **Yield:** 4 servings.

Spinach Swiss Pie

Phoebe Martin, Hampstead, Maryland

This egg dish has a wonderful flavor from the nutmeg, which combines well with the Swiss cheese.

1 package (10 ounces) frozen chopped spinach
1 cup (4 ounces) shredded Swiss cheese
2 tablespoons chopped onion
1-1/2 cups milk
3 eggs
3/4 cup biscuit/baking mix
1 teaspoon salt
1/4 teaspoon pepper
1/4 teaspoon ground nutmeg

1. Cook spinach according to package directions; drain well. In a bowl, combine cheese, onion and spinach. Transfer to a greased 9-in. pie plate.

2. In a blender, combine milk, eggs, biscuit mix, salt, pepper and nutmeg; cover and process until smooth. Pour over spinach mixture.

3. Bake at 350° for 45-50 minutes or until a knife inserted near the center comes out clean. **Yield:** 6-8 servings.

German Lasagna

Naomi Hochstetler, Woodburn, Indiana

Sausage and sauerkraut are a palate-pleasing pair, especially in lasagna. My family was a little skeptical when I first served this unusual dish, but in no time, they were clamoring for more.

3/4 cup butter
3/4 cup all-purpose flour
1 tablespoon beef bouillon granules
2 teaspoons onion salt
2 teaspoons pepper, *divided*
1/2 teaspoon white pepper, optional
2-1/4 cups milk
1 can (14-1/2 ounces) chicken broth
1 pound fully cooked kielbasa *or* Polish sausage, chopped
2 eggs
1 carton (12 ounces) small-curd cottage cheese
9 lasagna noodles, cooked and drained
1 jar (16 ounces) sauerkraut, rinsed and squeezed dry
2 cups (8 ounces) shredded Monterey Jack cheese, *divided*

1. In a saucepan, melt butter. Stir in flour, bouillon, onion salt, 1 teaspoon pepper and white pepper if desired until smooth. Gradually stir in milk and broth. Bring to a boil; cook and stir for 2 minutes or until thickened. Add sausage; heat through. Combine eggs, cottage cheese and remaining pepper.

2. Spread 1 cup sausage mixture in a greased 13-in. x 9-in. x 2-in. baking dish. Layer with three noodles, a third of the sausage mixture, half of the cottage cheese mixture and sauerkraut and 3/4 cup Monterey Jack. Repeat layers. Top with the remaining noodles and sausage mixture (dish will be full).

3. Cover and bake at 350° for 50-60 minutes or until bubbly. Sprinkle with remaining Monterey Jack. Bake 5 minutes longer or until cheese is melted. Let stand 15 minutes before cutting. **Yield:** 12 servings.

Fruit-Pecan Pork Roast

Gay Flynn, Bellevue, Nebraska

This spectacular roast was a huge hit with members of the cooking club I belong to. The sweet, tangy fruit glaze looks lovely.

1 rolled boneless pork loin roast (3-1/2 pounds)
1/2 cup chopped green onions
4 tablespoons butter, *divided*
1/4 cup orange juice
1 bay leaf
1 can (16 ounces) whole-berry cranberry sauce
1/2 cup chicken broth
1/2 cup chopped pecans
1 tablespoon red wine vinegar
1/4 teaspoon salt
1/8 teaspoon pepper
1/8 teaspoon sugar
1/4 cup apricot preserves

1. Place roast on a rack in a shallow roasting pan. Bake, uncovered, at 350° for 1 hour.

2. Meanwhile, in a skillet, saute onions in 1 tablespoon butter for 1 minute. Add orange juice and bay leaf; cook and stir over medium-high heat until thickened, about 4 minutes. Add cranberry sauce, broth, pecans and vinegar; cook and stir until slightly thickened, about 5 minutes. Reduce heat; stir in salt, pepper, sugar and remaining butter until butter is melted.

3. Discard bay leaf. Remove 1/4 cup sauce, stir in preserves and spoon over roast. Set remaining sauce aside.

4. Bake 45 minutes longer or until a meat thermometer reads 160°-170°. Let stand 10-15 minutes before slicing. Serve with reserved sauce. **Yield:** 10-12 servings.

Vegetable Lentil Stew

Vi Toews, Bluffton, Alberta

This stew is nothing but good for you! The chunky mixture is full of hearty beans, lentils and other veggies.

✓ Uses less fat, sugar or salt. Includes Nutritional Analysis and Diabetic Exchanges.

4 cups reduced-sodium V8 *or* tomato juice
2 cans (14-1/2 ounces *each*) Italian stewed tomatoes
1 can (16 ounces) kidney beans, rinsed and drained
1 can (15 ounces) garbanzo beans, rinsed and drained
2 medium carrots, thinly sliced
2 medium potatoes, cubed
1 large onion, chopped
1 green pepper, chopped
1 sweet red pepper, chopped
1 cup lentils
2 tablespoons minced parsley
2 tablespoons chili powder
2 teaspoons dried basil
1 teaspoon garlic powder
1 teaspoon ground cumin
1 package (10 ounces) frozen chopped spinach, thawed
1/2 cup reduced-fat sour cream
1/2 cup reduced-fat plain yogurt
2 tablespoons snipped chives

1. In a Dutch oven, combine the first 15 ingredients. Bring to a boil. Reduce heat; cover and simmer for 35-40 minutes or until lentils and vegetables are tender.

2. Stir in spinach. Combine last three ingredients; dollop 1 tablespoon on each serving. **Yield:** 13 servings.

Nutritional Analysis: One 1-cup serving equals 216 calories, 392 mg sodium, 4 mg cholesterol, 38 g carbohydrate, 12 g protein, 2 g fat, 12 g fiber. **Diabetic Exchanges:** 2 starch, 1 vegetable, 1/2 meat.

Traditional Lasagna

Lorri Foockle, Granville, Illinois

My family first tasted this rich, classic lasagna at a friend's home on Christmas Eve. We were so impressed that it became our own holiday tradition as well.

- **1 pound ground beef**
- **3/4 pound bulk pork sausage**
- **3 cans (8 ounces *each*) tomato sauce**
- **2 cans (6 ounces *each*) tomato paste**
- **2 garlic cloves, minced**
- **2 teaspoons sugar**
- **1 teaspoon Italian seasoning**
- **1 teaspoon salt**
- **1/2 teaspoon pepper**
- **3 eggs**
- **3 tablespoons minced fresh parsley**
- **3 cups (24 ounces) small-curd cottage cheese**
- **1 carton (8 ounces) ricotta cheese**
- **1/2 cup grated Parmesan cheese**
- **9 lasagna noodles, cooked and drained**
- **6 slices provolone cheese**
- **3 cups (12 ounces) shredded mozzarella cheese, *divided***

1. In a skillet, cook beef and sausage over medium heat until no longer pink; drain. Add the next seven ingredients. Simmer, uncovered, for 1 hour, stirring occasionally.

2. In a bowl, combine the eggs, parsley, cottage cheese, ricotta and Parmesan.

3. Spread 1 cup of meat sauce in an ungreased 13-in. x 9-in. x 2-in. baking dish. Layer with three noodles, provolone cheese, 2 cups cottage cheese mixture, 1 cup mozzarella, three noodles, 2 cups meat sauce, remaining cottage cheese mixture and 1 cup mozzarella. Top with the remaining noodles, meat sauce and mozzarella (dish will be full).

4. Cover and bake at 375° for 50 minutes. Uncover; bake 20 minutes longer. Let stand 15 minutes before cutting. **Yield:** 12 servings.

Chops with Mushroom Gravy

Loraine Van Broeck, Geneva, Illinois

These comforting pork chops come out great every time. We love the rich gravy over the chops and mashed potatoes.

1/2 cup all-purpose flour
1 to 2 teaspoons paprika
1-1/2 teaspoons salt
1/4 teaspoon pepper
6 to 8 boneless pork loin chops (1 inch thick)
1/4 cup butter
1 medium onion, chopped
1/2 cup chopped green pepper
1 can (4 ounces) mushroom stems and pieces, drained
2 cups milk
2 tablespoons lemon juice
Hot mashed potatoes

1. In a large resealable plastic bag, combine first four ingredients. Add pork chops, one at a time; toss to coat. Set remaining flour mixture aside. In a large skillet, saute chops in butter until golden brown; transfer to a greased 13-in. x 9-in. x 2-in. baking dish.

2. In the same skillet, saute onion, green pepper and mushrooms until tender. Stir in reserved flour mixture; gradually add milk. Bring to a boil; cook and stir for 2 minutes or until thickened. Remove from heat; stir in lemon juice. Pour over chops. Cover; bake at 350° for 50-60 minutes or until meat is no longer pink. Serve with potatoes. **Yield:** 6-8 servings.

Turkey Lattice Pie

Lorraine Naig, Emmetsburg, Iowa

With its pretty lattice crust, this cheesy baked dish is as eye-catching as it is delicious. It's easy to make, too, since it uses convenient crescent roll dough.

3 tubes (8 ounces *each*) refrigerated crescent rolls
4 cups cubed cooked turkey
1-1/2 cups (6 ounces) shredded cheddar *or* Swiss cheese
1 package (10 ounces) frozen chopped broccoli, thawed and drained
1 can (10-3/4 ounces) condensed cream of chicken soup, undiluted
1-1/3 cups milk
2 tablespoons Dijon mustard
1 tablespoon dried minced onion
1/2 teaspoon salt
Dash pepper
1 egg, lightly beaten

1. Unroll two tubes of crescent roll dough; separate into rectangles. Place rectangles in an ungreased 15-in. x 10-in. x 1-in. baking pan. Press onto the bottom and 1/4 in. up the sides of pan to form a crust, sealing seams and perforations. Bake at 375° for 5-7 minutes or until light golden brown.

2. Combine turkey, cheese, broccoli, soup, milk, mustard, onion, salt and pepper; mix well. Spoon over crust.

3. Unroll remaining dough; divide into rectangles. Seal perforations. Cut each rectangle into four 1-in. strips. Using strips, make a lattice design on top of turkey mixture. Brush with egg. Bake 17-22 minutes longer or until top crust is golden brown and filling is hot. **Yield:** 12-16 servings.

Bacon 'n' Egg Lasagna

Dianne Meyer, Graniteville, Vermont

My sister-in-law served this special dish for Easter breakfast one year, and our whole family loved the mix of bacon, eggs, noodles and cheese.

- **1 pound sliced bacon, diced**
- **1 large onion, chopped**
- **1/3 cup all-purpose flour**
- **1/2 to 1 teaspoon salt**
- **1/4 teaspoon pepper**
- **4 cups milk**
- **12 lasagna noodles, cooked and drained**
- **12 hard-cooked eggs, sliced**
- **2 cups (8 ounces) shredded Swiss cheese**
- **1/3 cup grated Parmesan cheese**
- **2 tablespoons minced fresh parsley**

1. In a skillet, cook bacon until crisp. Remove with a slotted spoon to paper towels. Drain, reserving 1/3 cup drippings. In the drippings, saute onion until tender. Stir in flour, salt and pepper until blended. Gradually stir in milk. Bring to a boil; cook and stir for 2 minutes. Remove from the heat.

2. Spread 1/2 cup sauce in a greased 13-in. x 9-in. x 2-in. baking dish. Layer with four noodles, a third of the eggs and bacon, Swiss cheese and white sauce. Repeat layers twice. Sprinkle with Parmesan cheese.

3. Bake, uncovered, at 350° for 35-40 minutes or until bubbly. Sprinkle with parsley. Let stand 15 minutes before cutting. **Yield:** 12 servings.

Calgary Stampede Ribs

Marian Misik, Sherwood Park, Alberta

"More, please!" is what I hear when I serve these zippy, finger-licking ribs to family or guests. The recipe has its roots in the Calgary Stampede, an annual Western and agricultural fair and exhibition in our province.

- **4 pounds pork back ribs, cut into serving-size pieces**
- **3 garlic cloves, minced**

- **1 tablespoon sugar**
- **1 tablespoon paprika**
- **2 teaspoons *each* salt, pepper, chili powder and ground cumin**

BARBECUE SAUCE:

- **1 small onion, finely chopped**
- **2 tablespoons butter**
- **1 cup ketchup**
- **1/4 cup packed brown sugar**
- **3 tablespoons lemon juice**
- **3 tablespoons Worcestershire sauce**
- **2 tablespoons vinegar**
- **1-1/2 teaspoons ground mustard**
- **1 teaspoon celery seed**
- **1/8 teaspoon cayenne pepper**

1. Rub ribs with garlic; place in a shallow roasting pan. Cover and bake at 300° for 2 hours. Cool slightly. Combine the seasonings and rub over ribs. Cover and refrigerate for 8 hours or overnight.

2. In a saucepan, saute onion in butter until tender. Stir in the remaining sauce ingredients. Bring to a boil. Reduce heat; cook and stir until thickened, about 10 minutes. Remove from the heat; set aside 3/4 cup. Brush ribs with some of the remaining sauce.

3. Grill, covered, over medium heat for 12 minutes, turning and basting with sauce. Serve with reserved sauce. **Yield:** 4 servings.

Open-Faced Omelet

Cynthia Hinkle, Front Royal, Virginia

This tasty breakfast dish is a snap to make with convenient frozen hash browns. It gets its colorful look and fresh flavor from broccoli, red pepper and green onions.

✓ Uses less fat, sugar or salt. Includes Nutritional Analysis and Diabetic Exchanges.

1 cup broccoli florets
1/2 cup chopped sweet red pepper
1/4 cup thinly sliced green onions
1-1/2 cups cubed reduced-sodium fully cooked ham
1 cup frozen shredded hash brown potatoes, thawed
Egg substitute equivalent to 10 eggs
1/4 teaspoon pepper
1/2 cup shredded reduced-fat cheddar cheese

1. In a 9-in. or 10-in. skillet coated with nonstick cooking spray, saute broccoli, red pepper and onions until crisp-tender. Add ham and hash browns. Cook for 2 minutes, stirring frequently.

2. In a bowl, whisk together the egg substitute and pepper. Pour over vegetable mixture. Reduce heat; cover and cook for 10-12 minutes or until set.

3. Remove from the heat. Sprinkle with cheese; cover and let stand for 5 minutes or until cheese is melted. Cut into wedges. **Yield:** 6 servings.

Nutritional Analysis: One serving equals 172 calories, 490 mg sodium, 15 mg cholesterol, 10 g carbohydrate, 21 g protein, 5 g fat, 1 g fiber. **Diabetic Exchanges:** 2-1/2 lean meat, 1/2 starch.

Chicken in Pear Sauce

Andrea Lunsford, Spokane, Washington

Pairing poultry with pears brought applause from my husband and four growing children. Simple enough for everyday meals and ideal for company, this dish is standout.

4 boneless skinless chicken breast halves
1/2 teaspoon salt
1/8 teaspoon white pepper
2 tablespoons vegetable oil
5 thick-cut bacon strips, diced
1 can (14-1/2 ounces) chicken broth
2 to 3 medium ripe pears, peeled and diced
2 tablespoons cornstarch
2 tablespoons cold water
1/4 cup snipped chives

1. Sprinkle chicken with salt and pepper. In a skillet over medium heat, cook chicken in oil on both sides for about 10 minutes or until juices run clear.

2. Meanwhile, in a saucepan, cook bacon until crisp. Drain, reserving 1 tablespoon drippings; set bacon aside. Gradually stir broth into the drippings, scraping pan to loosen browned bits. Bring to a boil. Boil, uncovered, for 5 minutes. Add pears; return to a boil. Boil, uncovered, for 5 minutes or until pears are tender.

3. Combine cornstarch and water until smooth; add the chives. Gradually stir into pear sauce; bring to a boil. Cook and stir for 2 minutes or until thickened and bubbly. Stir in bacon. Serve over the chicken. **Yield:** 4 servings.

Creamy Beef Lasagna

Jane Frawley, Charles Town, West Virginia

The creamy Stroganoff-like filling in this distinctive lasagna makes it a stick-to-your-ribs entree. My family loves the delicious taste, and I appreciate that it's inexpensive to fix.

1-1/2 pounds ground beef
2 cans (15 ounces *each*) tomato sauce
1/4 cup chopped onion
2 teaspoons sugar
2 teaspoons salt
2 teaspoons Worcestershire sauce
1/2 teaspoon garlic salt
2 packages (8 ounces *each*) cream cheese, softened
1 cup (8 ounces) sour cream
1/4 cup milk
18 lasagna noodles, cooked and drained
1 cup (4 ounces) shredded cheddar cheese
Minced fresh parsley, optional

1. In a skillet, cook beef over medium heat until no longer pink; drain. Stir in tomato sauce, onion, sugar, salt, Worcestershire sauce and garlic salt. In a mixing bowl, beat cream cheese, sour cream and milk until smooth.

2. In a greased 13-in. x 9-in. x 2-in. baking dish, layer a fourth of the meat sauce, six noodles and a third of cream cheese mixture. Repeat layers twice. Top with remaining meat sauce.

3. Cover and bake at 350° for 40 minutes. Uncover; sprinkle with cheddar cheese. Bake 5 minutes longer or until cheese is melted. Let stand 15 minutes before cutting. Sprinkle with parsley. **Yield:** 12 servings.

Turkey Ravioli Lasagna

Anne Plesmid, Sagamore Hills, Ohio

I came up with this "shortcut" lasagna one day when the dinner hour was fast approaching and all I had in the freezer was some frozen ravioli. Now I make it often, and my husband and son devour it.

1 pound ground turkey *or* beef
1/2 teaspoon garlic powder
Salt and pepper to taste
1 cup grated carrots
1 cup sliced fresh mushrooms
1 tablespoon olive oil
1 jar (28 ounces) spaghetti sauce
1 package (25 ounces) frozen cheese ravioli, cooked and drained
3 cups (12 ounces) shredded mozzarella cheese
1/2 cup grated Parmesan cheese
Minced fresh parsley, optional

1. In a skillet, cook turkey over medium heat until no longer pink; drain. Sprinkle with garlic powder, salt and pepper; set aside.

2. In a saucepan, cook carrots and mushrooms in oil until tender. Stir in the spaghetti sauce. Spread 1/2 cup sauce in a greased 13-in. x 9-in. x 2-in. baking dish. Layer with half of the ravioli, spaghetti sauce mixture, turkey and cheeses. Repeat layers. Sprinkle with parsley if desired.

3. Cover and bake at 375° for 25-30 minutes or until bubbly. Uncover; bake 10 minutes longer. Let stand 15 minutes before cutting. **Yield:** 12 servings.

Curried Ham and Fruit

Brenda DenHollander, Chilliwack, British Columbia

This dish tastes as good as it looks! The curry and fruit go well with the ham. We like to serve it over rice.

4 slices fully cooked ham (1/2 inch thick and 4 to 6 ounces *each*)
1 can (5-1/2 ounces) peach-orange nectar
1 can (20 ounces) pineapple tidbits, drained
1 can (15-1/4 ounces) sliced peaches, drained and halved
1 can (15-1/4 ounces) sliced pears, drained and halved
10 maraschino cherries
1/4 cup butter, melted
3/4 cup packed brown sugar
4 teaspoons curry powder

1. Place ham in a single layer in an ungreased 13-in. x 9-in. x 2-in. baking dish. Top with nectar. Bake, uncovered, at 350° for 20 minutes, basting once.

2. Combine fruits; spoon over ham. In a small bowl, combine butter, brown sugar and curry powder. Drop by spoonfuls over fruit. Bake 15-20 minutes longer, basting once. **Yield:** 4 servings.

Special Shrimp Bake

Kathy Houchen, Waldorf, Maryland

My husband and I entertain most weekends, and to me the easiest way of serving a crowd is a buffet. This dish can be put together the night before and baked the following day.

3 quarts water
1 tablespoon plus 1 teaspoon salt, *divided*
2-1/2 pounds uncooked medium shrimp, peeled and deveined
2 tablespoons vegetable oil
1 tablespoon lemon juice
1/4 cup finely chopped green pepper
1/4 cup finely chopped onion
2 tablespoons butter
1 can (10-3/4 ounces) condensed tomato soup, undiluted
1 cup heavy whipping cream
2-1/4 cups cooked rice
1/8 teaspoon *each* ground mace, pepper and cayenne pepper
1/2 cup slivered almonds, toasted, *divided*

1. In a Dutch oven, bring water and 1 tablespoon salt to a boil. Add shrimp; cook for 3 minutes or until pink. Drain. Sprinkle with oil and lemon juice; set aside.

2. In a skillet, saute green pepper and onion in butter for 5 minutes or until tender. Add soup, cream, rice, mace, pepper, cayenne, 1/4 cup of almonds and remaining salt. Set aside 1 cup of shrimp. Add remaining shrimp to the rice mixture.

3. Transfer to a greased 2-qt. baking dish. Bake, uncovered, at 350° for 30-35 minutes. Top with reserved shrimp and remaining almonds; bake 20 minutes longer or until the shrimp are lightly browned. **Yield:** 8-10 servings.

Creamy Mushroom Chicken

Sharmon McMillen, Park City, Montana

I call this meal "the easy chicken fix-in'" and love it that the leftovers are equally delicious heated up in the microwave.

6 boneless skinless chicken breast halves
1/4 teaspoon pepper
2 tablespoons vegetable oil
1 cup sliced fresh mushrooms
1/4 cup butter
4-1/2 teaspoons all-purpose flour
1 cup milk
3/4 cup grated Parmesan cheese, *divided*
Minced fresh parsley
Hot cooked pasta

1. Sprinkle chicken with pepper. In a large skillet over medium heat, brown chicken in oil until juices run clear. Remove to a serving platter and keep warm.

2. In the same skillet, saute mushrooms in butter until tender. Sprinkle with flour and stir until coated. Gradually add milk. Bring to a boil; cook and stir for 2 minutes or until thickened.

3. Remove from the heat; stir in 1/2 cup Parmesan cheese. Pour over chicken. Sprinkle with parsley and remaining cheese. Serve with pasta. **Yield:** 6 servings.

Italian Sausage Stew

Ann Erney, Middlebury Center, Pennsylvania

One day when I was preparing Italian sausages, I decided to do something different. After browning them, I put the sausages in a pot and added other ingredients, ending up with this stew that my husband and I like very much.

- **1-1/2 pounds Italian sausage links, cut into 1-inch pieces**
- **3 cups water**
- **4 medium potatoes, peeled and cut into chunks**
- **2 medium carrots, cut into chunks**
- **2 celery ribs, cut into chunks**
- **2 small onions, cut into wedges**
- **1/4 cup Worcestershire sauce**
- **1 teaspoon dried oregano**
- **1/2 teaspoon *each* dried basil, thyme and rosemary, crushed**
- **1 bay leaf**
- **Salt and pepper to taste**
- **3/4 cup ketchup**
- **1/2 large green *or* sweet red pepper, cut into chunks**
- **1 tablespoon minced fresh parsley**
- **1 tablespoon cornstarch**
- **1 tablespoon cold water**

1. In a soup kettle or Dutch oven over medium heat, brown sausage; drain. Add water, potatoes, carrots, celery, onions, Worcestershire sauce and seasonings. Bring to a boil. Reduce heat; cover and cook over low heat for 1 hour or until sausage is no longer pink and vegetables are tender.

2. Add the ketchup, green pepper and parsley; cook 12-15 minutes longer or until pepper is tender. Discard bay leaf.

3. Combine cornstarch and cold water until smooth; stir into stew. Bring to a boil; cook and stir for 2 minutes or until thickened. **Yield:** 6 servings.

Baked Chicken and Acorn Squash

Connie Svoboda, Elko, Minnesota

This eye-pleasing main dish is ideal for harvesttime with its colorful acorn squash and sweet peaches. The fragrance of rosemary-seasoned chicken baking is heavenly. My family says it tastes every bit as delicious as it smells.

- **2 small acorn squash (1-1/4 pounds *each*)**
- **2 to 4 garlic cloves, minced**
- **2 tablespoons vegetable oil, *divided***
- **4 chicken drumsticks**
- **4 chicken thighs**
- **1/4 cup packed brown sugar**
- **1 teaspoon salt**
- **1 tablespoon minced fresh rosemary**
- **1 can (15-1/4 ounces) sliced peaches, undrained**

1. Cut squash in half lengthwise; discard seeds. Cut each half widthwise into 1/2-in. slices; discard ends. Place slices in an ungreased 13-in. x 9-in. x 2-in. baking dish. Sprinkle with garlic and drizzle with 1 tablespoon oil.

2. In a large skillet, brown chicken in remaining oil. Arrange chicken over squash. Combine the brown sugar, salt and rosemary; sprinkle over chicken. Bake, uncovered, at 350° for 45 minutes, basting with pan juices twice.

3. Pour peaches over chicken and squash. Bake, uncovered, 15 minutes longer or until chicken juices run clear and peaches are heated through. **Yield:** 4 servings.

Orange-Glazed Pork Loin

Lynnette Miete, Alna, Maine

This is one of the best pork recipes I've ever tried. My family looks forward to this roast for dinner, and guests always want the recipe.

1 teaspoon salt
1 garlic clove, minced
1/4 teaspoon dried thyme
1/4 teaspoon ground ginger
1/4 teaspoon pepper
1 rolled boneless pork loin roast (about 5 pounds)

GLAZE:

1/4 cup packed brown sugar
1 tablespoon cornstarch
1 cup orange juice
1/3 cup water
1 tablespoon Dijon mustard

1. Combine the salt, garlic, thyme, ginger and pepper; rub over entire roast. Place roast with fat side up on a rack in a shallow roasting pan. Bake, uncovered, at 350° for 2 hours.

2. Meanwhile, in a saucepan, combine brown sugar and cornstarch. Stir in the remaining glaze ingredients until smooth. Bring to a boil; cook and stir for 2 minutes.

3. Brush some of the glaze over roast. Bake 1 hour longer or until a meat thermometer reads 160°, brushing occasionally with glaze. Let stand for 10 minutes before slicing; serve with remaining glaze. **Yield:** 12-16 servings.

Au Gratin Peas and Potatoes, p. 122

Grilled Dijon Summer Squash, p. 124

Lemon Butter Spread, p. 125

Side Dishes & Condiments

Turn to this chapter for all sorts of complementary side dishes and condiments to serve alongside or to top off main courses.

Tangy Barbecue Sauce, p. 129

Cheesy Zucchini Saute, p. 126

Au Gratin Peas and Potatoes

(Pictured on page 120)

Marie Peterson, De Forest, Wisconsin

While this delicious potato skillet is a wonderful side dish, we find it satisfying enough to be a main course, too. The skillet preparation takes less time than it does to bake an au gratin casserole or scalloped potatoes—but it's still good old-fashioned comfort food at its best!

- **6 bacon strips, diced**
- **1 medium onion, chopped**
- **4 cups sliced peeled cooked potatoes**
- **1/2 teaspoon salt**
- **1 package (10 ounces) frozen peas, cooked and drained**
- **2 cups (8 ounces) shredded sharp cheddar cheese, *divided***
- **1/2 cup mayonnaise**
- **1/2 cup milk**

1. In a skillet, cook bacon until crisp. Remove with a slotted spoon to paper towels. Drain, reserving 1 tablespoon drippings. In the drippings, saute the onion until tender.

2. Layer with potatoes, salt, peas, 1 cup of cheese and bacon. Reduce heat; cover and simmer for 10 minutes or until heated through.

3. Combine mayonnaise and milk until smooth; pour over bacon. Sprinkle with the remaining cheese. Remove from the heat; let stand for 5 minutes before serving. **Yield:** 4 servings.

Special Squash Casserole

Kathleen Cox, Wyoming, Michigan

Squash has traditionally been a food our family passes up, but this luscious casserole is an exception to the rule. It's one of the first dishes to return empty.

- **3 pounds butternut squash, peeled, seeded and cubed**
- **3/4 cup milk**
- **6 tablespoons butter, melted**
- **3 eggs, beaten**
- **1/2 teaspoon vanilla extract**
- **3/4 cup sugar**
- **3 tablespoons all-purpose flour**
- **1/2 teaspoon ground cinnamon**
- **1/8 teaspoon ground cloves**
- **1/8 teaspoon ground nutmeg**

TOPPING:

- **1/2 cup vanilla wafer crumbs (about 15 wafers)**
- **1/4 cup packed brown sugar**
- **2 tablespoons butter, melted**

1. Place squash in a large saucepan or Dutch oven; cover with water. Bring to a boil; cover and cook for 25-30 minutes or until tender. Drain and place in a mixing bowl; beat just until smooth.

2. Add milk, butter, eggs and vanilla; mix well. Combine the dry ingredients; add to squash mixture and mix well. Transfer to a greased 2-qt. baking dish. Cover and bake at 350° for 45 minutes.

3. Meanwhile, in a small bowl, combine topping ingredients until crumbly; sprinkle over squash. Bake, uncovered, for 12-15 minutes or until heated through. **Yield:** 8-10 servings.

Pickled Mushrooms

Linda Keiper-Quinn, Hazleton, Pennsylvania

Pennsylvania is known for its mushrooms. In the region where I live, mushrooms are used prominently in many recipes. This recipe is a favorite.

1/2 cup red wine vinegar
1/2 cup water
2 bay leaves
2 tablespoons sugar
1-1/2 teaspoons salt
1 garlic clove, minced
1 pound fresh mushrooms, quartered

1. In a saucepan over medium heat, combine vinegar, water, bay leaves, sugar, salt and garlic. Add mushrooms. Bring to a boil; boil for 2 minutes.

2. Transfer to a glass bowl; cover and refrigerate for 8 hours or overnight. Discard bay leaves before serving. **Yield:** about 2-1/2 cups.

Creamed Cauliflower

Peggie De Chick, Auburn, New York

This is a Hungarian recipe from my mother. It's easy to make and flavorful. Even those who don't normally care for cauliflower can't pass it up prepared this way.

1 medium head cauliflower, broken into florets (about 7 cups)
1-1/2 teaspoons salt, *divided*
1/2 cup dry bread crumbs, *divided*
1 cup half-and-half cream
1 tablespoon butter
Minced fresh parsley, optional

1. Place cauliflower in a saucepan; add 1 in. of water and 1 teaspoon salt. Bring to a boil. Reduce heat. Cover and simmer for 6-7 minutes or until crisp-tender; drain.

2. Grease the bottom and sides of a 2-qt. baking dish; sprinkle with 2 tablespoons bread crumbs. Add cauliflower. Pour cream over top. Dot with butter; sprinkle with remaining salt and bread crumbs.

3. Bake, uncovered, at 350° for 25-30 minutes or until cauliflower is tender. Garnish with parsley if desired. **Yield:** 6-8 servings.

Grilled Dijon Summer Squash

(Pictured on page 120)

Ruth Lee, Troy, Ontario

A niece gave this mustard-seasoned squash recipe to me. My husband, Doug, and our three grandchildren love the zesty flavor and slightly crunchy texture. The kabobs are perfect partners to any grilled meat and reheat easily.

- **1/2 cup olive oil**
- **1/4 cup red wine vinegar**
- **1 tablespoon minced fresh oregano *or* 1 teaspoon dried oregano**
- **1 tablespoon Dijon mustard**
- **2 garlic cloves, minced**
- **1/2 teaspoon salt**
- **1/4 teaspoon pepper**
- **4 medium zucchini, cut into 1/2-inch slices**
- **4 medium yellow squash, cut into 1/2-inch slices**
- **2 medium red onions, quartered**
- **1 large sweet red pepper, cut into 2-inch pieces**
- **1 large sweet yellow pepper, cut into 2-inch pieces**
- **12 to 16 whole fresh mushrooms**
- **12 cherry tomatoes**

1. In a jar with a tight-fitting lid, combine the oil, vinegar, oregano, mustard, garlic, salt and pepper. Place the vegetables in a shallow baking dish. Add marinade and toss to coat. Let stand for 15 minutes.

2. Drain and discard marinade; arrange vegetables on a vegetable grill rack. Grill, covered, over indirect heat for 10-12 minutes or until tender. **Yield:** 16-18 servings.

Zucchini Supreme

Bette Cimino, Vancouver, Washington

I'm always on the lookout for new zucchini recipes. This dish has a very pleasant flavor and nice combination of color and texture.

- **4 cups water**
- **6 cups sliced zucchini**
- **1 cup shredded carrot**
- **1/4 cup chopped onion**
- **1 teaspoon salt**
- **1 can (10-3/4 ounces) condensed cream of mushroom soup, undiluted**
- **1 cup (8 ounces) sour cream**
- **1/2 teaspoon garlic powder**
- **1/2 teaspoon pepper**
- **4 cups seasoned stuffing croutons**
- **1/2 cup butter, melted**

1. In a Dutch oven or soup kettle, bring water to a boil. Add the zucchini, carrot, onion and salt. Cook for 8-10 minutes or until vegetables are tender; drain.

2. In a large bowl, combine the soup, sour cream, garlic powder and pepper. Fold in vegetable mixture. Combine croutons and butter; place half in a greased 13-in. x 9-in. x 2-in. baking dish. Top with vegetable mixture and remaining croutons.

3. Cover and bake at 350° for 30 minutes. Uncover; bake 10 minutes longer or until golden brown. **Yield:** 8-10 servings.

Scalloped Potatoes And Carrots

Rosemary Wehinger, Monroe, Wisconsin

I feel this recipe represents our region because it contains dairy products. My husband and I farmed for more than 25 years.

2-1/2 pounds potatoes (about 9 medium), peeled and sliced
5 medium carrots, cut into 1/4-inch slices
1-1/2 cups sliced onions
2 cups boiling water
1 teaspoon salt

CHEESE SAUCE:

3 tablespoons butter
2 tablespoons all-purpose flour
1 teaspoon salt
1/8 teaspoon pepper
1-1/2 cups milk
1-1/2 cups (6 ounces) shredded cheddar cheese, *divided*

1. In a large Dutch oven, combine potatoes, carrots, onions, water and salt. Bring to a boil. Reduce heat; cover and cook for 10 minutes.

2. Meanwhile, in a saucepan, melt butter. Remove from the heat; stir in flour, salt and pepper until smooth. Gradually stir in milk. Bring to a boil over medium heat, stirring constantly. Cook and stir for 2 minutes. Stir in 1 cup cheese. Reduce heat; stir until cheese is melted.

3. Drain the vegetables; layer half in a greased 13-in. x 9-in. x 2-in. baking dish. Top with half of the cheese sauce. Repeat layers. Sprinkle with remaining cheese. Cover and bake at 375° for 20 minutes. Uncover and bake 10 minutes longer or until potatoes are tender. **Yield:** 6-8 servings.

Lemon Butter Spread

(Pictured on page 120)

Gloria Costes, West Hills, California

My grandmother, who was a great cook, brought this recipe with her from England. I use it as a spread on toast, for filling in a cake or on top of ice cream.

1 cup butter
2 cups sugar
3 eggs, lightly beaten
1/2 cup lemon juice
1 tablespoon grated lemon peel

1. In the top of a double boiler over boiling water, melt butter. Stir in sugar, eggs, lemon juice and peel. Cook over simmering water for 1 hour or until thickened, stirring occasionally.

2. Pour into containers. Store in the refrigerator. **Yield:** 3 cups.

Cheesy Zucchini Saute

(Pictured on page 121)

Doris Biggs, Felton, Delaware

Although I no longer have a garden of my own, friends and neighbors keep me amply supplied with squash. As a thank-you, I tell them how to make this refreshing zucchini saute. It's quick, easy and oh, so tasty!

- **1/2 cup chopped onion**
- **1/4 cup butter**
- **3 cups coarsely shredded zucchini**
- **2 teaspoons minced fresh basil *or* 1/2 teaspoon dried basil**
- **1/2 teaspoon salt**
- **1/8 teaspoon garlic powder**
- **1 cup (4 ounces) shredded cheddar cheese**
- **1 cup diced fresh tomato**
- **2 tablespoons sliced ripe olives**

1. In a large skillet, saute onion in butter until crisp-tender. Stir in zucchini, basil, salt and garlic powder. Cook and stir for 4-5 minutes or until zucchini is crisp-tender. Sprinkle with the cheese, tomato and olives.

2. Cover and cook for 4-5 minutes or until cheese is melted. Serve immediately. **Yield:** 6 servings.

Selecting Side Dishes

Your entree and side dishes should complement one another. If the entree has intense flavor, pair it with more mild-flavored side dishes and vice versa. If your entree has lots of garlic, onion or nuts, stay away from a side dish that's loaded with any of those same ingredients.

For ease of preparation, look for an oven-baked side dish that cooks at the same temperature as your oven entree.

If your oven will be full with the entree and other side dishes, choose another side dish that can be prepared on the stovetop or in a slow cooker. Or for a refreshing break from hot foods, turn to a tossed salad, an assortment of fresh fruit or a tried-and-true relish tray.

Parmesan Onion Bake

Linda Vail, Ballwin, Missouri

Dinner guests in my home know to expect the unexpected! I love experimenting with unusual combinations of ingredients. This cheesy onion bake adds flair to a meal.

- **6 medium onions, sliced**
- **1 cup diced celery**
- **8 tablespoons butter, *divided***
- **1/4 cup all-purpose flour**
- **1 teaspoon salt**
- **1/8 teaspoon pepper**
- **1-1/2 cups milk**
- **1/3 cup grated Parmesan cheese**
- **1/2 cup chopped pecans**

1. In a large skillet, saute onions and celery in 3 tablespoons butter until tender; drain and set aside.

2. In a saucepan, melt the remaining butter; stir in flour, salt and pepper until smooth. Gradually stir in milk. Bring to a boil; cook and stir for 2 minutes or until thickened. Pour over vegetables; toss to coat.

3. Pour into an ungreased 2-qt. baking dish. Sprinkle with cheese and pecans. Bake, uncovered, at 350° for 20-25 minutes or until heated through. **Yield:** 6-8 servings.

Crumb-Topped Broccoli Bake

Hope Huggins, Santa Cruz, California

Broccoli is one of the main crops grown in this area. This recipe has pleased just about everyone who has tried it, including some who said they didn't like broccoli.

1/4 cup chopped onion
2 tablespoons butter
2 tablespoons all-purpose flour
1/2 cup milk
1 jar (8 ounces) process cheese sauce
2 packages (10 ounces *each*) frozen broccoli cuts
3 eggs, beaten
1/2 cup crushed butter-flavored crackers (about 12 crackers), *divided*
Salt and pepper to taste

1. In a saucepan, saute onion in butter until tender. Stir in flour until blended. Gradually add milk. Bring to a boil; cook and stir for 2 minutes or until thickened. Reduce heat; stir in cheese sauce until smooth. Remove from the heat.

2. Cook broccoli according to package directions; drain and place in a bowl. Add cheese sauce mixture, eggs, 1/4 cup cracker crumbs, salt and pepper.

3. Transfer to a greased 1-1/2-qt. baking dish; sprinkle with remaining cracker crumbs. Place dish in a larger baking pan. Fill pan with hot water to a depth of 1 in. Bake, uncovered, at 350° for 50 minutes or until golden brown. **Yield:** 6 servings.

Creamy Herb Dressing

Brigitte Hinz, Des Plaines, Illinois

This dressing for vegetables is so easy, I make it the night before to save time. We like it over asparagus, but try serving it with green beans or broccoli for an equally delicious and eye-pleasing side dish.

1-1/2 cups mayonnaise
2/3 cup heavy whipping cream
1/2 cup chopped green onions
1/2 cup minced fresh parsley
1 can (2 ounces) anchovy fillets, drained, optional
2 tablespoons minced chives
2 tablespoons lemon juice
2 pounds fresh asparagus spears, trimmed

1. In a blender, combine the first seven ingredients; cover and process until smooth. Cover and refrigerate for at least 1 hour.

2. In a skillet, cook asparagus in a small amount of water for 3-4 minutes or until crisp-tender; drain well. Spoon dressing over asparagus. Store dressing in the refrigerator. **Yield:** 6 servings (2-1/2 cups dressing).

Wild Rice Stuffing

Connie Olson, Green River, Wyoming

Since trying this stuffing recipe from my sister, I haven't made any other kind. It's so moist and tasty. When a big bowlful starts circulating around the table, happy smiles get even bigger!

Turkey giblets
4 cups water
1 package (6 ounces) long grain and wild rice
1 celery rib, chopped
1 small onion, chopped
1/2 cup butter
2-1/2 cups crushed seasoned stuffing
1-1/2 cups chicken broth

1. Remove liver from giblets if desired. Place giblets and water in a saucepan. Cover and simmer for 2 hours or until tender.

2. Meanwhile, prepare the rice according to package directions. In a small skillet, saute celery and onion in butter; add to the rice.

3. Drain and dice giblets. Stir stuffing, broth and giblets into rice. Spoon into an ungreased 1-1/2-qt. baking dish. Bake, uncovered, at 350° for 25-30 minutes or until heated through. **Yield:** 8-10 servings.

Tangy Barbecue Sauce

(Also pictured on page 121)

Mary Kaye Rackowitz, Marysville, Washington

My mother-in-law created this recipe, and we just can't get enough of her delectable sauce! I always keep a little out of the basting dish prior to using it on the grill so we have some to serve at the table. It tastes terrific on any grilled meat.

1 cup ketchup
2 tablespoons lemon juice
2 tablespoons cider vinegar
1/4 cup packed brown sugar
2 teaspoons prepared mustard
1 teaspoon salt
1/2 to 1 teaspoon hot pepper sauce
1 bay leaf
1 garlic clove, minced
1/2 cup water
2 teaspoons Worcestershire sauce

1. Combine all of the ingredients in a small saucepan; bring to a boil, stirring occasionally. Reduce heat; cover and simmer for 30 minutes.

2. Discard bay leaf. Use as a basting sauce when grilling chicken, pork or beef. **Yield:** 1-1/2 cups.

Colorful Vegetable Saute

Regena Hofer, Meadows, Manitoba

This fresh-tasting mixture is so pretty and tasty—and a great way to enjoy your garden's bounty. A sprinkling of toasted sesame seeds adds a pleasant crunch to the savory saute. I love to cook and find that trying out new recipes for my large collection is one of my favorite "jobs!"

2 medium sweet red peppers, julienned
2 medium green peppers, julienned
2 medium zucchini, julienned
4 medium carrots, julienned
1 tablespoon olive oil
4 cups thinly sliced red cabbage
1/4 teaspoon salt
1/4 teaspoon pepper
4 teaspoons white wine vinegar
1/4 cup water
1 tablespoon sesame seeds, toasted

1. In a large skillet, saute peppers, zucchini and carrots in oil for 5 minutes. Add cabbage, salt and pepper; saute 1 minute longer.

2. Combine vinegar and water; pour over the vegetables. Saute 3 minutes more. Sprinkle with sesame seeds; cook and stir for 1 minute. **Yield:** 8-10 servings.

Corn Bread Casserole

Margaret Mayes, La Mesa, California

We live very close to the Mexican border, so recipes featuring corn and green chilies are popular here. This dish has always been a hit whenever I've taken it to a potluck dinner.

2 packages (8-1/2 ounces *each*) corn bread/muffin mix
1 can (15-1/4 ounces) whole kernel corn, drained
1 can (14-3/4 ounces) cream-style corn
1 can (4 ounces) chopped green chilies, drained
1 cup (4 ounces) shredded Monterey Jack cheese

1. Prepare corn bread mixes according to package directions. Pour half of the batter into a greased 11-in. x 7-in. x 2-in. baking pan. Combine corn and creamed corn; spread over batter. Top with chilies and cheese. Carefully spread with remaining corn bread batter.

2. Bake, uncovered, at 375° for 25-30 minutes or until a toothpick comes out clean. Serve warm. **Yield:** 12 servings.

Gingered Lime Carrots

Dorothy Swanson, St. Louis, Missouri

The produce manager at my grocery store suggested this memorable mixture of lightly sweet carrots, zippy ginger and tart lime. It's easy to fall in love with this recipe, which now has a permanent place among my favorites. My husband and I especially enjoy it with poultry or fish.

1 pound carrots, cut into 1/2-inch slices
1 tablespoon water
1 tablespoon lime juice
1 tablespoon butter
1 tablespoon honey
1 teaspoon grated lime peel
1 teaspoon grated fresh gingerroot
Lime slices

1. In a 1-1/2-qt. microwave-safe bowl, combine carrots and water. Cover and cook on high for 7-8 minutes or until crisp-tender, stirring once. Let stand for 5 minutes.

2. Meanwhile, in a small bowl, combine lime juice, butter, honey, peel and ginger. Cover and microwave on high for 1 minute. Drain carrots; stir in the lime mixture. Cover and cook on high for 1 minute. Garnish with lime. **Yield:** 4 servings.

Editor's Note: This recipe was tested in an 850-watt microwave.

Two-Tone Baked Potatoes

Sherree Stahn, Central City, Nebraska

One potato...two potato...this recipe is doubly wonderful as far as spud lovers are concerned. I have a reputation at home and at work for trying out new recipes. Everyone is glad I took a chance on this one.

- **6 medium russet potatoes**
- **6 medium sweet potatoes**
- **2/3 cup sour cream, *divided***
- **1/3 cup milk**
- **3/4 cup shredded cheddar cheese**
- **4 tablespoons minced chives, *divided***
- **1-1/2 teaspoons salt, *divided***

1. Pierce russet and sweet potatoes with a fork. Bake at 400° for 60-70 minutes or until tender. Set sweet potatoes aside.

2. Cut a third off the top of each russet potato; scoop out pulp, leaving skins intact. Place pulp in a bowl; mash with 1/3 cup sour cream, milk, cheese, 2 tablespoons chives and 3/4 teaspoon salt. Set aside.

3. Cut off the top of each sweet potato; scoop out pulp, leaving skins intact. Mash pulp with remaining sour cream, chives and salt.

4. Stuff mixture into half of each potato skin; spoon russet potato filling into other half. Place on a baking sheet. Bake at 350° for 15-20 minutes or until heated through. **Yield:** 12 servings.

Cabbage-Tomato Pasta Toss

Alcy Thorne, Los Molinos, California

Here's an unusual combination of ingredients that blend very well together. It's a nice side dish for any beef entree.

2 medium tomatoes, peeled and diced
2 tablespoons red wine vinegar
1 teaspoon dried basil
1/2 cup minced fresh parsley
8 ounces uncooked bow tie pasta
2 cups shredded cabbage
1-1/2 cups soft bread crumbs
1/2 cup slivered almonds
2 to 3 garlic cloves, minced
1/4 cup olive oil
1/4 cup butter

1. In a bowl, combine the tomatoes, vinegar, basil and parsley; set aside. Cook pasta according to package directions, adding the cabbage during the last 2 minutes.

2. Meanwhile, in a skillet, saute bread crumbs, almonds and garlic in oil and butter for 6 minutes or until golden brown.

3. Drain pasta and cabbage; place in a large bowl. Add tomato and crumb mixtures; toss and serve immediately. **Yield:** 6 servings.

Cherry-Almond Ham Glaze

Julie Sterchi, Fairfield, Illinois

I came across this recipe looking for an alternative to traditional sauces for holiday meats. Mostly, I serve it with ham, and it goes over well—probably because it is such a change of taste. But the glaze would be fine with almost any meat. And its cheery color adds a festive touch to the table.

- **1 jar (12 ounces) cherry preserves**
- **1/4 cup vinegar**
- **2 tablespoons corn syrup**
- **1/4 teaspoon ground cinnamon**
- **1/4 teaspoon ground cloves**
- **1/4 teaspoon ground nutmeg**
- **1/3 cup slivered almonds**
- **3 tablespoons water**

1. In a saucepan, combine the first six ingredients; bring to a boil. Reduce heat and simmer for 2 minutes, stirring frequently. Stir in the almonds.

2. About 15 minutes before ham is done, spoon 1/4 to 1/3 cup glaze over ham. Repeat if desired.

3. Stir water into remaining glaze; heat through and serve with ham. **Yield:** about 1-1/2 cups.

Cranberry Compote

Carole Dishman, Hampton, Virginia

This best-of-the-season dish adds to the beauty and bounty of any holiday spread. Whether served warm or cold, it's a delectable fruity treat for the taste buds as well as for the eyes when it's presented in a clear glass bowl.

- **2 medium tart apples, peeled and sliced**
- **1 package (12 ounces) fresh *or* frozen cranberries**
- **1-1/4 cups sugar**
- **1 cup golden raisins**
- **1/4 cup orange juice**
- **1 teaspoon grated orange peel**
- **1 teaspoon salt**
- **1/4 teaspoon ground allspice**
- **1/4 teaspoon ground cinnamon**
- **1 can (15-1/4 ounces) sliced peaches, drained**
- **1 can (15 ounces) apricot halves, drained**
- **1 cup chopped pecans**

1. In a saucepan, combine the first nine ingredients. Bring to a boil. Reduce heat; simmer, uncovered, for 10 minutes or until cranberries pop and apples are tender.

2. Add the peaches and apricots; heat through. Stir in pecans; serve warm or chilled. Store in the refrigerator. **Yield:** 6 cups.

Carrots in Almond Sauce

Carol Anderson, Salt Lake City, Utah

Here's an easy way to add elegance and flavor to a plain vegetable. The combination of tender carrots and crunchy nuts is different and delightful. Plus, the touch of dill lends just the right zip.

1 pound carrots, julienned
1/2 cup thinly sliced green onions
1/4 cup butter
1 teaspoon cornstarch
1/2 cup water
1/2 teaspoon chicken bouillon granules
1/2 teaspoon dill weed
1/8 teaspoon pepper
1/4 cup sliced almonds, toasted

1. In a saucepan, cook carrots in a small amount of water until crisp-tender; drain. Transfer to a serving bowl and keep warm.

2. In the same pan, saute onions in butter until tender. Combine cornstarch and water until smooth; stir into onions. Add bouillon, dill and pepper.

3. Bring to a boil over medium heat; cook and stir for 1 minute or until thickened and bubbly. Stir in almonds. Pour over carrots; stir to coat. **Yield:** 6 servings.

Creamy Hash Browns

Donna Downes, Las Vegas, Nevada

My mother often took this comforting side dish to social dinners because it was such a hit. Now I get the same compliments when I make it. Bacon and onion jazz up a creamy mixture that takes advantage of convenient frozen hash browns and canned soups.

1 package (2 pounds) frozen cubed hash brown potatoes
2 cups (8 ounces) cubed *or* shredded process cheese (Velveeta)
2 cups (16 ounces) sour cream
1 can (10-3/4 ounces) condensed cream of celery soup, undiluted
1 can (10-3/4 ounces) condensed cream of chicken soup, undiluted
1 pound sliced bacon, cooked and crumbled
1 large onion, chopped
1/4 cup butter, melted
1/4 teaspoon pepper

1. Place potatoes in an ungreased 5-qt. slow cooker. In a bowl, combine the remaining ingredients. Pour over potatoes and mix well.

2. Cover and cook on low for 4-5 hours or until potatoes are tender and heated through. **Yield:** 14 servings.

Asparagus Onion Casserole

Judy Fleetwood, Beulah, Michigan

This vegetable dish goes great with just about any meal. I've prepared it ahead of time, then popped it in the oven so it's ready with the meal.

- **1 pound fresh asparagus, cut into 1-inch pieces *or* 2 packages (10 ounces *each*) asparagus cuts, thawed**
- **2 medium onions, sliced**
- **5 tablespoons butter, *divided***
- **2 tablespoons all-purpose flour**
- **1 cup milk**
- **1 package (3 ounces) cream cheese, cubed**
- **1 teaspoon salt**
- **1/8 teaspoon pepper**
- **1/2 cup shredded cheddar cheese**
- **1 cup soft bread crumbs**

1. In a skillet, saute the asparagus and onions in 1 tablespoon of butter until crisp-tender, about 8 minutes. Transfer to an ungreased 1-1/2-qt. baking dish.

2. In a saucepan, melt 2 tablespoons butter. Stir in flour until smooth; gradually add milk. Bring to a boil; cook and stir for 2 minutes or until thickened.

3. Reduce heat. Add the cream cheese, salt and pepper; stir until cheese is melted. Pour over the vegetables. Sprinkle with cheddar cheese. Melt remaining butter; toss with bread crumbs. Sprinkle over casserole.

4. Bake, uncovered, at 350° for 35-40 minutes or until heated through. **Yield:** 4-6 servings.

Mushroom Wild Rice

Charlene Baert, Winnipeg, Manitoba

This colorful casserole is a standout from my mother's collection of family recipes. Excellent texture and taste guarantee it won't play second fiddle to the main dish!

4 cups water
1 cup uncooked wild rice
1 teaspoon butter
1-1/2 teaspoons salt, *divided*
1/2 cup uncooked brown rice
8 bacon strips, diced
2 cups sliced fresh mushrooms
1 large onion, chopped
1 medium green pepper, chopped
1 medium sweet red pepper, chopped
1 celery rib, thinly sliced
1 can (14-1/2 ounces) beef broth
2 tablespoons cornstarch
1/4 cup cold water
1/2 cup slivered almonds

1. In a large saucepan, bring water, wild rice, butter and 1/2 teaspoon salt to a boil. Reduce heat; cover and simmer for 40 minutes. Stir in brown rice. Cover and simmer 25-30 minutes longer or until rice is tender.

2. Meanwhile, in a large skillet, cook bacon until crisp. Remove bacon to paper towels; drain, reserving 2 tablespoons drippings. In the drippings, saute mushrooms, onion, peppers and celery until tender. Stir in broth and remaining salt. Bring to a boil.

3. Combine the cornstarch and cold water until smooth; stir into the mushroom mixture. Cook and stir for 2 minutes or until thickened and bubbly; stir in almonds and bacon. Drain rice; add mushroom mixture.

4. Transfer to a greased 13-in. x 9-in. x 2-in. baking dish. Cover and bake at 350° for 25 minutes. Uncover; bake 5-10 minutes longer or until heated through. **Yield:** 12 servings.

Slow-Simmered Kidney Beans

Sheila Vail, Long Beach, California

My husband always puts us down for this side dish when we're invited to a potluck. Canned beans cut down on prep time yet get plenty of zip from bacon, apple, red pepper and onion. I like simmering this mixture in the slow cooker because it blends the flavors and I don't have to stand over the stove.

6 bacon strips, diced
1/2 pound fully cooked Polish sausage *or* kielbasa, chopped
4 cans (16 ounces *each*) kidney beans, rinsed and drained
1 can (28 ounces) diced tomatoes, drained
2 medium sweet red peppers, chopped
1 large onion, chopped
1 cup ketchup
1/2 cup packed brown sugar
1/4 cup honey
1/4 cup molasses
1 tablespoon Worcestershire sauce
1 teaspoon salt
1 teaspoon ground mustard
2 medium unpeeled red apples, cored and cut into 1/2-inch pieces

1. In a skillet, cook bacon until crisp. Remove with a slotted spoon to paper towels. Add sausage to drippings; cook and stir for 5 minutes. Drain and set aside.

2. In an ungreased 5-qt. slow cooker, combine the beans, tomatoes, red peppers, onion, ketchup, brown sugar, honey, molasses, Worcestershire sauce, salt and mustard. Stir in the bacon and sausage.

3. Cover and cook on low for 4-6 hours. Stir in apples. Cover and cook 2 hours longer or until bubbly. **Yield:** 16 servings.

Fruity Cranberry Relish

Holly Cosentino, Templeton, Massachusetts

This recipe has been in my family for years. It has a zippy taste that everyone seems to enjoy.

2-1/2 cups cranberries
1 medium navel orange, peeled and sectioned
2 cups chopped peeled tart apples
1 can (8 ounces) crushed pineapple, drained
1 cup sugar
1/2 cup chopped green *or* red grapes
4 teaspoons grated orange peel
1/2 teaspoon salt
1/3 cup chopped walnuts

1. In a food processor, combine cranberries and orange sections. Cover and process until chopped.

2. Transfer to a bowl; add apples, pineapple, sugar, grapes, orange peel and salt. Cover and refrigerate overnight. Stir in the walnuts just before serving. **Yield:** 6-8 servings.

Zucchini Ricotta Bake

Eleanor Hauserman, Huntsville, Alabama

I have made this lasagna-like zucchini casserole frequently over the years. After my daughter had heart trouble, I adapted the recipe to cut fat and calories. We think this version is just as delicious.

✓ Uses less fat, sugar or salt. Includes Nutritional Analysis and Diabetic Exchanges.

2 pounds zucchini
1 carton (15 ounces) reduced-fat ricotta cheese
Egg substitute equivalent to 2 eggs
1/2 cup dry bread crumbs, *divided*
5 tablespoons grated Parmesan cheese, *divided*
1 tablespoon minced parsley
1/4 teaspoon dried oregano
1/4 teaspoon dried basil
1/8 teaspoon pepper
1 jar (26 ounces) reduced-sodium spaghetti sauce
1-1/2 cups (6 ounces) shredded part-skim reduced-fat mozzarella cheese

1. Cut zucchini lengthwise into 1/4-in. slices. Place in a basket over 1 in. of boiling water. Cover and steam for 5-6 minutes or until just tender. Drain; pat dry.

2. In a bowl, combine ricotta, egg substitute, 3 tablespoons bread crumbs, 3 tablespoons Parmesan, parsley, oregano, basil and pepper; set aside.

3. Spread a third of the spaghetti sauce in a 13-in. x 9-in. x 2-in. baking dish coated with nonstick cooking spray. Sprinkle with 2 tablespoons bread crumbs. Cover with half of the zucchini, ricotta mixture and mozzarella. Repeat layers of sauce, zucchini, ricotta mixture and mozzarella. Cover with the remaining sauce. Combine remaining crumbs and Parmesan; sprinkle over top.

4. Cover and bake at 350° for 45 minutes. Uncover; bake 15 minutes longer. Let stand 15 minutes before cutting. **Yield:** 12 servings.

Nutritional Analysis: One serving equals 201 calories, 237 mg sodium, 21 mg cholesterol, 18 g carbohydrate, 12 g protein, 9 g fat, 3 g fiber. **Diabetic Exchanges:** 1 starch, 1 meat, 1 fat, 1/2 vegetable.

Tangy Texas Salsa

Lois Kildahl, McAllen, Texas

I'm a "transplant" here from Wisconsin. Even after 25 years, I still can't get enough of our wonderful local citrus. This is one way to work it into a main dish. The combination of tangy fruit, spicy jalapeno and distinctive cilantro is perfect over any meat, poultry or fish. We also dip into it with chips.

1 medium grapefruit
1 large navel orange
1 *each* medium green, sweet red and yellow pepper, chopped
1 medium tomato, seeded and chopped
1 jalapeno pepper, seeded and chopped
3 tablespoons chopped red onion
1 tablespoon minced fresh cilantro
1-1/2 teaspoons sugar
1/2 teaspoon salt

1. Peel, section and dice grapefruit and orange, removing all membrane. Place in a bowl; add remaining ingredients and mix well.

2. Cover and refrigerate for at least 2 hours. **Yield:** about 5 cups.

Editor's Note: When cutting or seeding hot peppers, use rubber or plastic gloves to protect your hands. Avoid touching your face.

Colorful Apricot Chutney

Lucile Cline, Wichita, Kansas

This chutney is great served over a variety of meats. You can use it as an appetizer on crackers...or try mixing it with cream cheese into a spread. When the local Extension office held a "Pepper Day," I entered it in the recipe contest. It ended up winning first prize.

- **3 large sweet red peppers, diced**
- **12 ounces dried apricots, diced**
- **1 cup raisins**
- **1 cup sugar**
- **1 large onion, finely chopped**
- **3/4 cup red wine vinegar**
- **5 garlic cloves, minced**
- **1-1/2 teaspoons salt**
- **1-1/2 teaspoons crushed red pepper flakes**
- **1/4 teaspoon ground ginger**
- **1/4 teaspoon ground cumin**
- **1/4 teaspoon ground mustard**

1. In a large heavy saucepan, combine all ingredients; bring to a boil. Reduce heat; simmer, uncovered, for 25-30 minutes or until thickened, stirring occasionally. Cover and refrigerate.

2. Serve as an accompaniment to pork or chicken. Chutney may be stored in the refrigerator for up to 1 month. **Yield:** 4 cups.

Turkey Stuffing Bread, p. 152

Buttermilk Doughnuts, p. 146

Soft Italian Breadsticks, p. 142

Breads & Rolls

Only one thing can top the mouth-watering aroma of fresh bread baking, and that's its wonderful flavor! Ask anyone and they'll agree—bread is scrumptious served morning, noon and night.

Orange Crescents, p. 145

Pumpkin Streusel Muffins, p. 148

Soft Italian Breadsticks

(Pictured on page 140)

Christy Eichelberger, Jesup, Iowa

I use the "dough only" cycle on my bread machine to prepare these melt-in-your-mouth breadsticks that my family of five gobbles up! The soft, chewy breadsticks are irresistible when brushed with butter and sprinkled with Parmesan cheese. They're the perfect accompaniment to soups or Italian entrees.

1 cup water (70° to 80°)
3 tablespoons butter, softened
1-1/2 teaspoons salt
3 cups bread flour
2 tablespoons sugar
1 teaspoon Italian seasoning
1 teaspoon garlic powder
2-1/4 teaspoons active dry yeast

TOPPING:

1 tablespoon butter, melted
1 tablespoon grated Parmesan cheese

1. In bread machine pan, place the first eight ingredients in order suggested by manufacturer. Select dough setting (check dough after 5 minutes of mixing; add 1 to 2 tablespoons of water or flour if needed).

2. When cycle is completed, turn dough onto a lightly floured surface; divide in half. Cut each portion into 12 pieces; roll each into a 4-in. to 6-in. rope. Place 2 in. apart on greased baking sheets. Cover and let rise in a warm place until doubled, about 20 minutes.

3. Bake at 350° for 15-18 minutes or until golden brown. Immediately brush with butter; sprinkle with Parmesan cheese. Serve warm. **Yield:** 2 dozen.

Butternut Squash Dinner Rolls

Ula Kessler, Liberty Center, Ohio

These wholesome rolls are a pleasant addition to any entree. I get so many requests for them at holiday time, I make about 100 dozen in December.

2 tablespoons plus 1 teaspoon active dry yeast
3/4 teaspoon plus 1 cup sugar, *divided*
1/2 cup warm water (110° to 115°)
2 cups warm milk (110° to 115°)
1/4 cup butter, softened
2 cups mashed cooked butternut squash
2 teaspoons salt
1/4 cup wheat germ
10 to 11-1/2 cups all-purpose flour
Additional butter, melted

1. In a large mixing bowl, dissolve yeast and 3/4 teaspoon sugar in warm water; let stand for 5 minutes. Add the milk, butter, squash, salt and remaining sugar; mix until smooth. Add wheat germ and 4 cups flour; beat until smooth. Stir in enough remaining flour to form a soft dough.

2. Turn onto a floured surface; knead until smooth and elastic, about 6-8 minutes. Place in a greased bowl, turning once to grease top. Cover and let rise in a warm place until doubled, about 1 hour.

3. Punch dough down and divide into thirds; divide each portion into 20 pieces. Shape into balls. Place on greased baking sheets. Cover and let rise until doubled, about 30 minutes.

4. Bake at 350° for 15-17 minutes or until golden brown. Brush with butter. Remove to wire racks. **Yield:** 5 dozen.

Mango Nut Bread

Jo Sherley, Kahului, Hawaii

We live on the slopes of Haleakala, where carrots, potatoes, cabbage, bananas, litchis and mangoes are grown. This is my favorite recipe using mangoes.

2 cups all-purpose flour
1-1/2 cups sugar
1 teaspoon baking soda
1/2 teaspoon salt
1/2 teaspoon ground cinnamon
3 eggs
1/2 cup vegetable oil
1 teaspoon vanilla extract
2 cups chopped mangoes
1/2 cup chopped dates
1/2 cup chopped walnuts *or* macadamia nuts

1. In a large bowl, combine the first five ingredients. In another bowl, beat eggs, oil and vanilla. Stir into dry ingredients just until moistened. Fold in mangoes, dates and nuts (batter will be stiff).

2. Spoon into two greased 8-in. x 4-in. x 2-in. loaf pans. Bake at 350° for 50-55 minutes or until a toothpick inserted near the center comes out clean. Cool for 10 minutes before removing from pans to wire racks. **Yield:** 2 loaves.

Tangerine Muffins

Margaret Yerkes, New Port Richey, Florida

Here's a recipe that represents our state and region. We've lived in Florida since we retired in 1980. Before that, we lived in Alaska.

✓ Uses less fat, sugar or salt. Includes Nutritional Analysis and Diabetic Exchanges.

2 cups all-purpose flour
1/2 cup sugar
2 teaspoons baking powder
1 teaspoon baking soda
1/2 teaspoon salt
1 carton (8 ounces) vanilla yogurt
1 egg, lightly beaten
1/4 cup butter, melted
2 tablespoons milk
1 cup diced peeled tangerine
1 tablespoon grated tangerine peel

1. In a bowl, combine the first five ingredients. In a small bowl, combine the yogurt, egg, butter and milk until smooth; stir into dry ingredients just until moistened. Stir in tangerine and peel.

2. Fill greased or paper-lined muffin cups two-thirds full. Bake at 400° for 18-20 minutes or until a toothpick comes out clean. Cool for 5 minutes before removing from pan to a wire rack. **Yield:** 1 dozen.

Nutritional Analysis: One muffin (prepared with fat-free yogurt, egg substitute, margarine and fat-free milk) equals 172 calories, 352 mg sodium, trace cholesterol, 30 g carbohydrate, 4 g protein, 4 g fat, 1 g fiber. **Diabetic Exchanges:** 1 starch, 1 fruit, 1 fat.

Eggnog Bread

Ruth Bickel, Hickory, North Carolina

Someone always asks for the recipe when I make this rich bread for the holidays or to give as gifts. It's easy to make and quite delicious. The bread is a traditional part of the season at my home here in the foothills of the Blue Ridge Mountains.

1/4 cup butter, melted
3/4 cup sugar
2 eggs, beaten
2-1/4 cups all-purpose flour
2 teaspoons baking powder
1 teaspoon salt
1 cup eggnog
1/2 cup chopped pecans
1/2 cup raisins
1/2 cup chopped red and green candied cherries

1. In a large bowl, combine butter, sugar and eggs; mix well. Combine the flour, baking powder and salt. Stir into butter mixture alternately with eggnog, mixing just until moistened. Fold in pecans, raisins and cherries.

2. Spoon into a greased 8-1/2-in. x 4-1/2-in. x 2-1/2-in. loaf pan. Bake at 350° for 70 minutes or until a toothpick inserted near the center comes out clean. **Yield:** 1 loaf.

Editor's Note: This recipe was tested with commercially prepared eggnog.

Cinnamon Love Knots

Marlene Fetter, Alpena, Michigan

My sister-in-law and I enjoy these flavorful yeast rolls for breakfast, brunch or dessert, served with cups of steaming coffee and a hearty helping of love.

2 packages (1/4 ounce *each*) active dry yeast
1/2 cup warm water (110° to 115°)
1/2 cup warm milk (110° to 115°)
1/2 cup butter, softened
1/2 cup sugar
2 eggs, beaten
1 teaspoon salt
4-1/2 to 5 cups all-purpose flour
TOPPING:
2 cups sugar
2 tablespoons ground cinnamon
3/4 cup butter, melted

1. In a large mixing bowl, dissolve yeast in water. Let stand for 5 minutes. Add milk, butter, sugar, eggs and salt. Stir in enough flour to form a stiff dough.

2. Turn onto a floured surface; knead until smooth and elastic, about 6-8 minutes. Place in a greased bowl, turning once to grease top. Cover and let rise in a warm place until doubled, about 1-1/2 hours.

3. Punch dough down; divide into three portions. Cover two with plastic wrap. Shape one portion into 12 balls. Roll each ball into an 8-in. rope. Combine sugar and cinnamon. Dip rope into melted butter, then coat with cinnamon-sugar. Tie into a knot. Tuck and pinch ends under and place on ungreased baking sheets. Repeat with remaining dough. Cover and let rise until doubled, about 30 minutes.

4. Bake at 375° for 12-14 minutes or until golden brown. **Yield:** 3 dozen.

Herbed Tomato Bread

Sherry Letson, Trinity, Alabama

I added my favorite herbs to another recipe to create this savory tomato loaf. For extra flavor, I serve it with a garlic chive spread my family loves. In fact, my sister confiscated all the leftovers at our last gathering! Slices of this moist bread also make great grilled cheese sandwiches.

1/2 cup plus 2 tablespoons milk (70° to 80°)
1 can (6 ounces) tomato paste
1 egg
2 tablespoons olive oil
1/2 teaspoon salt
2 tablespoons minced fresh parsley
1 tablespoon sugar
2 teaspoons dried minced onion
1/2 teaspoon garlic powder
1/2 teaspoon dried tarragon
3 cups bread flour
2-1/4 teaspoons active dry yeast

GARLIC CHIVE SPREAD:

1/2 cup butter, softened
1 tablespoon minced chives
1 garlic clove, minced

1. In bread machine pan, place the first 12 ingredients in order suggested by manufacturer. Select basic bread setting. Choose crust color and loaf size if available. Bake according to bread machine directions (check dough after 5 minutes of mixing; add 1 to 2 tablespoons of water or flour if needed).

2. In a bowl, combine spread ingredients. Serve with bread. **Yield:** 1 loaf (1-1/2 pounds) and 1/2 cup spread.

Editor's Note: Use of the timer feature is not recommended for this recipe.

Orange Crescents

(Pictured on page 141)

Dianne Brooks, Augusta, Kansas

The bold orange flavor of these sweet rolls satisfies at breakfast, brunch, dessert or snacktime. My family and friends love them and often request that I make a batch. We consider them a real treat!

1 package (1/4 ounce) active dry yeast
1/4 cup warm water (110° to 115°)
3/4 cup sugar, *divided*
1 teaspoon salt
2 eggs
1/2 cup sour cream
8 tablespoons butter, melted, *divided*
3-1/4 to 3-3/4 cups all-purpose flour
2 tablespoons grated orange peel

GLAZE:

3/4 cup sugar
1/4 cup butter
2 tablespoons orange juice
1/2 cup sour cream

1. In a mixing bowl, dissolve yeast in water. Add 1/4 cup sugar, salt, eggs, sour cream and 6 tablespoons butter; mix well. Beat in 2 cups flour until smooth. Add enough remaining flour to form a soft dough.

2. Turn onto a floured surface; knead until smooth and elastic, about 6-8 minutes. Place in a greased bowl, turning once to grease top. Cover and let rise in a warm place until doubled, about 1-1/2 hours.

3. Punch dough down; divide in half. Roll each portion into a 12-in. circle. Brush each with 1 tablespoon butter. Combine orange peel and remaining sugar; sprinkle over dough. Cut each into 12 wedges. Roll up, starting with the wide side. Place point side down in two greased 13-in. x 9-in. x 2-in. baking pans, curving ends slightly to form a crescent. Cover and let rise in a warm place for 45 minutes or until doubled.

4. Bake at 350° for 20-30 minutes or until golden brown. In a saucepan, combine glaze ingredients. Bring to a boil; cook and stir for 3 minutes. Pour over warm rolls. Store in the refrigerator. **Yield:** 2 dozen.

Buttermilk Doughnuts

(Pictured on page 140)

Betty Rauschendorfer, Sidney, Montana

It doesn't take long for a platter of these doughnuts to vanish. Our grandkids go for them in a big way! They're great for munching at breakfast or brunch.

4 eggs
2 cups sugar
1/3 cup butter, melted
1 teaspoon vanilla extract
5-1/2 to 6 cups all-purpose flour
2 teaspoons baking powder
2 teaspoons baking soda
1 teaspoon salt
1 teaspoon ground nutmeg
2 cups buttermilk
Oil for frying
Additional sugar, cinnamon-sugar *or* confectioners' sugar, optional

1. In a mixing bowl, beat eggs and sugar until light and lemon-colored. Add butter and vanilla; mix well. Combine the flour, baking powder, baking soda, salt and nutmeg; add to egg mixture alternately with buttermilk. Cover and refrigerate for 2-3 hours.

2. On a lightly floured surface, roll dough to 1/2-in. thickness. Cut with a 3-in. doughnut cutter.

3. In an electric skillet or deep-fat fryer, heat oil to 375°. Fry doughnuts, a few at a time, for 1 minute on each side or until golden. Drain on paper towels. Roll in sugar if desired. **Yield:** 4 dozen.

Cinnamon-Swirl Pear Bread

Joan Anderson, Winnipeg, Manitoba

Pears add moisture to this delightful bread. I've been making it for over 25 years, and it's become a favorite of my family and friends. Try slices of the bread toasted to go along with Sunday brunch.

3 cups chopped peeled ripe pears (about 3 medium)
1/2 cup water
1-1/4 cups plus 1 teaspoon sugar, *divided*
3 packages (1/4 ounce *each*) active dry yeast
1/2 cup warm water (110° to 115°)
4 eggs, lightly beaten
1/2 cup butter, softened
1/2 cup honey
2 teaspoons salt
1 teaspoon almond extract
10 to 11 cups all-purpose flour
1 tablespoon ground cinnamon

1. In a saucepan, combine pears, water and 1/2 cup sugar. Simmer, uncovered, for 10-12 minutes or until tender. Drain well, reserving syrup. Add cold water if necessary to syrup to measure 1 cup; set aside.

2. In a mixing bowl, dissolve yeast in warm water. Add 1 teaspoon sugar; let stand for 10 minutes. Add eggs, butter, honey, salt, extract, 4 cups flour and reserved pears and syrup. Beat until smooth. Add enough remaining flour to form a soft dough.

3. Turn onto a floured surface; knead until smooth and elastic, about 6-8 minutes. Place in a greased bowl, turning once to grease top. Cover and let rise in a warm place until doubled, about 1-1/4 hours.

4. Punch dough down; divide into thirds. Roll each portion into a 16-in. x 8-in. rectangle. Combine cinnamon and remaining 3/4 cup sugar; sprinkle over dough to within 1/2 in. of edges. Roll up jelly-roll style, starting with a short side; pinch seams to seal. Place, seam side down, in three greased 9-in. x 5-in. x 3-in. loaf pans. Cover and let rise until doubled, about 45 minutes.

5. Bake at 375° for 20 minutes. Cover loosely with foil. Bake 15-20 minutes longer or until bread tests done. Remove from pans to wire racks to cool. **Yield:** 3 loaves.

Mashed Potato Rolls

Glenda Suit, Boise, Idaho

Potatoes are synonymous with our state. My grandmother always made these rolls, which everyone loved. Because it makes such a large batch, this recipe is great for company.

1 package (1/4 ounce) active dry yeast
1/4 cup warm water (110° to 115°)
1-3/4 cups warm milk (110° to 115°)
1/4 cup butter, softened
1/4 cup vegetable oil
6 tablespoons sugar
1 egg
1/2 cup warm mashed potatoes (prepared with milk and butter)
1-1/2 teaspoons salt
1 teaspoon baking powder
1/2 teaspoon baking soda
6 cups all-purpose flour
Melted butter, optional

1. In a mixing bowl, dissolve yeast in water. Add milk, butter, oil, sugar, egg and mashed potatoes; mix well. Stir in the salt, baking powder, baking soda and enough flour to form a soft dough.

2. Turn onto a floured surface; knead until smooth and elastic, about 6-8 minutes. Place in a greased bowl, turning once to grease top. Cover and let rise in a warm place until doubled, about 1-1/2 hours.

3. Punch dough down. Turn onto a lightly floured surface; divide in half. Cover one piece. Shape the other piece into 16 balls. Place 2 in. apart on greased baking sheets. Repeat with the remaining dough. Cover and let rise until doubled, about 30 minutes.

4. Bake at 375° for 15-18 minutes or until golden brown. Brush with butter if desired. **Yield:** 32 rolls.

Pumpernickel Caraway Bread

Lorraine Darocha, Berkshire, Massachusetts

This rich, dark bread has an old-fashioned homemade taste that's oh-so-satisfying. Made with molasses and caraway seeds, it's moist and flavorful. My family prefers slices of it slathered with apple butter or cream cheese.

3/4 cup water (70° to 80°)
2 tablespoons molasses
4-1/2 teaspoons butter
1 teaspoon salt
1 cup bread flour
2/3 cup rye flour
1/3 cup whole wheat flour
2 tablespoons cornmeal
5 teaspoons baking cocoa
4-1/2 teaspoons sugar
3 teaspoons nonfat dry milk powder
1 teaspoon caraway seeds

1/4 teaspoon instant coffee granules
1-1/2 teaspoons active dry yeast

1. In bread machine pan, place all ingredients in order suggested by manufacturer. Select basic bread setting. Choose crust color and loaf size if available.

2. Bake according to bread machine directions (check dough after 5 minutes of mixing; add 1 to 2 tablespoons of water or flour if needed). **Yield:** 1 loaf (1 pound).

Pumpkin Streusel Muffins

(Pictured on page 141)

Connie Pietila, Atlantic Mine, Michigan

These nicely spiced muffins are a great accompaniment to any meal—or try them for breakfast, dessert or a snack. The pumpkin flavor is complemented by a sweet brown sugar topping. You'll never know they're made with egg substitute.

✓ Uses less fat, sugar or salt. Includes Nutritional Analysis and Diabetic Exchanges.

1/4 cup margarine, softened
1/2 cup sugar
1/4 cup packed brown sugar
2/3 cup canned pumpkin
1/2 cup buttermilk
Egg substitute equivalent to 2 eggs
2 tablespoons molasses
1 teaspoon grated orange peel
2 cups all-purpose flour
2 teaspoons baking powder
1 teaspoon baking soda
1 teaspoon pumpkin pie spice
1/4 teaspoon salt

STREUSEL TOPPING:
1/3 cup all-purpose flour
3 tablespoons brown sugar
2 tablespoons cold margarine

1. In a mixing bowl, cream margarine and sugars. Add pumpkin, buttermilk, egg substitute, molasses and orange peel; mix well. Combine dry ingredients; gradually add to pumpkin mixture just until blended.

2. Use paper liners or coat muffin cups with nonstick cooking spray; fill two-thirds full.

3. For topping, combine flour and brown sugar; cut in margarine until crumbly. Sprinkle over batter.

4. Bake at 375° for 20-25 minutes or until a toothpick comes out clean. Cool in pan for 5 minutes before removing to a wire rack. **Yield:** 1 dozen.

Nutritional Analysis: One muffin equals 229 calories, 336 mg sodium, trace cholesterol, 39 g carbohydrate, 4 g protein, 6 g fat, 1 g fiber. **Diabetic Exchanges:** 2 starch, 1 fat, 1/2 fruit.

Pineapple Zucchini Bread

Shirley Boulet, Whitefield, New Hampshire

Meals are even more memorable when I complement them with this light garden-fresh bread. The zucchini makes it so moist and tender...and the pineapple lends a delicate tropical twist to every delicious slice.

3 eggs
2 cups finely shredded zucchini
1 cup vegetable oil
1 can (8 ounces) crushed pineapple, drained
2 teaspoons vanilla extract
3 cups all-purpose flour
2 cups sugar
2 teaspoons baking soda
1-1/2 teaspoons ground cinnamon
1 teaspoon salt
3/4 teaspoon ground nutmeg
1/2 teaspoon baking powder
1 cup chopped nuts
1 cup raisins *or* currants, optional

1. In a bowl, combine eggs, zucchini, oil, pineapple and vanilla. Combine dry ingredients; stir into egg mixture just until moistened. Fold in nuts and raisins if desired.

2. Pour into two greased 8-in. x 4-in. x 2-in. loaf pans. Bake at 350° for 50-60 minutes or until a toothpick inserted near the center comes out clean. Cool for 10 minutes before removing from pans to wire racks. **Yield:** 2 loaves.

Orange Swirl Coffee Cake

Barbara Daniel, Ducor, California

My family and I look forward to warm slices of this citrus-flavored coffee cake every Christmas and Easter morning. It's a tasty tradition we've been sharing for a number of years.

1 package (1/4 ounce) active dry yeast
1/4 cup warm water (110° to 115°)
1 cup sugar, *divided*
2 eggs
1/2 cup sour cream
8 tablespoons butter, *divided*
1 teaspoon salt
3-1/4 to 3-1/2 cups all-purpose flour
3/4 cup flaked coconut, toasted
2 tablespoons grated orange peel

ORANGE GLAZE:

6 tablespoons sugar
1-1/2 teaspoons cornstarch
1/4 cup sour cream
2 tablespoons butter
1 tablespoon orange juice
1/4 cup flaked coconut, toasted

1. In a mixing bowl, dissolve yeast in warm water. Add 1/4 cup sugar, eggs, sour cream, 6 tablespoons butter and salt; mix well. Stir in enough flour to form a soft dough.

2. Turn onto a floured surface; knead until smooth and elastic, about 6-8 minutes. Place in a greased bowl, turning once to grease top. Cover and let rise in a warm place until doubled, about 1 hour.

3. Meanwhile, combine coconut, orange peel and remaining sugar; set aside. Punch dough down. Turn onto a floured surface; roll into an 18-in. x 10-in. rectangle. Melt remaining butter; brush over dough. Spread coconut mixture over dough. Roll up jelly-roll style, starting with a long side; pinch seam to seal. Place seam side near the top and facing the center tube in a greased fluted 10-in. tube pan; pinch ends together. Cover and let rise in a warm place until doubled, about 1 hour.

4. Bake at 350° for 30 minutes or until golden brown. Cool for 10 minutes before removing from pan to a wire rack.

5. For glaze, combine sugar, cornstarch, sour cream, butter and orange juice in a saucepan. Bring to a boil; boil and stir for 2 minutes. Spoon or brush over warm coffee cake. Sprinkle with coconut. **Yield:** 16-20 servings.

Focaccia Bread Squares

Kay King, Dyersville, Iowa

Looking for an alternative to garlic bread? Try this golden focaccia bread. The dough is easy to whip up in the bread machine, then season with rosemary, garlic salt and Parmesan cheese.

3/4 cup plus 3 tablespoons water (70° to 80°)
3 tablespoons butter, softened
2 tablespoons nonfat dry milk powder
3 tablespoons sugar
1-1/2 teaspoons salt
3 cups bread flour
2-1/4 teaspoons active dry yeast

TOPPING:

2 tablespoons olive oil
3 tablespoons grated Parmesan cheese
2 teaspoons minced fresh rosemary *or* 3/4 teaspoon dried rosemary, crushed
1/2 teaspoon garlic salt

1. In bread machine pan, place the first seven ingredients in order suggested by manufacturer. Select dough setting (check dough after 5 minutes of mixing; add 1 to 2 tablespoons of water or flour if needed).

2. When cycle is completed, turn the dough onto a lightly floured surface. Cover and let rest for 15 minutes. Knead for 1 minute. Roll dough into a 15-in. x 10-in. rectangle.

3. Transfer to a greased 15-in. x 10-in. x 1-in. baking pan. Press dough 1/4 in. up the sides of pan. Cover and let rise in a warm place for 20-30 minutes or until slightly risen.

4. With a wooden spoon handle, make indentations at 1-in. intervals. Brush dough with oil; sprinkle with Parmesan cheese, rosemary and garlic salt.

5. Bake at 400° for 13-15 minutes or until lightly browned. Cool slightly. Cut into squares; serve warm.
Yield: 2 dozen.

Cranberry Biscuits

Debra Fulenwider, Colfax, California

I like the texture and nutrition of potato rolls and the taste of orange-cranberry bread, so I combined them in these yummy breakfast biscuits. These treats are a family favorite.

1-2/3 cups milk (70° to 80°)
2 eggs
3 tablespoons butter, softened
3/4 cup mashed potato flakes
1/4 cup sugar
2 teaspoons salt
1-1/4 teaspoons ground cinnamon
1 teaspoon grated orange peel
4 cups bread flour
1 tablespoon active dry yeast
1 cup dried cranberries

ORANGE GLAZE:
1 cup confectioners' sugar
2 to 3 tablespoons orange juice
3 tablespoons chopped dried cranberries, optional

1. In bread machine pan, place the first 10 ingredients in order suggested by manufacturer. Select dough setting (check dough after 5 minutes of mixing; add 1 to 2 tablespoons of water or flour if needed). Just before final kneading (your machine may audibly signal this), add cranberries.

2. When cycle is completed, turn dough onto a lightly floured surface. Cover and let rest for 15 minutes. Roll or pat to 1/2-in. thickness. Cut with a 2-1/2-in. biscuit cutter. Place in a greased 15-in. x 10-in. x 1-in. baking pan. Cover and let rise in a warm place until almost doubled, about 40 minutes.

3. Bake at 375° for 10-15 minutes or until golden brown. Combine confectioners' sugar and enough orange juice to achieve a glaze consistency. Drizzle over warm biscuits. Sprinkle with chopped cranberries if desired. **Yield:** about 1-1/2 dozen.

Editor's Note: Use of the timer feature is not recommended for this recipe.

Grilled Cheese Loaf

Debbi Baker, Green Springs, Ohio

Generally, I serve this with steaks and salads. The loaf's so quick to make, in fact, I often grill two of them.

1 package (3 ounces) cream cheese, softened
2 tablespoons butter, softened
1 cup (4 ounces) shredded mozzarella cheese
1/4 cup chopped green onions with tops
1/2 teaspoon garlic salt
1 loaf (1 pound) French bread, sliced

1. In a mixing bowl, beat cream cheese and butter. Add cheese, onions and garlic salt; mix well. Spread on both sides of each slice of bread.

2. Wrap loaf in a large piece of heavy-duty foil (about 28 in. x 18 in.); seal tightly. Grill, covered, over medium heat for 8-10 minutes, turning once. Unwrap foil; grill 5 minutes longer. **Yield:** 10-12 servings.

Turkey Stuffing Bread

(Pictured on page 140)

Gayl Koster, Nunica, Michigan

My father-in-law had a ball experimenting with his bread machine to come up with this unique bread that tastes just like real turkey stuffing. It's fabulous served with a chicken or turkey dinner...and works well with all of those Thanksgiving leftovers, too.

- **1 cup plus 1 tablespoon milk (70° to 80°)**
- **1 egg**
- **1 tablespoon butter, softened**
- **2 tablespoons brown sugar**
- **1-1/2 teaspoons salt**
- **1/3 cup cornmeal**
- **3 cups bread flour**
- **4-1/2 teaspoons dried minced onion**
- **1-1/2 teaspoons celery seed**
- **3/4 teaspoon poultry seasoning**
- **1/2 teaspoon rubbed sage**
- **1/2 teaspoon pepper**
- **2-1/4 teaspoons active dry yeast**

1. In bread machine pan, place all ingredients in order suggested by manufacturer. Select basic bread setting. Choose crust color and loaf size if available.

2. Bake according to bread machine directions (check dough after 5 minutes of mixing; add 1 to 2 tablespoons of water or flour if needed). **Yield:** 1 loaf (1-1/2 pounds).

Editor's Note: Use of the timer feature is not recommended for this recipe.

Sour Cream Lemon Bread

Barbara Strickler, Syracuse, Indiana

My family always requests this light, tender bread with a hint of lemon. This loaf is so scrumptious that it complements almost any meal. I serve slices with a creamy lemon spread for an early-morning treat or late-night snack that's simply dreamy.

- **1/4 cup sour cream**
- **2 tablespoons lemon juice**
- **2 to 3 tablespoons milk (70° to 80°)**
- **2 tablespoons butter, softened**
- **1 egg**
- **2 teaspoons grated lemon peel**
- **2 tablespoons sugar**
- **1 teaspoon salt**
- **1/4 teaspoon baking soda**
- **2 cups bread flour**
- **1-1/2 teaspoons active dry yeast**

LEMON SPREAD:

- **1 package (3 ounces) cream cheese, softened**
- **1/4 cup confectioners' sugar**
- **1 tablespoon lemon juice**
- **1 teaspoon lemon peel**

1. In a measuring cup, combine sour cream and lemon juice. Add enough milk to measure 1/2 cup.

2. In bread machine pan, place the sour cream mixture, butter, egg, lemon peel, sugar, salt, baking soda, flour and yeast in order suggested by manufacturer. Select sweet bread setting. Choose the crust color and loaf size if available.

3. Bake according to bread machine directions (check dough after 5 minutes of mixing; add 1 to 2 tablespoons of water or flour if needed).

4. In a mixing bowl, beat spread ingredients until smooth; serve with the bread. **Yield:** 1 loaf (1 pound) and about 1/2 cup spread.

Editor's Note: Use of the timer feature is not recommended for this recipe. If your bread machine does not have a sweet bread setting, follow the manufacturer's directions using the basic setting.

Sweet Potato Crescents

Rebecca Bailey, Fairbury, Nebraska

My family agrees that our Thanksgiving feast would not be complete without these light-as-air crescent rolls. They're a nice accompaniment to any menu. Baking them always puts me in the holiday spirit.

2 packages (1/4 ounce *each*) active dry yeast
1 cup warm water (110° to 115°)
1 can (15 ounces) cut sweet potatoes, drained and mashed
1/2 cup sugar
1/2 cup shortening
1 egg
1-1/2 teaspoons salt
5 to 5-1/2 cups all-purpose flour
1/4 cup butter, melted

1. In a large mixing bowl, dissolve yeast in water; let stand for 5 minutes. Beat in the sweet potatoes, sugar, shortening, egg, salt and 3 cups flour. Add enough remaining flour to form a stiff dough.

2. Turn onto a floured surface; knead until smooth and elastic, about 6-8 minutes. Place in a greased bowl, turning once to grease top. Cover and let rise in a warm place until doubled, about 1 hour.

3. Punch dough down; divide into thirds. Roll each portion into a 12-in. circle; cut each into 12 wedges. Brush with butter. Roll up from the wide end and place, pointed end down, 2 in. apart on greased baking sheets. Cover and let rise until doubled, about 40 minutes.

4. Bake at 375° for 13-15 minutes or until golden brown. Remove from pans to wire racks. **Yield:** 3 dozen.

Garlic Herb Bubble Loaf

Katie Crill, Priest River, Idaho

I adapted an old sour cream bread recipe to make the dough for this deliciously different pull-apart loaf that smells heavenly while baking. It has a light crust, tender interior and lots of herb and butter flavor.

1/2 cup water (70° to 80°)
1/2 cup sour cream
2 tablespoons butter, softened
3 tablespoons sugar
1-1/2 teaspoons salt
3 cups bread flour
2-1/4 teaspoons active dry yeast

GARLIC HERB BUTTER:
1/4 cup butter, melted
4 garlic cloves, minced
1/4 teaspoon *each* dried oregano, thyme and rosemary, crushed

1. In bread machine pan, place the first seven ingredients in order suggested by manufacturer. Select dough setting (check dough after 5 minutes of mixing; add 1 to 2 tablespoons of water or flour if needed).

2. When cycle is completed, divide dough into 36 pieces. Shape each into a ball.

3. In a bowl, combine butter, garlic and herbs. Dip each ball in mixture; place in an ungreased 9-in. x 5-in. x 3-in. loaf pan. Cover and let rise in a warm place until doubled, about 45 minutes.

4. Bake at 375° for 35-40 minutes or until golden brown. Serve warm. **Yield:** 1 loaf.

Best Ever Banana Bread

Gert Kaiser, Kenosha, Wisconsin

Whenever I pass a display of bananas in the grocery store, I can almost smell the wonderful aroma of this bread. It really is good!

1-3/4 cups all-purpose flour
1-1/2 cups sugar
1 teaspoon baking soda
1/2 teaspoon salt
2 eggs
2 medium ripe bananas, mashed (about 1 cup)
1/2 cup vegetable oil
1/4 cup plus 1 tablespoon buttermilk
1 teaspoon vanilla extract
1 cup chopped walnuts

1. In a large bowl, combine flour, sugar, baking soda and salt. In another bowl, combine eggs, bananas, oil, buttermilk and vanilla; add to flour mixture, stirring just until combined. Fold in nuts.

2. Pour into a greased 9-in. x 5-in. x 3-in. baking pan. Bake at 325° for 1 hour and 20 minutes or until a toothpick inserted near the center comes out clean. Cool on a wire rack. **Yield:** 1 loaf.

Frosted Cinnamon Rolls

Velma Horton, La Grange, California

These pretty cinnamon rolls are absolutely marvelous and taste just like the ones sold at the mall. Topped with a sweet cream cheese frosting, they're best served warm with steaming cups of coffee. Or reheat leftover rolls in the microwave and enjoy any time of day.

1 cup milk (70° to 80°)
1/4 cup water (70° to 80°)
1/4 cup butter, softened
1 egg
1 teaspoon salt
4 cups bread flour
1/4 cup instant vanilla pudding mix
1 tablespoon sugar
1 tablespoon active dry yeast

FILLING:
1/4 cup butter, softened
1 cup packed brown sugar
2 teaspoons ground cinnamon

FROSTING:
4 ounces cream cheese, softened
1/4 cup butter, softened
1-1/2 cups confectioners' sugar
1-1/2 teaspoons milk
1/2 teaspoon vanilla extract

1. In bread machine pan, place first nine ingredients in order suggested by manufacturer. Select dough setting (check dough after 5 minutes of mixing; add 1 to 2 tablespoons water or flour if needed).

2. When cycle is completed, turn dough onto lightly floured surface. Roll into a 17-in. x 10-in. rectangle. Spread with butter; sprinkle with brown sugar and cinnamon. Roll up jelly-roll style, starting from a long side; pinch seam to seal. Cut into 21 slices. Place 12 slices, cut side down, in a greased 13-in. x 9-in. x 2-in. baking pan and nine rolls in a 9-in. square baking pan. Cover; let rise in a warm place until doubled, about 45 minutes.

3. Bake at 350° for 20-25 minutes or until golden brown. Cool on wire racks for 5 minutes.

4. In a mixing bowl, beat frosting ingredients. Frost warm rolls. Store in refrigerator. **Yield:** 21 rolls.

Editor's Note: Use of the timer feature is not recommended for this recipe.

Cardamom Braids

Walter Dust, Rapid City, Michigan

This is an old recipe that I like to make for breakfast. The bread is great for dunking in a cup of coffee.

1 package (1/4 ounce) active dry yeast
1-1/2 cups warm milk (110° to 115°), *divided*
1 cup sugar, *divided*
3 egg yolks, beaten
1/2 cup butter, softened
1 tablespoon ground cardamom
1/2 teaspoon salt
5 to 6 cups all-purpose flour
2 tablespoons milk

1. In a large mixing bowl, dissolve yeast in 1/2 cup warm milk. Add 3/4 cup sugar, egg yolks, butter, cardamom, salt, 3 cups of flour and remaining warm milk; beat until smooth. Stir in enough remaining flour to form a soft dough.

2. Turn onto a floured surface; knead until smooth and elastic, about 6-8 minutes. Place in a greased bowl, turning once to grease top. Cover and let rise in a warm place until doubled, about 1-1/4 hours.

3. Punch dough down; divide into six pieces. Shape each piece into a 16-in. rope. Place three ropes on a greased baking sheet; braid. Pinch ends firmly and tuck under. Repeat with remaining three ropes on another baking sheet. Cover and let rise until doubled, about 45 minutes.

4. Brush braids with milk and sprinkle with remaining sugar. Bake at 350° for 25-30 minutes or until golden brown. Remove to wire racks to cool. **Yield:** 2 loaves.

Multigrain Bread

Michele MacKinlay, Madoc, Ontario

It's hard to get a good whole-grain bread where I live, so my bread machine comes in very handy when making this hearty loaf. I adapted it from an old recipe, and the cornmeal and wheat germ give it a wonderful texture and nutty flavor I love.

1 cup water (70° to 80°)
2 tablespoons vegetable oil
2 egg yolks
1/4 cup molasses
1 teaspoon salt
1-1/2 cups bread flour
1 cup whole wheat flour
1/2 cup rye flour
1/2 cup nonfat dry milk powder
1/4 cup quick-cooking oats
1/4 cup wheat germ
1/4 cup cornmeal
2-1/4 teaspoons active dry yeast

1. In bread machine pan, place all ingredients in order suggested by manufacturer. Select basic bread setting. Choose crust color and loaf size if available.

2. Bake according to bread machine directions (check dough after 5 minutes of mixing; add 1 to 2 tablespoons water or flour if needed). **Yield:** 1 loaf (2 pounds).

Editor's Note: Use of the timer feature is not recommended for this recipe.

Golden Honey Pan Rolls

Sara Wing, Philadelphia, Pennsylvania

A cousin in North Carolina gave me the recipe for these delicious honey-glazed rolls. Using my bread machine to make the dough saves me about 2 hours compared to the traditional method. The rich, buttery taste of these rolls is so popular with family and friends that I usually make two batches so I have enough!

1 cup milk (70° to 80°)
1 egg
1 egg yolk
1/2 cup vegetable oil
2 tablespoons honey
1-1/2 teaspoons salt
3-1/2 cups bread flour
2-1/4 teaspoons active dry yeast
GLAZE:
1/3 cup sugar
2 tablespoons butter, melted
1 tablespoon honey
1 egg white
Additional honey, optional

1. In bread machine pan, place the first eight ingredients in order suggested by manufacturer. Select dough setting (check dough after 5 minutes of mixing; add 1 to 2 tablespoons of water or flour if needed.)

2. When cycle is completed, turn dough onto a lightly floured surface. Punch down; cover and let rest for 10 minutes. Divide into 24 pieces; shape each into a ball. Place 12 balls each in two greased 8-in. baking pans. Cover and let rise in a warm place until doubled, about 30 minutes.

3. For glaze, combine sugar, butter, honey and egg white; drizzle over dough. Bake at 350° for 20-25 minutes or until golden brown. Brush with additional honey if desired. **Yield:** 2 dozen.

Editor's Note: Use of the timer feature is not recommended for this recipe.

Cranberry Orange Scones

Karen McBride, Indianapolis, Indiana

Moist and scrumptious, these fruity scones come out perfect every time I make them. I savor the chewy dried cranberries inside and sweet orange glaze drizzled over the top. There's nothing better than serving these remarkable scones warm with delicate orange butter.

2 cups all-purpose flour
10 teaspoons sugar, *divided*
1 tablespoon grated orange peel
2 teaspoons baking powder
1/2 teaspoon salt
1/4 teaspoon baking soda
1/3 cup cold butter
1 cup dried cranberries
1/4 cup orange juice
1/4 cup half-and-half cream
1 egg
1 tablespoon milk

GLAZE (optional):
1/2 cup confectioners' sugar
1 tablespoon orange juice

ORANGE BUTTER:
1/2 cup butter, softened
2 to 3 tablespoons orange marmalade

1. In a bowl, combine flour, 7 teaspoons sugar, orange peel, baking powder, salt and baking soda. Cut in butter until the mixture resembles coarse crumbs; set aside.

2. In a small bowl, combine cranberries, orange juice, cream and egg. Add to flour mixture and stir until a soft dough forms.

3. On a floured surface, gently knead 6-8 times. Pat dough into an 8-in. circle. Cut into 10 wedges. Separate wedges and place on an ungreased baking sheet. Brush with milk; sprinkle with remaining sugar.

4. Bake at 400° for 12-15 minutes or until lightly browned. Combine glaze ingredients if desired; drizzle over scones. Combine orange butter ingredients; serve with warm scones. **Yield:** 10 scones.

Granola Raisin Bread

Patricia Nelson, Kenosha, Wisconsin

Made with granola, oats, raisins and honey, this bread has a subtle sweetness. It's so delightful that friends often request the recipe. Slices of the crusty loaf are especially good toasted. If you prefer a softer crust, rub butter on the loaf while it's still warm.

1-2/3 cups water (70° to 80°)
1/3 cup honey
2 tablespoons butter
1-1/2 teaspoons salt
3-1/2 cups bread flour
1 cup quick-cooking oats
1 tablespoon active dry yeast
1 cup granola cereal
3/4 cup golden raisins

1. In bread machine pan, place the first seven ingredients in order suggested by manufacturer. Select basic bread setting. Choose crust color and loaf size if available.

2. Bake according to bread machine directions (check dough after 5 minutes of mixing; add 1 to 2 tablespoons of water or flour if needed). Just before the final kneading (your machine may audibly signal this), add the granola and raisins. **Yield:** 1 loaf (2 pounds).

Pumpkin Pecan Loaves

Brenda Jackson, Garden City, Kansas

Among all my pumpkin bread recipes, this caramel-glazed creation is the pick of the crop. Often, I'll wrap up a lovely loaf as a homemade gift for teachers.

3-1/3 cups all-purpose flour
3 cups sugar

2 teaspoons baking soda
1-1/2 teaspoons salt
1 teaspoon ground cinnamon
1 teaspoon ground nutmeg
1 can (15 ounces) solid-pack pumpkin
1 cup vegetable oil
4 eggs, lightly beaten
2/3 cup water
1/2 cup chopped pecans

CARAMEL GLAZE:

1/4 cup butter
1/4 cup sugar
1/4 cup packed brown sugar
1/4 cup heavy whipping cream
2/3 cup confectioners' sugar
1 teaspoon vanilla extract

1. In a bowl, combine the first six ingredients. Combine the pumpkin, oil, eggs and water; mix well. Stir into dry ingredients just until combined; fold in the pecans.

2. Spoon into two greased 9-in. x 5-in. x 3-in. loaf pans. Bake at 350° for 60-65 minutes or until a toothpick inserted near the center comes out clean. Cool for 10 minutes before removing from pans to wire racks.

3. For glaze, combine butter, sugars and cream in a saucepan. Cook until sugar is dissolved. Cool for 20 minutes. Stir in the confectioners' sugar and vanilla until smooth. Drizzle over cooled loaves. **Yield:** 2 loaves.

Cranberry Date Bars, p. 162

Mint Brownie Cupcakes, p. 170

Peanut Butter Sandwich Cookies, p. 171

Zucchini Dessert Squares, p. 165

Brownies, Bars & Cookies

Scottish Shortbread, p. 163

A cookie jar packed with homemade mmm…morsels or a platter piled high with bars and brownies will brighten anyone's day. Just bake a batch and watch the smiles appear!

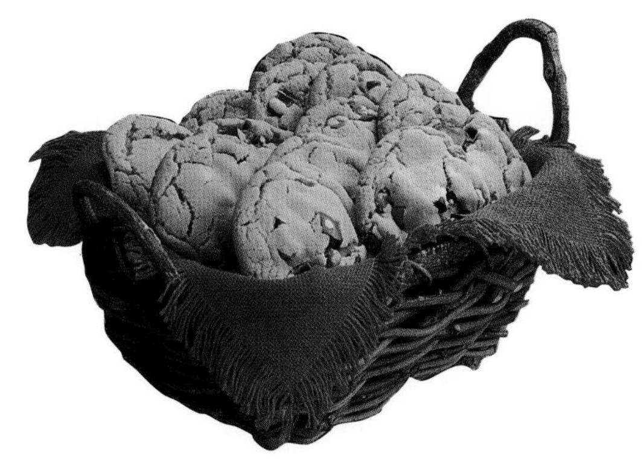
Chocolate Malted Cookies, p. 167

Watermelon Cookies

A. Ruth Witmer, Stevens, Pennsylvania

Shaped to look like watermelon slices, these cute cookies are especially fun to serve at summer picnics and family gatherings.

3/4 cup butter
3/4 cup sugar
1 egg
1/2 teaspoon almond extract
2-1/4 cups all-purpose flour
1/4 teaspoon salt
1/4 teaspoon baking powder
Red and green food coloring
Dried currants *or* raisins
Sesame seeds

1. In a mixing bowl, cream butter, sugar, egg and extract until light and fluffy. Combine flour, salt and baking powder; stir into creamed mixture and mix well.

2. Remove 1 cup of dough; set aside. At low speed, beat in enough red food coloring to tint dough deep red. Roll into a 3-1/2-in.-long tube; wrap in plastic wrap and refrigerate until firm, about 2 hours.

3. Divide 1 cup of reserved dough into two pieces. To one piece, add enough green food coloring to tint dough deep green. Do not tint remaining piece of dough. Wrap each piece separately in plastic wrap; chill until firm, about 1 hour.

4. On a floured sheet of waxed paper, roll untinted dough into an 8-1/2-in. x 3-1/2-in. rectangle. Place red dough along short end of rectangle. Roll up and encircle red dough with untinted dough; set aside.

5. On floured waxed paper, roll the green dough into a 10-in. x 3-1/2-in. rectangle. Place tube of red/untinted dough along the short end of green dough. Roll up and encircle tube with green dough. Cover tightly with plastic wrap; refrigerate at least 8 hours or overnight.

6. Unwrap dough and cut into 1/8-in. slices. Place 1 in. apart on ungreased baking sheets. Lightly press dried currants and sesame seeds into each slice to resemble watermelon seeds.

7. Bake at 375° for 6-8 minutes or until cookies are firm but not brown. While still warm, cut each cookie in half or into pie-shaped wedges. Remove to a wire rack to cool. **Yield:** 3 dozen.

Cranberry Date Bars

(Pictured on page 160)

Bonnie Nieter, Warsaw, Indiana

I first discovered this recipe at Christmas a couple years ago, but it's a great way to use frozen cranberries throughout the year. I help out at the school our sons attend and am active at our church. It seems I'm always baking a batch of these moist bars for some event.

1 package (12 ounces) fresh *or* frozen cranberries, thawed
1 package (8 ounces) chopped dates
2 tablespoons water
1 teaspoon vanilla extract
2 cups all-purpose flour
2 cups old-fashioned oats
1-1/2 cups packed brown sugar
1/2 teaspoon baking soda
1/2 teaspoon salt
1 cup butter, melted

GLAZE:

2 cups confectioners' sugar
2 to 3 tablespoons orange juice
1/2 teaspoon vanilla extract

1. In a covered saucepan over low heat, simmer cranberries, dates and water for 15 minutes, stirring occasionally until the cranberries have popped. Remove from the heat; stir in vanilla and set aside.

2. In a large bowl, combine the flour, oats, brown sugar, baking soda and salt. Stir in butter until well blended. Pat half into an ungreased 13-in. x 9-in. x 2-in. baking pan. Bake at 350° for 8 minutes.

3. Spoon cranberry mixture over crust. Sprinkle with the remaining oat mixture. Pat gently. Bake at 350° for 25-30 minutes or until browned. Cool. Combine glaze ingredients; drizzle over bars. **Yield:** 3 dozen.

Scottish Shortbread

(Pictured on page 161)

Rose Mabee, Selkirk, Manitoba

Scottish settlers first came to this area over 150 years ago. My mother was Scottish, and—as with most of my favorite recipes—she passed this on to me. I make a triple batch of it each year at Christmas, to enjoy and to give as gifts.

1 pound butter, softened
1 cup packed brown sugar
4 to 4-1/2 cups all-purpose flour

1. In a mixing bowl, cream the butter and brown sugar. Add 3-3/4 cups flour; mix well.

2. On a floured surface, knead the dough for 5 minutes, adding enough remaining flour to make a soft, nonsticky dough. Roll to 1/2-in. thickness. Cut into 3-in. x 1-in. strips. Place 1 in. apart on ungreased baking sheets. Prick with a fork.

3. Bake at 325° for 20-25 minutes or until cookies are lightly browned. **Yield:** about 4 dozen.

Mocha Truffle Brownies

Margaret Roberts, Kuna, Idaho

My husband is a chocolate lover, so I bake brownies about once a week. This mouth-watering variety is one of his favorites and so simple to make.

1-1/4 cups semisweet chocolate chips
1/2 cup butter
1 teaspoon instant coffee granules
2 tablespoons hot water
2 eggs
3/4 cup packed brown sugar
3/4 cup all-purpose flour
1/2 teaspoon baking powder

FILLING:

1 tablespoon instant coffee granules
1 tablespoon hot water
1 package (8 ounces) cream cheese, softened
1/3 cup confectioners' sugar
1 cup (6 ounces) semisweet chocolate chips, melted

GLAZE:

1/4 cup semisweet chocolate chips
1 teaspoon shortening

1. In a heavy saucepan or microwave, melt chips and butter. Stir until smooth; cool for 5 minutes. Dissolve coffee granules in hot water; set aside.

2. In a mixing bowl, combine eggs and brown sugar; beat on medium for 1 minute. Stir in chocolate mixture and coffee. Combine flour and baking powder; gradually add to chocolate mixture.

3. Transfer to a greased 9-in. square baking pan. Bake at 350° for 30-35 minutes or until a toothpick inserted near the center comes out with moist crumbs. Cool completely on a wire rack.

4. Dissolve coffee granules in water; set aside. In a mixing bowl, beat cream cheese until smooth. Beat in confectioners' sugar, melted chocolate and coffee. Spread over brownies.

5. For glaze, melt the chips and shortening; stir until smooth. Drizzle over filling. Refrigerate for at least 2 hours before cutting. **Yield:** about 6-1/2 dozen.

Cinnamon Sugar Cookies

Leah Costigan, Otto, North Carolina

My mom always had these cookies on hand. They're so good with a cup of hot chocolate, coffee or milk.

1 cup butter, softened
1 cup sugar
1 cup confectioners' sugar
1 cup vegetable oil
2 eggs
1 teaspoon vanilla extract
4-1/3 cups all-purpose flour
1 teaspoon salt
1 teaspoon baking soda
1 teaspoon ground cinnamon
1 teaspoon cream of tartar
1 cup finely chopped pecans, optional
Colored sugar, optional

1. In a large mixing bowl, cream butter, sugars and oil. Add eggs and vanilla; mix well. Add flour, salt, baking soda, cinnamon and cream of tartar. Stir in pecans if desired.

2. Roll into 1-in. balls. Place on greased baking sheets; flatten with the bottom of a glass dipped in sugar. Sprinkle with colored sugar if desired. Bake at 375° for 10-12 minutes. **Yield:** about 8 dozen.

Cooling Cookies

If cookies seem to crumble when you remove them from the baking sheet, let them cool for 1 to 2 minutes first. But beware that if cookies cool too long, they become hard and can break when removed. If this happens, return the baking sheet to the oven to warm the cookies slightly so they'll release more easily.

Zucchini Dessert Squares

(Pictured on page 160)

Nancy Morelli, Livonia, Michigan

We planted one too many zucchini plants a few summers ago and harvested a lot of zucchinis that year. I was looking for ways to use them...these delicious bars are the result.

4 cups all-purpose flour
2 cups sugar
1/2 teaspoon ground cinnamon
1/2 teaspoon salt
1-1/2 cups cold butter

FILLING:

8 to 10 cups cubed seeded peeled zucchini (4 to 5 pounds)
2/3 cup lemon juice
1 cup sugar
1 teaspoon ground cinnamon
1/2 teaspoon ground nutmeg

1. In a bowl, combine flour, sugar, cinnamon and salt. Cut in butter until crumbly; reserve 3 cups. Pat remaining crumb mixture into the bottom of a greased 13-in. x 9-in. x 2-in. baking pan. Bake at 375° for 12 minutes.

2. Meanwhile, for filling, place zucchini and lemon juice in a saucepan; bring to a boil. Reduce heat; cover and cook for 6-8 minutes or until zucchini is crisp-tender. Stir in sugar, cinnamon and nutmeg; cover and simmer for 5 minutes (mixture will be thin).

3. Spoon over crust; sprinkle with the reserved crumb mixture. Bake at 375° for 40-45 minutes or until golden. **Yield:** 16-20 servings.

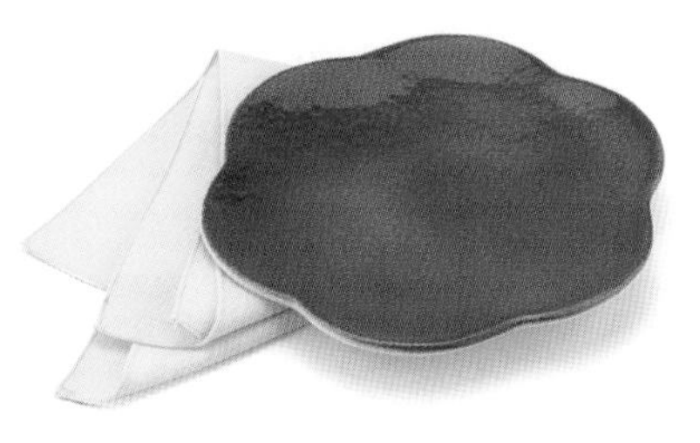

Macaroon Brownies

Christine Foust, Stoneboro, Pennsylvania

My mother-in-law made these coconut-filled brownies for my bridal shower and wedding reception. After the first bite, I knew why my husband loves them!

1 cup butter, softened
2 cups sugar
4 eggs
1 teaspoon vanilla extract
2 cups all-purpose flour
1/2 cup baking cocoa
1/2 teaspoon cream of tartar
1/2 cup chopped walnuts

MACAROON FILLING:

1 package (14 ounces) flaked coconut
1 can (14 ounces) sweetened condensed milk
2 teaspoons vanilla extract

FROSTING:

3/4 cup sugar
1/4 cup milk
2 tablespoons butter
1 cup miniature marshmallows
1 cup (6 ounces) semisweet chocolate chips
1 teaspoon vanilla extract

1. In a mixing bowl, cream butter and sugar. Add eggs and vanilla; mix well. Combine flour, cocoa and cream of tartar; gradually add to creamed mixture. Stir in nuts. Spread half into a greased 13-in. x 9-in. x 2-in. baking pan.

2. Combine coconut, condensed milk and vanilla; carefully spread over chocolate layer. Top with the remaining chocolate mixture. Bake at 350° for 40-45 minutes or until a toothpick inserted near the center comes out clean. Cool on a wire rack.

3. For frosting, combine sugar, milk and butter in a saucepan; cook and stir until sugar is dissolved. Add the remaining ingredients. Cook and stir until marshmallows and chips are melted. Cool until mixtures reaches spreading consistency, about 25 minutes. Spread over the cooled brownies. Cut into bars. **Yield:** 4 dozen.

Chewy Peanut Butter Bars

Mrs. Sanford Wickham, Holbrook, Nebraska

This recipe combines three of my favorite foods—peanut butter, coconut and chocolate—into one mouth-watering dessert. It's very rich and filling, so a small piece usually satisfies even a real sweet tooth.

1 cup all-purpose flour
1/3 cup sugar
1/2 cup butter

FILLING:

2 eggs
1/2 cup corn syrup
1/2 cup sugar
1/4 cup crunchy peanut butter
1/4 teaspoon salt
1/2 cup flaked coconut
1/2 cup semisweet chocolate chips

1. In a bowl, combine flour and sugar; cut in the butter until crumbly. Press into a greased 13-in. x 9-in. x 2-in. baking pan. Bake at 350° for 14-16 minutes or until lightly browned.

2. In a mixing bowl, mix eggs, corn syrup, sugar, peanut butter and salt until smooth. Fold in coconut and chocolate chips. Pour over crust. Return to the oven for 15-20 minutes or until golden. **Yield:** 3 dozen.

Macadamia Chip Brownies

Lucile Cline, Wichita, Kansas

With two kinds of chocolate, plus the macadamia nuts, there's no need to frost these scrumptious bars! I like to make them for special occasions. I'm a retired home economist and love to bake for fun and relaxation.

1/3 cup butter
4 squares (1 ounce *each*) white baking chocolate
2 eggs
1 cup sugar
1 teaspoon vanilla extract
1 cup all-purpose flour
1/4 teaspoon salt
1/2 cup chopped macadamia nuts
1/2 cup milk chocolate chips

1. In a saucepan over low heat, melt butter and white chocolate; remove from the heat. In a bowl, combine the eggs, sugar and vanilla. Add the chocolate mixture, flour and salt; mix well. Stir in nuts and chocolate chips.

2. Pour into a greased 9-in. square baking pan. Bake at 325° for 30-35 minutes or until top is lightly browned. Cool on a wire rack. Cut into bars. **Yield:** 1-1/2 dozen.

Chocolate Malted Cookies

(Pictured on page 161)

Teri Rasey-Bolf, Cadillac, Michigan

These cookies are the next best thing to a good old-fashioned malted milk. With malted milk powder, chocolate syrup plus chocolate chips and chunks, these are the best cookies I've ever tasted...and with six kids, I've made a lot of cookies over the years.

1 cup butter-flavored shortening
1-1/4 cups packed brown sugar

1/2 cup malted milk powder
2 tablespoons chocolate syrup
1 tablespoon vanilla extract
1 egg
2 cups all-purpose flour
1 teaspoon baking soda
1/2 teaspoon salt
1-1/2 cups semisweet chocolate chunks
1 cup (6 ounces) milk chocolate chips

1. In a mixing bowl, combine the first five ingredients; beat for 2 minutes. Add egg. Combine the flour, baking soda and salt; gradually add to creamed mixture, mixing well after each addition. Stir in chocolate chunks and chips.

2. Shape into 2-in. balls; place 3 in. apart on ungreased baking sheets. Bake at 375° for 12-14 minutes or until golden brown. Cool for 2 minutes before removing to a wire rack. **Yield:** about 1-1/2 dozen.

Glazed Chocolate Chip Brownies

Dawn Berg, Budd Lake, New Jersey

Shortly after we married, my husband asked if I would bake up a pan of brownies for him to take to work. I said, "Sure—I have the best recipe." He liked to cook, too, and said he had the best recipe. To settle the matter, we each baked a batch and let his co-workers decide. My recipe won!

2/3 cup butter, melted
2 eggs, lightly beaten
1 teaspoon vanilla extract
2 cups sugar
1-1/3 cups all-purpose flour
3/4 cup baking cocoa
1/2 teaspoon baking soda
1/4 teaspoon salt
1/2 cup water
1 cup (6 ounces) semisweet chocolate chips

GLAZE:

3/4 cup semisweet chocolate chips
1/4 cup milk
2 tablespoons butter
1-1/4 cups confectioners' sugar
1 teaspoon vanilla extract

1. In a bowl, combine the butter, eggs and vanilla. Combine the dry ingredients; add to the butter mixture and mix well. Stir in water and chocolate chips until combined. Pour into a greased 13-in. x 9-in. x 2-in. baking pan. Bake at 350° for 30-35 minutes or until brownies pull away from the sides of the pan. Cool on a wire rack.

2. In a saucepan, combine the chips, milk and butter until chips and butter are melted. Remove from the heat; whisk in the confectioners' sugar and vanilla until smooth.

3. Cover and refrigerate until frosting is room temperature, about 20 minutes; frost brownies. Cut into bars. **Yield:** 4 dozen.

Caramel Cashew Brownies

Judy High, Berryville, Arkansas

I always have my eye out for a good recipe, like the one for these marvelous golden brownies. It's hard to eat just one!

- **18 caramels**
- **1/3 cup butter**
- **2 tablespoons milk**
- **3/4 cup sugar**
- **2 eggs**
- **1/2 teaspoon vanilla extract**
- **1 cup all-purpose flour**
- **1/2 teaspoon baking powder**
- **1/4 teaspoon salt**
- **1 cup chopped salted cashews**

1. In a saucepan, cook and stir caramels, butter and milk over low heat until the caramels are melted and mixture is smooth.

2. Remove from the heat; stir in sugar. Combine eggs and vanilla; stir into caramel mixture. Combine flour, baking powder and salt; stir into caramel mixture until blended. Fold in cashews.

3. Transfer to a greased 9-in. square baking pan. Bake at 350° for 24-28 minutes or until a toothpick inserted near the center comes out clean. Cool on a wire rack. Cut into bars. **Yield:** 25 brownies.

Valentine Butter Cookies

Eleanor Slimak, Chicago, Illinois

These cookies are my grandchildren's favorite. I've even shaped the dough in the form of their initials for special occasions. They make a great dessert anytime.

2 cups butter, softened
2 cups sugar
3 eggs
1 tablespoon vanilla extract
6 cups all-purpose flour
2 teaspoons baking powder
Red decorators' sugar, optional

1. In a mixing bowl, cream butter and sugar. Add eggs and vanilla; mix well. Combine flour and baking powder; gradually add to creamed mixture and mix well.

2. Shape with a cookie press. Place on ungreased cookie sheets. Decorate with sugar if desired. Bake at 350° for 10-12 minutes or until edges are light brown. **Yield:** 18-19 dozen (1-inch cookies).

Chewy Pecan Pie Bars

Judy Taylor, Shreveport, Louisiana

This is one of my husband's favorite recipes, and I've been making it for many years. If you like pecan pie, you'll love the flavor of these bars.

1/4 cup butter, melted
2 cups packed brown sugar
2/3 cup all-purpose flour
4 eggs
2 teaspoons vanilla extract
1/4 teaspoon baking soda
1/4 teaspoon salt
2 cups chopped pecans
Confectioners' sugar

1. Pour butter into a 13-in. x 9-in. x 2-in. baking pan; set aside. In a mixing bowl, combine brown sugar, flour, eggs, vanilla, baking soda and salt; mix well. Stir in pecans. Spread over butter.

2. Bake at 350° for 30-35 minutes. Remove from the oven; immediately dust with confectioners' sugar. Cool before cutting. **Yield:** about 2 dozen.

Banana Squares

Susan Miller, Raleigh, North Carolina

When we were first married, my husband was in the Navy. Stationed in Puerto Rico, we had banana trees growing in our yard, so I found ways to use dozens of ripe bananas at a time. I made these squares often. They freeze well and make a great snack to have on hand.

2 eggs, *separated*
2/3 cup shortening
1-1/2 cups sugar
1 cup mashed ripe bananas (2 to 3 medium)
1-1/2 cups all-purpose flour
1 teaspoon baking soda
1/4 cup sour milk
1/2 teaspoon vanilla extract
1/2 cup chopped walnuts, optional
Whipped cream and sliced bananas, optional

1. In a small mixing bowl, beat egg whites until soft peaks form; set aside. In a large mixing bowl, cream shortening and sugar. Beat in egg yolks; mix well. Add bananas. Combine flour and baking soda; add to creamed mixture alternately with milk, beating well after each addition. Add vanilla. Fold in egg whites. Fold in nuts if desired.

2. Pour into a greased 13-in. x 9-in. x 2-in. baking pan. Bake at 350° for 45-50 minutes or until a toothpick inserted near the center comes out clean. Cool on a wire rack.

3. If desired, garnish with a dollop of whipped cream and a few banana slices. **Yield:** 12-16 servings.

Editor's Note: To sour milk, place 1 teaspoon white vinegar in a measuring cup. Add enough milk to equal 1/4 cup.

Mint Brownie Cupcakes

(Pictured on page 160)

Carol Maertz, Spruce Grove, Alberta

"Are they a brownie or are they a cupcake?" There's no wrong answer to this question, I tell my first-grade students. I found the recipe when I began teaching over 20 years ago.

1 cup mint chocolate chips
1/2 cup butter
1/2 cup sugar
2 eggs
1/2 cup all-purpose flour
1 teaspoon baking powder

TOPPING:

4 cups miniature marshmallows
3/4 cup milk
1-1/2 teaspoons peppermint extract
Green *or* red food coloring, optional
1-1/2 cups heavy whipping cream, whipped
Additional chocolate chips, optional

1. In a heavy saucepan, melt chips and butter; stir until smooth. Remove from the heat. Stir in sugar and eggs. Combine flour and baking powder; gradually stir into chocolate mixture until smooth. Fill paper-lined muffin cups half full. Bake at 350° for 15-20 minutes or until a toothpick comes out clean (cupcakes will fall in center). Remove to a wire rack.

2. In a saucepan, cook and stir marshmallows and milk over low heat until smooth. Remove from the heat; stir in extract and food coloring if desired. Cover and refrigerate until cool, about 15 minutes.

3. Fold in whipped cream. Spread over cupcakes or top each with a dollop of topping. Chill for at least 1 hour. Sprinkle with chocolate chips if desired. Store in the refrigerator. **Yield:** 16 cupcakes.

Editor's Note: If mint chocolate chips are not available, substitute semisweet chocolate chips and add 1/4 teaspoon peppermint extract.

Peanut Butter Sandwich Cookies

(Pictured on page 160)

Debbie Kokes, Tabor, South Dakota

I'm a busy mother of two young children. I work in our school office and help my husband on our hog and cattle farm. When I find time to bake a treat, I like it to be special. The creamy filling gives traditional peanut butter cookies a new twist in this scrumptious recipe.

- **1 cup butter-flavored shortening**
- **1 cup creamy peanut butter**

- **1 cup sugar**
- **1 cup packed brown sugar**
- **1 teaspoon vanilla extract**
- **3 eggs**
- **3 cups all-purpose flour**
- **2 teaspoons baking soda**
- **1/4 teaspoon salt**

FILLING:

- **1/2 cup creamy peanut butter**
- **3 cups confectioners' sugar**
- **1 teaspoon vanilla extract**
- **5 to 6 tablespoons milk**

1. In a mixing bowl, cream the shortening, peanut butter and sugars. Add vanilla. Add eggs, one at a time, beating well after each addition. Combine flour, baking soda and salt; add to creamed mixture.

2. Shape into 1-in. balls and place 2 in. apart on ungreased baking sheets. Flatten to 3/8-in. thickness with a fork. Bake at 375° for 7-8 minutes or until golden. Cool on wire racks.

3. In a mixing bowl, beat filling ingredients until smooth. Spread on half of the cookies and top each with another cookie. **Yield:** about 4 dozen.

Coconut Pecan Blondies

Anna Tokash Henry, Keller, Texas

Here's a classic white chocolate brownie that I've entered in the state fair and frequently make for the men I work with—I'm a landscaper.

- **1 egg**
- **3/4 cup plus 2 tablespoons packed brown sugar**
- **1/2 cup butter, melted and cooled**
- **1-1/2 teaspoons vanilla extract**
- **3/4 cup plus 2 tablespoons all-purpose flour**
- **1/2 teaspoon baking soda**
- **1/8 teaspoon salt**
- **3/4 cup coarsely chopped pecans, toasted**
- **2/3 cup flaked coconut**
- **4 squares (1 ounce *each*) white baking chocolate, coarsely chopped**

1. In a mixing bowl, beat egg and brown sugar for 3 minutes. Add butter and vanilla; mix well. Combine flour, baking soda and salt; gradually add to the brown sugar mixture, beating just until blended. Stir in pecans, coconut and white chocolate.

2. Spread into a greased 8-in. square baking pan. Bake at 325° for 30-40 minutes or until a toothpick inserted near the center comes out with moist crumbs (do not overbake). Cool on a wire rack. Cut into bars. **Yield:** 16 brownies.

Treasured Brownies

Marianne Wolfe, Westlock, Alberta

This terrific treat is included in a book of good-but-easy recipes my sister compiled as a wedding present for me. She refers to them as "money-back guarantee" brownies. And I can confirm that they turn out delicious every single time.

1 cup butter, melted and cooled
3 eggs
1-1/2 teaspoons vanilla extract
1 cup all-purpose flour
1 cup sugar
1 cup packed brown sugar
3/4 cup baking cocoa
1-1/2 teaspoons baking powder
1 cup chopped nuts
ICING:
1/2 cup butter, softened
1-1/4 cups confectioners' sugar
2/3 cup baking cocoa
2 tablespoons milk
2 tablespoons hot brewed coffee
1 teaspoon vanilla extract

1. In a mixing bowl, combine butter, eggs and vanilla. Combine the dry ingredients; gradually add to butter mixture. Stir in nuts (do not overmix).

2. Spread into a greased 13-in. x 9-in. x 2-in. baking pan. Bake at 350° for 25-30 minutes or until a toothpick inserted near the center comes out clean. Cool on a wire rack.

3. Combine icing ingredients in a mixing bowl; beat until smooth. Spread over cooled brownies. Cut into bars. **Yield:** 1-1/2 dozen.

Peanut Butter Chocolate Cookies

June Formanek, Belle Plaine, Iowa

This recipe was featured in our Sunday paper and I just had to try it. Kids of all ages really love the peanut butter surprise inside the cookie.

1/2 cup butter, softened
1/2 cup sugar
1/2 cup packed brown sugar
1 cup creamy peanut butter, *divided*
1 egg, lightly beaten
1 teaspoon vanilla extract
1-1/2 cups all-purpose flour
1/2 cup baking cocoa
1/2 teaspoon baking soda
3/4 cup confectioners' sugar

1. In a large mixing bowl, cream butter, sugars and 1/4 cup peanut butter. Add egg and vanilla; mix well. Combine flour, cocoa and baking soda; add to creamed mixture and mix well.

2. Blend confectioners' sugar with remaining peanut butter until smooth. Roll into 24 balls, 1 in. each. Divide dough into 24 pieces; flatten each into a 3-in. circle. Place one peanut butter ball on each circle; bring edges over to completely cover it. (Dough may crack; reshape cookies as needed.)

3. Place cookies with seam side down on ungreased baking sheets. Flatten each cookie slightly with the bottom of a glass dipped in sugar. Bake at 375° for 7-9 minutes or until set. **Yield:** 2 dozen.

Sour Cream Raisin Squares

Leona Eash, McConnelsville, Ohio

My aunt shared this recipe with me, and my family has always enjoyed it. I love to make these bars for friends who visit or give them away as gifts.

1 cup butter, softened
1 cup packed brown sugar
2 cups all-purpose flour
2 cups quick-cooking oats
1 teaspoon baking powder
1 teaspoon baking soda
1/8 teaspoon salt

FILLING:

4 egg yolks
2 cups (16 ounces) sour cream
1-1/2 cups raisins
1 cup sugar
1 tablespoon cornstarch

1. In a mixing bowl, cream the butter and brown sugar. Beat in flour, oats, baking powder, baking soda and salt (mixture will be crumbly).

2. Set aside 2 cups; pat remaining crumbs into a greased 13-in. x 9-in. x 2-in. baking pan. Bake at 350° for 15 minutes. Cool.

3. Meanwhile, combine the filling ingredients in a saucepan. Bring to a boil; cook and stir constantly for 5-8 minutes. Pour over crust; sprinkle with reserved crumbs. Return to the oven for 15 minutes. **Yield:** 12-16 servings.

Triple Chocolate Kisses

Evelyn Lindburg, Shenandoah, Iowa

These crisp meringue cookies with a chocolate center are easy to make but look like you spent a lot of time on them. When our son and daughter-in-law moved into their first home on Valentine's Day, I prepared them a nice dinner and gave them a batch of these cute treats.

2 egg whites
1/4 teaspoon cream of tartar
1/2 cup sugar
1/4 teaspoon almond extract
1 square (1 ounce) semisweet chocolate, grated
42 milk chocolate kisses
Baking cocoa

1. In a mixing bowl, beat egg whites until foamy. Add cream of tartar; beat until soft peaks form, about 6 minutes. Gradually add sugar, one tablespoon at a time, beating until stiff peaks form, about 6 minutes. Beat in extract. Fold in grated chocolate.

2. Insert a medium open-star tip in a pastry or plastic bag. Fill with the meringue. On lightly greased baking sheets, pipe forty-two 1-in. circles. Press a chocolate kiss into the center of each. Pipe meringue around each kiss in continuous circles from the base to the top until kiss is completely covered. Dust with cocoa.

3. Bake at 325° for 15-18 minutes or until the edges are lightly browned. Immediately remove to wire racks to cool. **Yield:** 3-1/2 dozen.

Jewel Nut Bars

Joyce Fitt, Listowel, Ontario

These colorful bars, with the eye-catching appeal of candied cherries and the crunchy goodness of mixed nuts, are certain to become a holiday favorite year after year. I get lots of compliments on the rich, chewy crust and the combination of sweet and salty flavors.

1-1/4 cups all-purpose flour
2/3 cup packed brown sugar, *divided*
3/4 cup cold butter
1 egg
1/2 teaspoon salt
1-1/2 cups salted mixed nuts
1-1/2 cups halved green and red candied cherries
1 cup (6 ounces) semisweet chocolate chips

1. In a bowl, combine flour and 1/3 cup brown sugar; cut in butter until mixture resembles coarse crumbs. Press into a lightly greased 13-in. x 9-in. x 2-in. baking pan. Bake at 350° for 15 minutes.

2. Meanwhile, in a mixing bowl, beat egg. Add salt and remaining brown sugar. Stir in the nuts, cherries and chocolate chips. Spoon evenly over crust. Bake at 350° for 20 minutes. Cool on a wire rack. Cut into bars. **Yield:** 3 dozen.

Fudgy Nut Brownies

Ruth Sparer Stern, Shadow Hills, California

I've prepared this special recipe for many an open house and potluck dinner. It came from an old roommate, who is now a grandmother. While in our early 20s, we never imagined we'd be sharing brownie recipes after all these years.

2-1/2 cups semisweet chocolate chips
1 cup butter
1 cup sugar
1/4 teaspoon salt
4 eggs, lightly beaten
2 teaspoons vanilla extract
3/4 cup all-purpose flour
1 cup coarsely chopped hazelnuts *or* almonds, toasted

TOPPING:

12 squares (1 ounce *each*) semisweet chocolate
1 tablespoon shortening
3 squares (1 ounce *each*) white baking chocolate

1. In a saucepan over low heat, melt chocolate chips and butter; remove from the heat. Add sugar and salt; stir until dissolved. Cool for 10 minutes. Stir in eggs, vanilla, flour and nuts. Spread into a greased 15-in. x 10-in. x 1-in. baking pan. Bake at 350° for 25-30 minutes or until a toothpick inserted near the center comes out with moist crumbs (do not overbake). Cool completely on a wire rack.

2. For topping, in a heavy saucepan or microwave, heat semisweet chocolate and shortening just until melted. Spread over brownies.

3. Melt white chocolate. Pour into a small heavy-duty resealable plastic bag; cut a small hole in corner of bag. Pipe thin lines 1 in. apart widthwise. Beginning about 1 in. from a wide side, gently pull a toothpick through the lines to the opposite side. Wipe toothpick clean. Then pull toothpick through lines in opposite direction. Repeat over entire top at 1-in. intervals. Cut into bars. **Yield:** about 2-1/2 dozen.

Pumpkin Bars

Brenda Keller, Andalusia, Alabama

What could be more appropriate for a Halloween treat than a pan of pumpkin-flavored bars? Actually, they're a hit with my family any time of the year.

4 eggs
1-2/3 cups sugar
1 cup vegetable oil
1 can (16 ounces) pumpkin
2 cups all-purpose flour
2 teaspoons ground cinnamon
2 teaspoons baking powder
1 teaspoon baking soda
1 teaspoon salt

ICING:

1 package (3 ounces) cream cheese, softened
2 cups confectioners' sugar
1/4 cup butter, softened
1 teaspoon vanilla extract
1 to 2 tablespoons milk

1. In a mixing bowl, beat eggs, sugar, oil and pumpkin. Combine flour, cinnamon, baking powder, baking soda and salt; gradually add to pumpkin mixture.

2. Pour into an ungreased 15-in. x 10-in. x 1-in. baking pan. Bake at 350° for 25-30 minutes. Cool completely.

3. For icing, beat cream cheese, confectioners' sugar, butter and vanilla in a small mixing bowl. Add enough milk to achieve desired spreading consistency. Spread over bars. **Yield:** 2 dozen.

Shortbread Lemon Bars

Margaret Peterson, Forest City, Iowa

I've put together two family cookbooks over the years, and this recipe ranks among my favorites. These special lemon bars have a yummy shortbread crust and a refreshing flavor. I'm never afraid to make this dessert for guests since I know it will be a hit with everyone.

1-1/2 cups all-purpose flour
1/2 cup confectioners' sugar
1 teaspoon grated lemon peel
1 teaspoon grated orange peel
3/4 cup cold butter

FILLING:

4 eggs
2 cups sugar
1/3 cup lemon juice
1/4 cup all-purpose flour
2 teaspoons grated lemon peel
2 teaspoons grated orange peel
1 teaspoon baking powder

TOPPING:

2 cups (16 ounces) sour cream
1/3 cup sugar
1/2 teaspoon vanilla extract

1. In a food processor, combine flour, confectioners' sugar, and lemon and orange peel. Cut in butter until crumbly; process until mixture forms a ball. Pat into a greased 13-in. x 9-in. x 2-in. baking pan. Bake at 350° for 12-14 minutes or until set and the edges are lightly browned.

2. Meanwhile, in a mixing bowl, combine the filling ingredients; mix well. Pour over hot crust. Bake for 14-16 minutes or until set and lightly browned.

3. Meanwhile, in a bowl, combine topping ingredients. Spread over filling. Bake 7-9 minutes longer or until topping is set. Cool on a wire rack. Refrigerate overnight. Cut into bars just before serving. **Yield:** 3 dozen.

Almond Coconut Brownies

Wendy Wilkins, Prattville, Alabama

I combined a couple of my favorite brownie recipes and came up with this. My family has always enjoyed brownies, and this has become a special treat.

1-1/2 cups butter
4 squares (1 ounce *each*) unsweetened chocolate
2-1/4 cups sugar
3 eggs, beaten
1 cup all-purpose flour
3/4 cup chopped slivered almonds
1 teaspoon vanilla extract

FILLING:
1 cup sugar
1 cup milk
24 large marshmallows
1 package (14 ounces) flaked coconut

TOPPING:
1 cup (6 ounces) semisweet chocolate chips
3/4 cup sugar
1/4 cup butter
1/4 cup milk
1/4 cup chopped slivered almonds, toasted

1. In a saucepan over low heat, melt butter and chocolate; cool slightly. Add sugar. Stir in the eggs, flour, almonds and vanilla. Transfer to a greased 13-in. x 9-in. x 2-in. baking pan. Bake at 350° for 30 minutes or until a toothpick inserted in the center comes out clean. Cool on a wire rack.

2. In a large saucepan, combine filling ingredients; bring to a boil. Pour over cooled brownies.

3. In another saucepan, combine chocolate chips, sugar, butter and milk; bring to a boil. Spoon over the filling. Sprinkle with almonds. Chill for 2 hours or until set. Store in the refrigerator. **Yield:** 4 dozen.

Holiday Brownies

Erna Madsen, Bothell, Washington

Folks always ask me for this recipe whenever I make these brownies. I make batches and batches of this tasty treat before the holidays and give them as gifts.

1/2 cup butter
4 squares (1 ounce *each*) unsweetened chocolate
2 cups sugar
1-1/4 cups all-purpose flour
2 teaspoons ground cinnamon
1/2 teaspoon salt
4 eggs, beaten
1 teaspoon vanilla extract
1-1/2 cups halved red *and/or* green candied cherries, *divided*
1 cup chopped walnuts

1. In a heavy saucepan, melt butter and chocolate over low heat. Cool for 10 minutes. In a bowl, combine the sugar, flour, cinnamon and salt. Stir in the cooled chocolate mixture, eggs and vanilla until smooth. Fold in 1-1/4 cups cherries and the walnuts.

2. Transfer to a greased 13-in. x 9-in. x 2-in. baking pan. Arrange remaining cherries over top. Bake at 350° for 35 minutes or until a toothpick inserted near the center comes out clean. Cool on a wire rack. Cut into bars. **Yield:** 2 dozen.

Chocolate Mint Cookies

Christina Burbage, Spartanburg, South Carolina

My dad sandwiches mint patties between two tender chocolate cookies to create these chewy treats. The blend of chocolate and mint is a big hit at our house. Best of all, these cookies are easy and fun to make.

1-1/4 cups butter, softened
2 cups sugar
2 eggs
2 teaspoons vanilla extract
2 cups all-purpose flour
3/4 cup baking cocoa
1 teaspoon baking soda
1/2 teaspoon salt
32 round thin chocolate-covered mint patties

1. In a mixing bowl, cream butter and sugar. Add eggs, one at a time, beating well after each addition. Beat in vanilla. Combine the flour, cocoa, baking soda and salt; gradually add to the creamed mixture, beating until well combined.

2. Drop by tablespoonfuls 2 in. apart onto ungreased baking sheets. Bake at 350° for 8-9 minutes or until puffy and tops are cracked.

3. Invert half of the cookies onto wire racks. Immediately place a mint patty on each, then top with remaining cookies. Press lightly to seal. Cool completely. **Yield:** 32 sandwich cookies.

Frosted Fudge Brownies

Sue Soderlund, Elgin, Illinois

A neighbor brought over a pan of these rich brownies along with the recipe when I came home from the hospital with our baby daughter over 15 years ago. I've made them ever since for family occasions, potlucks and parties at work.

1 cup plus 3 tablespoons butter
3/4 cup baking cocoa
4 eggs
2 cups sugar
1-1/2 cups all-purpose flour
1 teaspoon baking powder
1 teaspoon salt
1 teaspoon vanilla extract

FROSTING:

6 tablespoons butter, softened
2-2/3 cups confectioners' sugar
1/2 cup baking cocoa
1 teaspoon vanilla extract
1/4 to 1/3 cup milk

1. In a saucepan, melt butter. Remove from the heat. Stir in cocoa; cool. In a mixing bowl, beat eggs and sugar. Combine flour, baking powder and salt; gradually add to egg mixture. Stir in vanilla and the cooled chocolate mixture; mix well.

2. Spread into a greased 13-in. x 9-in. x 2-in. baking pan. Bake at 350° for 25-28 minutes or until a toothpick inserted near the center comes out clean (do not overbake). Cool on a wire rack.

3. For frosting, in a mixing bowl, cream butter, confectioners' sugar, cocoa and vanilla. Add enough milk until the frosting achieves spreading consistency. Spread over brownies. Cut into bars. **Yield:** 2 dozen.

Lemon Snowballs

Audrey Thibodeau, Fountain Hills, Arizona

These crunchy little cookies are great for a light dessert. The bright taste of lemon makes them a winner!

1/2 cup butter, softened
2/3 cup sugar
1 egg
1/4 cup lemon juice
1 tablespoon grated lemon peel
1-3/4 cups all-purpose flour
1/4 teaspoon baking soda
1/4 teaspoon cream of tartar
1/4 teaspoon salt
1/2 cup finely chopped almonds
Confectioners' sugar

1. In a mixing bowl, cream butter, sugar and egg until well blended. Add lemon juice and peel. Combine flour, baking soda, cream of tartar and salt; stir into creamed mixture. Add almonds. Cover and refrigerate the dough for at least 1 hour or overnight.

2. Roll into 1-in. balls. Place on ungreased baking sheets. Bake at 350° for 10-12 minutes or until bottoms are lightly browned (cookies will not brown on the top).

3. Remove immediately to wire racks; cool for 5 minutes, then roll in confectioners' sugar. **Yield:** about 3 dozen.

Apricot Bars

Jill Moritz, Irvine, California

This recipe is down-home baking at its best. It's won blue ribbons at county fairs and cookie contests in several states! This treat is easy to make, and it's perfect for potluck suppers, bake sales, lunch boxes or just plain snacking.

3/4 cup butter
1 cup sugar
1 egg
2 cups all-purpose flour
1/4 teaspoon baking powder
1-1/3 cups flaked coconut
1/2 cup chopped walnuts
1/2 teaspoon vanilla extract
1 jar (12 ounces) apricot preserves

1. In a mixing bowl, cream butter and sugar. Add egg and mix well. Combine flour and baking powder; gradually add to butter mixture. Add coconut, walnuts and extract; mix thoroughly.

2. Press two-thirds of dough into a greased 13-in. x 9-in. x 2-in. baking pan. Spread with preserves; crumble remaining dough over preserves.

3. Bake at 350° for 30-35 minutes or until golden brown. Cool in pan on wire rack. Cut into bars. **Yield:** 36 bars.

Apple Snack Squares

Julia Quintrell, Sumerco, West Virginia

As soon as I was old enough to stand on a chair, I started cooking. This recipe came from my sister-in-law and it's a favorite at our large family gatherings. Our five children are grown. My husband and I have six grandchildren.

2 cups sugar
2 eggs
3/4 cup vegetable oil
2-1/2 cups self-rising flour
1 teaspoon ground cinnamon
3 cups diced peeled tart apples
1 cup chopped walnuts
3/4 cup butterscotch chips

1. In a bowl, combine sugar, eggs and oil; mix well. Stir in flour and cinnamon (batter will be thick). Stir in apples and nuts. Spread into a greased 13-in. x 9-in. x 2-in. baking pan. Sprinkle with chips.

2. Bake at 350° for 35-40 minutes or until golden and a toothpick inserted near the center comes out clean. Cool before cutting. **Yield:** 2 dozen.

Editor's Note: As a substitute for *each* cup of self-rising flour, place 1-1/2 teaspoons of baking powder and 1/2 teaspoon of salt in a measuring cup. Add all-purpose flour to equal 1 cup.

Licorice Cookie Strips

Dolores Hurtt, Florence, Montana

If you like the flavor of licorice, you'll love these crispy cookies. When our six children were young, I often made them for lunches or after-school snacks. Flattening the dough logs with a fork gives them a pretty look. Once they're baked, it's a breeze to cut them into strips.

1 cup butter, softened
1 cup sugar
1 cup packed brown sugar
1 egg
2-1/2 cups all-purpose flour
2 teaspoons aniseed
1 teaspoon baking soda
1/2 teaspoon salt
1/2 teaspoon ground cinnamon
1/2 teaspoon ground nutmeg
1/2 cup chopped nuts

1. In a mixing bowl, cream butter and sugars. Beat in egg. Combine the next six ingredients; add to creamed mixture and mix well. Stir in nuts.

2. Divide dough into 10 portions; shape each into a 12-in. log. Place 3 in. apart on ungreased baking sheets. Flatten with a fork to 1/4-in. thickness. Bake at 350° for 8-10 minutes or until golden brown. Cool for 5 minutes; cut diagonally into 1-in. slices. Remove to wire racks to cool completely. **Yield:** about 8 dozen.

Chocolate Cherry Bars

Tina Dierking, Canaan, Maine

These tempting bars are simple to make with cherry pie filling, crunchy almonds and chocolate chips. I took them to a church supper and everyone wanted the recipe. Some people said the sweet treats reminded them of chocolate-covered cherries.

1-3/4 cups all-purpose flour
1 cup sugar
1/4 cup baking cocoa
1 cup cold butter
1 egg, lightly beaten
1 teaspoon almond extract
1 can (21 ounces) cherry pie filling
2 cups (12 ounces) semisweet chocolate chips
1 cup chopped almonds

1. In a bowl, combine the flour, sugar and cocoa. Cut in butter until crumbly. Add egg and almond extract until blended; set aside 1 cup for topping.

2. Press remaining crumb mixture into a greased 13-in. x 9-in. x 2-in. baking pan. Carefully top with pie filling. Combine chocolate chips, almonds and reserved crumb mixture; sprinkle over pie filling.

3. Bake at 350° for 35-40 minutes or until a toothpick inserted near the center comes out clean. Cool; refrigerate for at least 2 hours before cutting. **Yield:** 3 dozen.

Pear Custard Bars

Jeannette Nord, San Juan Capistrano, California

When I take this crowd-pleasing treat to a potluck, I come home with an empty pan every time. Cooking and baking come naturally for me—as a farm girl, I helped my mother feed my 10 siblings.

1/2 cup butter, softened
1/3 cup sugar
3/4 cup all-purpose flour
1/4 teaspoon vanilla extract
2/3 cup chopped macadamia nuts

FILLING/TOPPING:

1 package (8 ounces) cream cheese, softened
1/2 cup sugar
1 egg
1/2 teaspoon vanilla extract
1 can (15-1/4 ounces) pear halves, drained
1/2 teaspoon sugar
1/2 teaspoon ground cinnamon

1. In a mixing bowl, cream butter and sugar. Beat in the flour and vanilla until combined. Stir in the nuts. Press into a greased 8-in. square baking pan. Bake at 350° for 20 minutes or until lightly browned. Cool on a wire rack.

2. Increase heat to 375°. In a mixing bowl, beat cream cheese until smooth. Add sugar, egg and vanilla; mix until combined. Pour over crust. Cut pears into 1/8-in. slices; arrange in a single layer over filling. Combine sugar and cinnamon; sprinkle over pears.

3. Bake at 375° for 28-30 minutes (center will be soft set and will become firmer upon cooling). Cool on a wire rack for 45 minutes. Cover and refrigerate for at least 2 hours before cutting. Store in the refrigerator. **Yield:** 16 bars.

Scandinavian Pecan Cookies

Laurie Knoke, DeKalb, Illinois

We enjoyed these rich, buttery cookies at a bed-and-breakfast in Galena, Illinois, and the hostess was kind enough to share her simple recipe. The pretty nut-topped treats are so special you could give a home-baked batch as a gift.

1 cup butter, softened
3/4 cup packed brown sugar
1 egg, *separated*
2 cups all-purpose flour
1/2 cup finely chopped pecans

1. In a mixing bowl, cream butter, brown sugar and egg yolk. Gradually add flour. Shape into 1-in. balls.

2. In a small bowl, beat egg white. Dip balls in egg white, then roll in pecans. Place 2 in. apart on ungreased baking sheets; flatten slightly.

3. Bake at 375° for 8-12 minutes or until edges are lightly browned. Cool on wire racks. **Yield:** 4-5 dozen.

Out-of-This-World Brownies

Jeannette Haley, Council, Idaho

For company and every time there is a bake sale, I bake a batch of these fabulous brownies. Most everyone who tastes them says, "Yum! These are the best brownies I have ever eaten!"

1 cup butter, softened
2 cups sugar
4 eggs
2 teaspoons vanilla extract
2 cups all-purpose flour
1/4 cup plus 3 tablespoons baking cocoa
1/8 teaspoon salt

BROWN BUTTER FROSTING:
1/2 cup butter
4 cups confectioners' sugar
1/4 cup plus 2 teaspoons half-and-half cream
2 teaspoons vanilla extract

GLAZE:
1 square (1 ounce) unsweetened chocolate
1 tablespoon butter

1. In a mixing bowl, cream butter and sugar. Add the eggs, one at a time, beating well after each addition. Beat in vanilla. Combine flour, cocoa and salt; gradually add to the creamed mixture.

2. Spread into an ungreased 13-in. x 9-in. x 2-in. baking pan. Bake at 350° for 25-30 minutes or until a toothpick inserted near the center comes out clean (do not overbake). Cool on wire rack.

3. For frosting, in a heavy saucepan, cook and stir butter over medium heat for 5-7 minutes or until golden brown. Pour into a mixing bowl; beat in the confectioners' sugar, cream and vanilla. Frost cooled brownies.

4. For glaze, melt chocolate and butter; drizzle over the frosting. Cut into bars. **Yield:** 3 dozen.

Old-Fashioned Gingersnaps

Francis Stoops, Stoneboro, Pennsylvania

I discovered this recipe many years ago, and it's been a favorite among our family and friends since.

3/4 cup butter
1 cup sugar
1 egg
1/4 cup molasses
2 cups all-purpose flour
2 teaspoons baking soda
1/4 teaspoon salt
1 teaspoon ground cinnamon
1 teaspoon ground cloves
1 teaspoon ground ginger
Additional sugar

1. In a mixing bowl, cream butter and sugar. Add egg and molasses; beat well. Combine flour, baking soda, salt, cinnamon, cloves and ginger; gradually add to creamed mixture. Chill dough.

2. Roll into 1-1/4-in. balls and dip in sugar. Place 2 in. apart on ungreased baking sheets. Bake at 375° for 10 minutes or until set and surface cracks. Cool on wire racks. **Yield:** about 4 dozen.

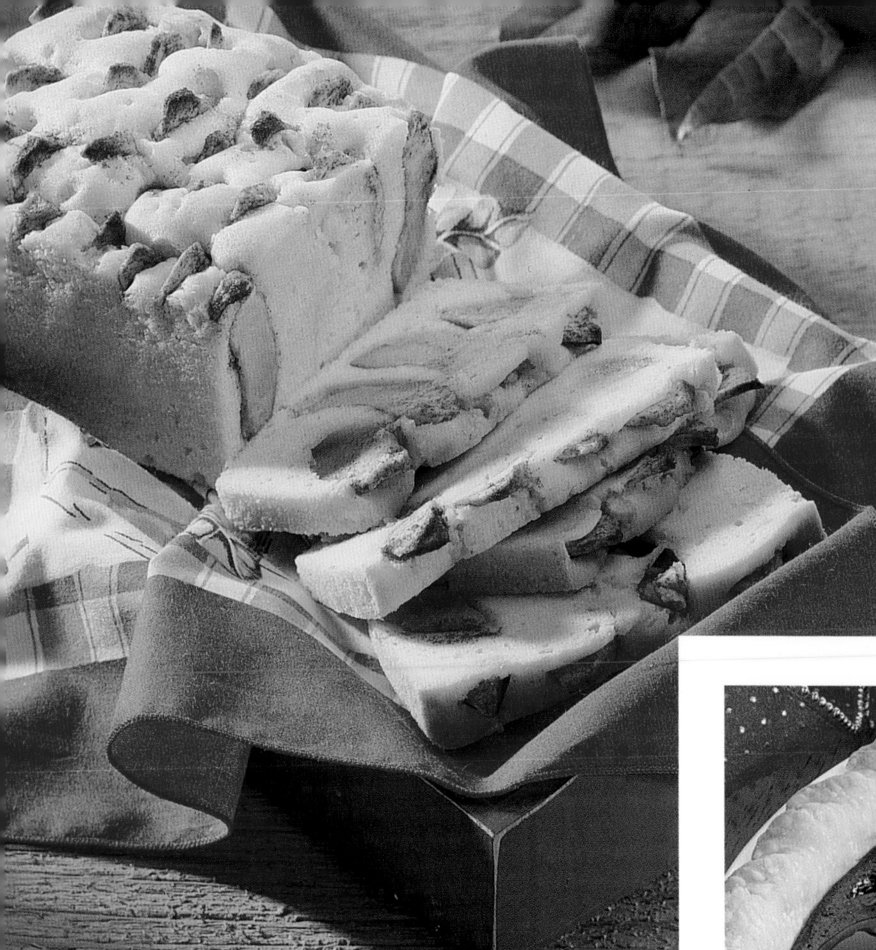

Dutch Apple Cake, p. 194

Black Forest Pie, p. 186

Chocolate Cookie Torte, p. 188

Cakes & Pies

Any way you slice it, this chapter's appealing assortment of cakes and pies is simply scrumptious! So end your meals on a sweet note with some of them soon!

Fancy Cream Cupcakes, p. 190

Very Raspberry Pie, p. 193

Black Forest Pie

(Pictured on page 184)

Trudy Black, Dedham, Massachusetts

With three active children, I don't usually fuss with fancy desserts. This one is simple but impressive—it's the one I make to show how much I care. The tempting combination of chocolate and tangy red cherries is guaranteed to make someone feel special.

3/4 cup sugar
1/3 cup baking cocoa
2 tablespoons all-purpose flour
1/3 cup milk
1/4 cup butter
2 eggs, lightly beaten
1 can (21 ounces) cherry pie filling, *divided*
1 unbaked pastry shell (9 inches)
Whipped topping, optional

1. In a saucepan, combine sugar, cocoa, flour and milk until smooth. Add butter. Bring to a boil; cook and stir for 2 minutes or until thickened. Remove from the heat.

2. Stir a small amount of hot mixture into eggs. Return all to the pan. Fold in half of the pie filling. Pour into pastry shell. Bake at 350° for 35-40 minutes or until filling is almost set. Cool completely on a wire rack.

3. Just before serving, top with remaining pie filling and whipped topping if desired. **Yield:** 6-8 servings.

Carrot Cake

Melanie Habener, Santa Maria, California

We have enjoyed this scrumptious cake for years. Whenever there's a gathering of family and friends, it seems my cake is always requested.

3 eggs, beaten
3/4 cup vegetable oil
3/4 cup buttermilk
2 cups sugar
2 teaspoons vanilla extract
2 cups all-purpose flour
2 teaspoons ground cinnamon
2 teaspoons baking soda
1/2 teaspoon salt
1 can (8 ounces) crushed pineapple, undrained
2 cups grated carrots
1 cup raisins
1 cup chopped nuts
1 cup flaked coconut
CREAM CHEESE FROSTING:
1/2 cup butter, softened
1 package (8 ounces) cream cheese, softened
1 teaspoon vanilla extract
4 cups confectioners' sugar
2 tablespoons heavy whipping cream

1. In a mixing bowl, combine eggs, oil, buttermilk, sugar and vanilla; mix well. Combine flour, cinnamon, baking soda and salt; stir into egg mixture. Stir in pineapple, carrots, raisins, nuts and coconut.

2. Pour into a greased and floured 13-in. x 9-in. x 2-in. baking pan. Bake at 350° for 50-55 minutes or until a toothpick inserted near the center comes out clean. Do not overbake. Remove to a wire rack to cool.

3. In another mixing bowl, combine all frosting ingredients; beat until creamy. Spread on cooled cake. Store in the refrigerator **Yield:** 12-16 servings.

Golden Squash Pie

Patricia Hardin, Seymour, Tennessee

Whether you take this yummy pie to a party or potluck, be prepared to share the recipe. An alternative to pumpkin pie, it bakes up high and flavorful.

4 eggs
4 cups mashed cooked butternut squash
1 cup buttermilk
1/4 cup butter, melted
2 teaspoons vanilla extract
2 cups sugar
2 tablespoons all-purpose flour
1 teaspoon salt
1/2 teaspoon baking soda
2 unbaked pastry shells (9 inches)
Ground nutmeg, optional

1. In a bowl, combine the eggs, squash, buttermilk, butter and vanilla. Combine the dry ingredients; add to the squash mixture and mix until smooth. Pour into pastry shells. Cover edges loosely with foil.

2. Bake at 350° for 35 minutes. Remove foil. Bake 25 minutes longer or until a knife inserted near the center comes out clean. Cool on a wire rack. Sprinkle with nutmeg if desired. Store in the refrigerator. **Yield:** 2 pies (6-8 servings each).

Lime Angel Food Cake

Nancy Foust, Stoneboro, Pennsylvania

It's fun to start with a purchased angel food cake and turn out a pretty and special dessert. A lovely lime-cream frosting is the key to this dressy, flavorful creation. It went over big at my husband's family reunion.

2 eggs
2 egg yolks
1/2 cup plus 3 tablespoons sugar, *divided*
6 tablespoons lime juice
2 teaspoons grated lime peel
1/2 cup cold butter, cubed
1 cup heavy whipping cream
1/2 teaspoon vanilla extract
1 prepared angel food cake (10 inches)
1 cup flaked coconut, toasted

1. In the top of a double boiler, beat eggs and yolks. Stir in 1/2 cup of sugar, lime juice and peel. Cook over simmering water while gradually whisking in butter. Cook and stir until mixture is thickened and reaches 160°. Strain; refrigerate until completely cool.

2. In a mixing bowl, beat cream and vanilla until stiff peaks form; gradually beat in remaining sugar. Gently fold into lime mixture.

3. Split cake horizontally into three layers. Place bottom layer on a serving plate. Spread with 2/3 cup lime mixture. Repeat. Place top layer on cake. Frost top and sides with remaining lime mixture. Sprinkle with coconut. Refrigerate for at least 30 minutes before slicing. **Yield:** 12 servings.

Caramel Pear Pie

Mary Kaehler, Lodi, California

A dear friend gave me the recipe for this attractive pie. The caramel drizzle and streusel topping make it almost too pretty to eat. Knowing this dessert is waiting is great motivation for our children to eat all their vegetables.

6 cups sliced peeled ripe pears (about 6 medium)
1 tablespoon lemon juice
1/2 cup plus 3 tablespoons sugar, *divided*
2 tablespoons quick-cooking tapioca
3/4 teaspoon ground cinnamon
1/4 teaspoon salt
1/4 teaspoon ground nutmeg
1 unbaked pastry shell (9 inches)
3/4 cup old-fashioned oats
1 tablespoon all-purpose flour
1/4 cup cold butter
18 caramels
5 tablespoons milk
1/4 cup chopped pecans

1. In a large bowl, combine pears and lemon juice. In another bowl, combine 1/2 cup sugar, tapioca, cinnamon, salt and nutmeg. Add to pears; stir gently. Let stand for 15 minutes. Pour into pastry shell.

2. In a bowl, combine the oats, flour and remaining sugar. Cut in butter until crumbly. Sprinkle over pears. Bake at 400° for 45 minutes.

3. Meanwhile, in a saucepan over low heat, melt caramels with milk. Stir until smooth; add pecans. Drizzle over pie. Bake 8-10 minutes longer or until crust is golden brown and filling is bubbly. Cool on a wire rack. **Yield:** 6-8 servings.

Chocolate Cookie Torte

(Pictured on page 184)

Irene Bigler, New Cumberland, Pennsylvania

This recipe has been used many times in our family for get-togethers. It's easy to make and beautiful when served.

1/2 cup butter, softened
1 cup sugar
1 egg
1 egg yolk
1/2 teaspoon vanilla extract
2 cups all-purpose flour
1 teaspoon baking powder
1/2 teaspoon salt
Additional sugar
FROSTING:
2 cups (12 ounces) semisweet chocolate chips
1/2 cup half-and-half cream
2 cups heavy whipping cream, whipped
2 teaspoons vanilla extract
Chocolate sprinkles

1. In a mixing bowl, cream butter and sugar. Beat in the egg, yolk and vanilla. Combine flour, baking powder and salt; gradually add to the creamed mixture and mix well.

2. Form into a long log; cut into eight equal pieces. Shape each into a ball; wrap in plastic wrap. Refrigerate for 1 hour.

3. Roll balls in additional sugar; place between two sheets of waxed paper. Roll each into a 6-in. circle. Remove top sheet of waxed paper; flip the circles onto ungreased baking sheets. Remove waxed paper; prick dough with a fork. Bake at 350° for 10-12 minutes or until lightly browned. Carefully loosen cookies and cool on paper towels.

4. For frosting, melt chocolate chips with half-and-half in a heavy saucepan, stirring occasionally. Cool. Combine whipped cream and vanilla; fold into chocolate mixture.

5. Layer cookies, spreading 1/4 cup frosting between each layer. Spread remaining frosting over sides and top. Decorate with chocolate sprinkles. Refrigerate overnight before cutting. **Yield:** 8-10 servings.

Blueberry Oat Cake

Linda Police, Dover, New Jersey

This is my favorite blueberry recipe. Everyone in my family likes it, so I make it rather frequently. It's moist, nutritious and very easy to make.

2 eggs
2 cups buttermilk
1 cup packed brown sugar
1/2 cup vegetable oil
2 cups all-purpose flour
2 teaspoons baking powder
1 teaspoon baking soda
1 teaspoon ground cinnamon
1/2 teaspoon salt
2 cups quick-cooking oats
2 cups fresh *or* frozen blueberries
1 cup chopped walnuts, optional
Confectioners' sugar

1. In a mixing bowl, beat the eggs, buttermilk, brown sugar and oil. Combine the flour, baking powder, baking soda, cinnamon and salt; add to batter. Beat on low speed for 2 minutes. Fold in oats, blueberries and walnuts if desired.

2. Transfer to a greased and floured 10-in. fluted tube pan. Bake at 375° for 45-50 minutes or until a toothpick comes out clean. Cool for 10 minutes before removing from pan to a wire rack to cool completely. Dust with confectioners' sugar. **Yield:** 12-16 servings.

Editor's Note: If using frozen blueberries, do not thaw them before adding to batter.

County Fair Pie

Judy Acuff, Lathrop, Missouri

This quick and easy recipe is one of my family's favorites. I've taken it to lots of potlucks and have been asked for the recipe many times.

1/2 cup butter, melted
1 cup sugar
1/2 cup all-purpose flour
2 eggs
1 teaspoon vanilla extract
1 cup coarsely chopped walnuts
1 cup (6 ounces) semisweet chocolate chips
1/2 cup butterscotch chips
1 unbaked pastry shell (9 inches)

1. In a mixing bowl, beat the butter, sugar, flour, eggs and vanilla until well blended. Stir in nuts and chips.

2. Pour into pie shell. Bake at 325° for 1 hour or until golden brown. Cool on a wire rack. **Yield:** 6-8 servings.

Fancy Cream Cupcakes

(Pictured on page 185)

Merrilee Chambers, Haines Junction, Yukon Territory

These cute, tender cupcakes are creamy and not too sweet. They look fancy but are quick to fix...and even a big platter of these timeless treats disappears in no time. I've been making desserts since I was a youngster, the oldest of seven sisters.

1/2 cup shortening
1-1/2 cups sugar
4 egg whites
1 teaspoon vanilla extract
2 cups all-purpose flour
3-1/2 teaspoons baking powder
1 teaspoon salt
1 cup milk
1 cup heavy whipping cream
2 tablespoons confectioners' sugar
4 to 5 drops red food coloring, optional
1/4 teaspoon almond extract

1. In a mixing bowl, cream shortening and sugar. Add egg whites, one at a time, beating well after each addition. Beat in vanilla. Combine dry ingredients; add to creamed mixture alternately with milk.

2. Fill paper- or foil-lined muffin cups two-thirds full. Bake at 350° for 15-20 minutes or until a toothpick comes out clean. Cool for 10 minutes; remove to wire racks to cool completely.

3. For filling, in a mixing bowl, beat cream until soft peaks form. Gradually beat in confectioners' sugar and food coloring if desired until stiff peaks form. Beat in almond extract.

4. Cut a 1-in. cone shape from the center of each cupcake; set cone aside. Fill indentation with filling. Cut each cone in half from top to bottom; place two halves on filling for butterfly wings. If desired, pipe a thin strip of filling between wings for butterfly body. **Yield:** 22 cupcakes.

Farm Apple Pan Pie

Dolores Skrout, Summerhill, Pennsylvania

You'll find this pie's very convenient for taking to a covered-dish supper, picnic, etc. But be prepared—people always ask for a copy of the recipe!

EGG YOLK PASTRY:
5 cups all-purpose flour
4 teaspoons sugar
1/2 teaspoon salt
1/2 teaspoon baking powder
1-1/2 cups shortening
2 egg yolks, lightly beaten
3/4 cup cold water

FILLING:
5 pounds tart apples, peeled and thinly sliced
4 teaspoons lemon juice
3/4 cup sugar
3/4 cup packed brown sugar
1 teaspoon ground cinnamon
1/2 teaspoon ground nutmeg
1/4 teaspoon salt
Milk
Additional sugar

1. In a bowl, combine flour, sugar, salt and baking powder; cut in shortening until the mixture resembles coarse crumbs. Combine yolks and cold water. Sprinkle over dry ingredients; toss with fork. If needed, add additional water, 1 tablespoon at a time, until the mixture can be formed into a ball.

2. Divide dough in half. On a lightly floured surface, roll half of dough to fit a 15-in. x 10-in. x 1-in. baking pan.

3. Sprinkle apples with lemon juice; arrange half of them over dough. Combine the sugars, cinnamon, nutmeg and salt; sprinkle half over apples. Top with remaining apples; sprinkle with remaining sugar mixture.

4. Roll remaining pastry to fit pan; place on top of filling and seal edges. Brush with milk and sprinkle with sugar. Cut vents in top pastry. Bake at 400° for 50 minutes or until crust is golden brown and filling is bubbly. **Yield:** 18-24 servings.

Old-Fashioned Chess Pie

Christine Batts, Murray, Kentucky

This recipe dates back many years and has certainly stood the test of time. It's very rich, so small servings might be in order.

1 cup butter, softened
2 cups sugar
6 egg yolks
1 egg
1/3 cup cornmeal
1/4 cup all-purpose flour
1/3 cup milk
1 teaspoon vanilla extract
1 unbaked deep-dish pastry shell (9 inches)
TOPPING:
2 cups sugar, *divided*
2/3 cup milk
1/2 cup butter

1. In a mixing bowl, cream butter and sugar. Beat in egg yolks and egg. Add the cornmeal and flour; mix well. Beat in milk and vanilla (do not overbeat). Pour into the pastry shell. Bake at 325° for 55-65 minutes or until the filling is almost set. Cool on a wire rack.

2. In a heavy saucepan, heat 1/2 cup sugar over low heat without stirring until partially melted, about 5 minutes. Cook and stir with a metal spoon until syrup is completely melted and golden, about 5 minutes. Stir in milk, butter and remaining sugar (mixture will be lumpy). Cook over medium heat, stirring until a candy thermometer reads 234° (soft-ball stage).

3. Remove from the heat. Pour into a mixing bowl without stirring. Cool, without stirring, to 190°. Beat on high speed until mixture turns light brown and creamy and a candy thermometer reads 130°-137°, about 5 minutes. Immediately spread over pie. Store in the refrigerator. **Yield:** 8-10 servings.

Strawberry Cream Cake Roll

Laura Hagedorn, Fort Branch, Indiana

There are plenty of strawberry patches near my hometown, so I like to put those pretty red berries to delicious use. I discovered this recipe a few summers ago and have made it often. Believe me, it tastes as good as it looks!

4 eggs
1 teaspoon vanilla extract
3/4 cup sugar
3/4 cup cake flour
1 teaspoon baking powder
1/4 teaspoon salt
Confectioners' sugar
CREAM FILLING:
1 cup heavy whipping cream
1/4 cup sugar
1/2 teaspoon vanilla extract
2 cups fresh *or* frozen strawberries, cut up
Confectioners' sugar
Additional whole strawberries
Whipped cream, optional

1. In a mixing bowl, beat eggs and vanilla on high speed for 5 minutes or until lemon-colored. Gradually add sugar, beating until dissolved. Combine flour, baking powder and salt; fold gently into egg mixture just until combined. Pour into a greased and waxed paper-lined jelly roll pan. Spread batter evenly over pan. Bake at 375° for 10-12 minutes or until light brown.

2. Turn out onto a clean kitchen towel that has been sprinkled with confectioners' sugar. Peel off waxed paper from cake; roll up towel and cake. Cool.

3. For filling, whip cream, sugar and vanilla. Unroll cake and spread filling over it; sprinkle with strawberries. Roll up the cake again and chill 2 hours before serving.

4. Sprinkle with confectioners' sugar; garnish with whole strawberries and whipped cream if desired. **Yield:** 10 servings.

🎗🎗🎗

Sweetheart Walnut Torte

Gladys Jenik, Orland Park, Illinois

I always donate one of these heart-shaped tortes for our church bake sale. The congregation never gets to see it, however—the ladies in charge quickly put it aside for one of them to buy!

1/2 cup butter, softened
1/2 cup sugar
4 egg yolks
1/3 cup milk
1/2 teaspoon vanilla extract
1 cup all-purpose flour
2 teaspoons baking powder
1/8 teaspoon salt

MERINGUE:

4 egg whites
1/8 teaspoon cream of tartar
3/4 cup sugar
1 cup chopped walnuts
Walnut halves

FILLING:

1 cup cold milk
1 package (3.9 ounces) instant chocolate pudding mix
1 cup heavy whipping cream, whipped

1. Grease two 9-in. heart-shaped pans. Line with waxed paper and grease the paper; set aside. In a mixing bowl, cream butter and sugar. Add egg yolks, milk and vanilla; mix well. Combine flour, baking powder and salt; gradually add to creamed mixture. Pour into prepared pans.

2. In a mixing bowl, beat egg whites and cream of tartar until soft peaks form. Gradually add sugar, one tablespoon at a time; beat until stiff and glossy. Fold in chopped nuts. Spread evenly over batter, sealing edges to sides of pan. Arrange walnut halves over meringue in one pan.

3. Bake at 300° for 55 minutes or until golden brown. Cool for 10 minutes; remove to wire racks. Invert so meringue side is up; cool completely.

4. In a mixing bowl, beat milk and pudding mix until thickened. Fold in whipped cream. Place plain cake, meringue side up, on serving plate. Spread with half of the filling; top with remaining cake. Frost sides with remaining filling. **Yield:** 12-16 servings.

Very Raspberry Pie

(Pictured on page 185)

Kathy Jones, West Winfield, New York

We live along a 130-year-old railroad track (our house once was a train station) edged a couple weeks a year with wild raspberries that I pick for my pie.

RASPBERRY TOPPING:
- **6 cups fresh raspberries, *divided***
- **1 cup sugar**
- **3 tablespoons cornstarch**
- **1/2 cup water**

CREAM FILLING:
- **1 package (8 ounces) cream cheese, softened**
- **1 cup whipped topping**
- **1 cup confectioners' sugar**
- **1 graham cracker crust (9 inches)**

Fresh mint, optional

1. Mash about 2 cups raspberries to measure 1 cup; place in a saucepan. Add sugar, cornstarch and water. Bring to a boil, stirring constantly; cook and stir 2 minutes longer. Strain to remove berry seeds if desired. Cool to room temperature, about 20 minutes.

2. Meanwhile, for filling, beat cream cheese, whipped topping and confectioners' sugar in a mixing bowl. Spread in bottom of crust. Top with remaining raspberries. Pour cooled raspberry sauce over top. Refrigerate until set, about 3 hours. Store in the refrigerator. Garnish with mint if desired. **Yield:** 6-8 servings.

Granny's Rhubarb Pie

Blanche Baninski, Minto, North Dakota

This recipe originated with my grandmother, who baked many different rhubarb desserts. This pie was always a favorite of mine.

- **3 cups all-purpose flour**
- **1-1/2 teaspoons salt**
- **1 cup shortening**
- **5 tablespoons water**
- **1 egg**
- **1 teaspoon vinegar**

FILLING:
- **3 cups cut fresh *or* frozen rhubarb (1/2-inch pieces)**
- **2 cups sliced peeled tart apples**
- **1 can (8 ounces) crushed pineapple, drained**
- **1/4 cup honey**
- **1 tablespoon lemon juice**
- **1 cup sugar**
- **3 tablespoons all-purpose flour**
- **1 tablespoon butter**

1. In a bowl, combine flour and salt; cut in shortening until the mixture resembles coarse crumbs. Combine the water, egg and vinegar; stir into flour mixture until a ball forms. Divide dough in half. Roll out one portion on a lightly floured surface; transfer to a 9-in. pie plate. Trim pastry even with edge.

2. In a bowl, combine the rhubarb, apples, pineapple, honey and lemon juice. Combine sugar and flour; add to rhubarb mixture. Pour into crust. Dot with butter. Roll out remaining pastry to fit top of pie. Place over filling; trim, seal and flute edges. Cut slits in pastry.

3. Bake at 350° for 1-1/4 hours or until the pastry is golden brown and the the apples are tender. **Yield:** 6-8 servings.

Dutch Apple Cake

(Pictured on page 184)

Elizabeth Peters, Martintown, Ontario

My husband and I came to Canada more than 50 years ago from Holland. This recipe, a family favorite, is one I found in a Dutch cookbook. It frequently goes along with me to potluck suppers and other gatherings.

- **3 medium peeled tart apples, sliced 1/4 inch thick (3 cups)**
- **3 tablespoons plus 1 cup sugar, *divided***
- **1 teaspoon ground cinnamon**
- **2/3 cup butter, softened**
- **4 eggs**
- **1 teaspoon vanilla extract**
- **2 cups all-purpose flour**
- **1/8 teaspoon salt**

1. In a bowl, combine the apples, 3 tablespoons sugar and cinnamon; let stand for 1 hour.

2. In a mixing bowl, cream butter and remaining sugar. Add eggs, one at a time, beating well after each. Add vanilla. Combine flour and salt; gradually add to creamed mixture and beat until smooth.

3. Pour into a greased 9-in. x 5-in. x 3-in. loaf pan. Push apple slices vertically into batter, placing them close together. Bake at 300° for 1 hour and 40 minutes or until a toothpick inserted near the center comes out clean. Cool for 10 minutes on a wire rack. Remove from pan. Serve warm. **Yield:** 10-12 servings.

Golden Peach Pie

Shirley Olson, Polson, Montana

Over 15 years ago, I entered this beautiful lattice-top pie in the Park County Fair in Livingston. It won a first-place blue ribbon plus a purple ribbon for "Best All Around!" My large family and many friends agree with the judges that it's very delicious.

Pastry for double-crust pie (9 inches)

- **1 cup sugar**
- **1/4 cup cornstarch**
- **1/4 teaspoon ground nutmeg**
- **1/8 teaspoon salt**
- **2 teaspoons lemon juice**
- **1/2 teaspoon grated orange peel**
- **1/8 teaspoon almond extract**
- **5 cups sliced peeled fresh peaches (about 5 medium)**
- **2 tablespoons butter**

Milk

1. Line a 9-in. pie plate with bottom pastry; trim even with edge of plate. Set aside. In a bowl, combine sugar, cornstarch, nutmeg and salt; stir in lemon juice, orange peel and extract. Add the peaches; toss gently. Pour into crust; dot with butter.

2. Roll out remaining pastry to make a lattice crust or to fit top of pie; make decorative cutouts in pastry. Set cutouts aside. Place top crust over filling. Trim, seal and flute edges. Brush pastry and cutouts with milk; place cutouts on top of pie. Cover the edges loosely with foil.

3. Bake at 400° for 40 minutes. Remove foil; bake 10-15 minutes longer or until crust is golden brown and filling is bubbly. Cool on a wire rack. **Yield:** 6-8 servings.

Low-Fat Devil's Food Cake

Nancy Lambert, Jacksonville, Florida

I adjusted the original recipe for this cake so my father, who's on a low-fat diet, can enjoy it. This moist bundt cake is a breeze to make because it starts with convenient reduced-fat cake mix. It's terrific for parties...no one believes it's low in fat.

✓ Uses less fat, sugar or salt. Includes Nutritional Analysis and Diabetic Exchanges.

1 package (18-1/4 ounces) reduced-fat devil's food cake mix
1 carton (8 ounces) nonfat plain yogurt
1/2 cup orange juice
1/2 cup water
Egg substitute equivalent to 2 eggs
2 tablespoons unsweetened applesauce
2 tablespoons grated orange peel
1 teaspoon ground cinnamon

GLAZE:
1 cup confectioners' sugar
2 tablespoons baking cocoa
2 tablespoons orange juice
1/2 teaspoon vanilla extract

1. In a mixing bowl, combine the first eight ingredients; beat on low speed for 1 minute, scraping the bowl constantly. Coat a 10-in. fluted tube pan with nonstick cooking spray and dust with flour. Pour batter into pan.

2. Bake at 350° for 50-55 minutes or until a toothpick comes out clean. Cool for 10 minutes before removing to a wire rack to cool completely. Combine the glaze ingredients; drizzle over cake. **Yield:** 12 servings.

Nutritional Analysis: One serving equals 243 calories, 368 mg sodium, trace cholesterol, 48 g carbohydrate, 5 g protein, 4 g fat, 2 g fiber. **Diabetic Exchanges:** 2 starch, 1 fruit, 1 fat.

Macaroon Cherry Pie

Lori Daniels, Beverly, West Virginia

I use homegrown cherries in this bountiful pie with its unique crunchy coconut topping. But I've found that purchased tart cherries yield a dessert that's nearly as delicious. I always bake this pie around Presidents' Day or Valentine's Day, but it's popular with my family in any season.

Pastry for single-crust pie (9 inches)
3 cans (14-1/2 ounces *each*) pitted tart cherries
1 cup sugar
1/3 cup cornstarch
1/2 teaspoon ground cinnamon
1/4 teaspoon red food coloring, optional

TOPPING:
1 egg, lightly beaten
2 tablespoons milk
1 tablespoon butter, melted
1/4 teaspoon almond extract
1/4 cup sugar
1/8 teaspoon salt
1 cup flaked coconut
1/2 cup sliced almonds

1. Line a 9-in. deep-dish pie plate with pastry. Trim to 1/2 in. beyond edge of plate; flute edges. Bake at 400° for 6 minutes; set aside.

2. Drain cherries, reserving 1 cup juice. Set cherries aside. In a saucepan, combine sugar and cornstarch; gradually stir in cherry juice until blended. Bring to a boil over medium heat; cook and stir for 2 minutes or until thickened. Remove from the heat; stir in cinnamon and food coloring if desired. Gently fold in cherries. Pour into crust. Cover edges loosely with foil. Bake at 400° for 20 minutes.

3. Meanwhile, in a bowl, combine the first six topping ingredients. Stir in coconut and almonds. Remove foil from pie; spoon topping over pie. Bake at 350° for 20 minutes or until topping is lightly browned. Cool on a wire rack for 1 hour. Chill for 4 hours or overnight before cutting. **Yield:** 6-8 servings.

Cupid's Chocolate Cake

Shelaine Duncan, North Powder, Oregon

I'm pleased to share the recipe for the very best chocolate cake I have ever tasted. I prepare this treat every year on Valentine's Day. It's rich, delectable and absolutely irresistible.

1 cup butter, softened
2-1/2 cups sugar
4 eggs
2-1/2 teaspoons vanilla extract, *divided*
2-3/4 cups all-purpose flour
1 cup baking cocoa
2 teaspoons baking soda
1/2 teaspoon baking powder
1/2 teaspoon salt
2 cups water
1 cup heavy whipping cream
1/4 cup confectioners' sugar
4 cups buttercream frosting of your choice

1. In a mixing bowl, cream butter and sugar. Add the eggs, one at a time, beating well after each addition. Beat on high speed until light and fluffy. Stir in 1-1/2 teaspoons vanilla. Combine dry ingredients; add to the creamed mixture alternately with water.

2. Pour into three greased and floured 9-in. round baking pans. Bake at 350° for 25-30 minutes or until a toothpick inserted near the center comes out clean. Cool for 10 minutes before removing from pans to wire racks to cool completely.

3. For filling, in a mixing bowl, beat cream until stiff peaks form. Beat in confectioners' sugar and remaining vanilla. Place bottom cake layer on a serving plate; spread with half of the filling. Repeat. Place top layer on cake; frost top and sides of cake with buttercream frosting. Store in the refrigerator. **Yield:** 12-14 servings.

Fresh Plum Kuchen

Anna Daley, Montague, Prince Edward Island

In late summer when plums are in season, this tender fruit-topped cake is delectable! The plum slices look so appealing arranged in circles on top. For variety, I sometimes substitute fresh pear or apple slices instead.

1/4 cup butter, softened
3/4 cup sugar
2 eggs
1 cup all-purpose flour
1 teaspoon baking powder
1/4 cup milk
1 teaspoon grated lemon peel
2 cups sliced fresh plums (about 4 medium)
1/2 cup packed brown sugar
1 teaspoon ground cinnamon

1. In a mixing bowl, cream butter and sugar; beat in eggs. Combine flour and baking powder; add to the creamed mixture alternately with milk. Add lemon peel.

2. Pour into a greased 10-in. springform pan. Arrange plums on top, overlapping slices. Gently press into batter. Sprinkle with brown sugar and cinnamon. Bake at 350° for 40-50 minutes or until top is golden and a toothpick inserted near the center comes out clean. Cool for 10 minutes. Run a knife around edge of pan; remove sides. Cool on a wire rack. **Yield:** 10-12 servings.

Old-Fashioned Custard Pie

Maxine Linkenauger, Montverde, Florida

This recipe came from the best cook in West Virginia—my mother! I just added a little to her ingredients. Mostly I make my custard pie for church and club functions. It's the most different pie of all the ones in my collection.

Pastry for single- *or* double-crust pie (9 inches)
4 eggs
2-1/2 cups milk
1/2 cup sugar
1 teaspoon vanilla extract
1 teaspoon almond extract
1 teaspoon salt
1 teaspoon ground nutmeg

1. Line pie plate with bottom pastry; flute edges or prepare a braided crust (see Editor's Note). Bake at 400° for 10 minutes.

2. Meanwhile, beat eggs in a large bowl. Add remaining ingredients; mix well. Pour into crust. Cover edges with foil. Bake for 20-25 minutes or until a knife inserted near the center comes out clean. Cool completely. Store in the refrigerator. **Yield:** 6-8 servings.

Editor's Note: Pastry for a double crust is needed only if a braided crust is desired. To prepare braided crust: Trim pastry even with the edge of the pie plate; brush with water. From the top pastry, cut 12 strips, each 1/4 in. thick. Using three strips at a time, braid pastry on edge of crust, attaching ends together. Press down gently. Bake as directed.

Homemade Chocolate Cake

Cindy Miller, Riverside, Iowa

A rich chocolate frosting is the flavorful finishing touch to this moist from-scratch cake that's mixed in one bowl. It always turns out and is quickly gobbled up by friends and family. I'm asked to fix this favorite so often that the recipe card is an absolute mess!

3 cups all-purpose flour
2 cups sugar
1/3 cup baking cocoa
2 teaspoons baking soda
1 teaspoon salt
2 cups water
3/4 cup vegetable oil
2 teaspoons vanilla extract
2 teaspoons vinegar

CHOCOLATE CREAM CHEESE FROSTING:
1 package (3 ounces) cream cheese, softened
1/4 cup butter, softened
2 cups confectioners' sugar
1/3 cup baking cocoa
Dash salt
3 tablespoons milk
1/2 teaspoon vanilla extract

1. In a mixing bowl, combine the first five ingredients. Add the water, oil, vanilla and vinegar; mix well (batter will be thin). Pour into a greased 13-in. x 9-in. x 2-in. baking pan. Bake at 350° for 25-30 minutes or until a toothpick inserted near the center comes out clean. Cool completely.

2. For frosting, in a mixing bowl, beat the cream cheese and butter. Add the confectioners' sugar, cocoa, salt, milk and vanilla; mix well. Spread over the cake. Store in the refrigerator. **Yield:** 12-15 servings.

Editor's Note: This recipe contains no egg.

Fudgy Raspberry Torte

Dolores Hurtt, Florence, Montana

Guests will think you fussed when you serve this torte made with convenient cake and pudding mixes, a bit of jam and fresh raspberries. It looks elegant for most any special occasion.

1 package (18-1/4 ounces) chocolate fudge cake mix
1-1/3 cups water
3 eggs
1/3 cup vegetable oil
3/4 cup ground pecans
1-1/2 cups cold milk
1 package (3.9 ounces) instant chocolate fudge *or* chocolate pudding mix
1/2 cup seedless raspberry jam
1-1/2 cups whipped topping
1/4 cup finely chopped pecans
Fresh raspberries

1. In a mixing bowl, combine dry cake mix, water, eggs and oil; mix well. Add ground pecans; mix just until combined. Pour into three greased and floured 9-in. round baking pans.

2. Bake at 350° for 15-20 minutes or until a toothpick inserted near the center comes out clean. Cool for 10 minutes before removing from pans to wire racks to cool completely.

3. In a mixing bowl, beat milk and pudding mix on low speed for 2 minutes or until thickened. In a saucepan, melt jam. Brush over the top of each cake.

4. Place one cake on a serving plate; spread with half of the pudding. Repeat layers. Top with third cake layer; spread top with whipped topping. Sprinkle with chopped pecans. Garnish with raspberries. Store in the refrigerator. **Yield:** 12 servings.

Lemon Sour Cream Pie

Nancy Beran, St. Peter, Minnesota

One bite and people marvel over this pie. Some even say it reminds them of cheesecake. The recipe was shared by a friend; now, I'm glad to do the same.

1 cup sugar
1/4 cup cornstarch
1/8 teaspoon salt
1 cup milk
3 egg yolks, beaten
1/4 cup butter
1/4 cup fresh lemon juice
1 teaspoon grated lemon peel
1 cup (8 ounces) sour cream
1 pastry shell (9 inches), baked

MERINGUE:
3 egg whites
1/2 teaspoon vanilla extract
1/4 teaspoon cream of tartar
6 tablespoons sugar
Lemon peel strips, optional

1. In a saucepan, combine sugar, cornstarch and salt. Gradually stir in milk. Bring to a boil over medium heat, stirring constantly. Cook and stir for 2 minutes.

2. Blend a small amount into egg yolks; mix well. Return all to pan; mix well. Cook and stir for 2 minutes. Remove from the heat. Add butter, lemon juice and peel; mix well. Set aside.

3. For meringue, beat egg whites until foamy. Add vanilla and cream of tartar. Add sugar, 1 tablespoon at a time, beating until stiff peaks form; set aside. Fold sour cream into the lemon mixture; pour into pastry shell. Cover with meringue, sealing to edges of pastry.

4. Bake at 350° for 12-15 minutes or until golden. Garnish with lemon peel strips if desired. Cool completely. Store in the refrigerator. **Yield:** 6-8 servings.

Mocha Cupcakes

Lorna Smith, New Hazelton, British Columbia

This recipe is one that I have called on over the years for numerous occasions—birthdays, PTA meetings, for serving to company, etc. Everyone likes it.

1 cup boiling water
1 cup mayonnaise
1 teaspoon vanilla extract
2 cups all-purpose flour
1 cup sugar
1/2 cup baking cocoa
2 teaspoons baking soda

MOCHA FROSTING:

3/4 cup confectioners' sugar
1/4 cup baking cocoa
1/2 to 1 teaspoon instant coffee granules
Pinch salt
1-1/2 cups heavy whipping cream

1. In a mixing bowl, combine water, mayonnaise and vanilla. Combine flour, sugar, cocoa and baking soda; add to the mayonnaise mixture and beat until well mixed.

2. Fill greased or paper-lined muffin cups two-thirds full. Bake at 350° for 20-25 minutes or until a toothpick inserted near the center comes out clean. Cool 10 minutes before removing to wire racks to cool completely.

3. For frosting, combine confectioners' sugar, cocoa, coffee and salt in a mixing bowl. Stir in cream; cover and chill with beaters for 30 minutes. Beat frosting until stiff peaks form. Frost the cupcakes. **Yield:** about 1-1/2 dozen.

Editor's Note: Reduced-fat or fat-free mayonnaise is not recommeded for this recipe.

Spring and Fall Pie

Laura Collins, Rapid City, South Dakota

Every spring, I have a good crop of rhubarb in my garden, and one of my favorite ways to use it is in this pie. I adapted this version from a recipe I received from our county Extension service.

1-1/2 cups sugar
3 tablespoons all-purpose flour
1-1/2 cups diced fresh *or* frozen rhubarb, thawed and drained
1-1/2 cups fresh *or* frozen cranberries, halved
1-1/2 cups chopped peeled tart apples
Pastry for double-crust pie (9 inches)

1. In a large bowl, combine sugar and flour; stir in rhubarb, cranberries and apples. Line a 9-in. pie plate with the bottom pastry; add filling. Cover with a lattice crust; seal and flute edges.

2. Bake at 450° for 10 minutes. Reduce heat to 350°; bake 40 minutes longer or until filling is bubbly. Cover edges with foil to prevent overbrowning if necessary. **Yield:** 6-8 servings.

Orange Date Pound Cake

Ruth Bartz, Suring, Wisconsin

Loaded with chewy dates and crunchy pecans, this cake is a "must" to take to family gatherings. The sweet and zesty orange sauce tops it off just right. This cake slices nicely and looks so appetizing served on a pretty plate.

1 cup butter, softened
3 cups sugar, *divided*
4 eggs
1 tablespoon orange peel, *divided*
3 cups all-purpose flour
1 teaspoon baking soda
1-1/3 cups buttermilk
1 pound chopped dates
1 cup coarsely chopped pecans
1/2 cup orange juice

1. In a mixing bowl, cream butter and 2 cups sugar. Add the eggs, one at a time, beating well after each addition. Add 2 teaspoons orange peel. Combine flour and baking soda; add to the creamed mixture alternately with buttermilk. Stir in dates and pecans.

2. Pour into a greased and floured 10-in. tube pan; spread evenly. Bake at 325° for 70-75 minutes or until a toothpick inserted near the center comes out clean.

3. Combine the orange juice and remaining sugar and orange peel; pour over cake. Cool for 30 minutes before removing from pan to a wire rack to cool completely. **Yield:** 12-16 servings.

Walnut Mincemeat Pie

Laverne Kamp, Kutztown, Pennsylvania

As a cold and tasty finishing touch, my husband and I usually put a scoop of ice cream on top of this pie. The recipe's from my mother—each year, I make it for Christmas, and then for my sister-in-law's New Year's party besides.

2 eggs
1 cup sugar
2 tablespoons all-purpose flour
1/8 teaspoon salt
2 cups prepared mincemeat
1/2 cup chopped walnuts
1/4 cup butter, melted
1 unbaked pastry shell (9 inches)

1. In a mixing bowl, lightly beat eggs. Combine sugar, flour and salt; gradually add to eggs. Stir in mincemeat, nuts and butter; pour into pie shell.

2. Bake at 400° for 15 minutes. Reduce heat to 325°; bake 35-40 minutes or until a knife inserted near the center comes out clean. Cool completely. Store in refrigerator. **Yield:** 6-8 servings.

Cream Puff Pie

Holly Camozzi, Rohnert Park, California

When I was a girl, my mother, sister and I made mini cream puffs. Now, instead of several little puffs, I make one big pie for big appetites.

CRUST:

- **1/2 cup water**
- **1/4 cup butter**
- **1/2 teaspoon salt**
- **1/2 cup all-purpose flour**
- **2 eggs**

FILLING:

- **3/4 cup sugar**
- **1/3 cup all-purpose flour**
- **1/8 teaspoon salt**
- **2 cups milk**
- **2 eggs, lightly beaten**
- **1 teaspoon vanilla extract**
- **2 cups whipped cream, *divided***

Chocolate sauce *and/or* fresh raspberries, optional

1. In a large saucepan, bring water, butter and salt to a boil. Add flour all at once and stir until a smooth ball forms. Remove from the heat; let stand for 5 minutes. Add eggs, one at a time, beating well after each addition. Continue beating until the mixture is smooth and shiny.

2. Spread in the bottom and halfway up the sides of a well-greased 9-in. pie plate. Bake at 400° for 35-40 minutes. Cool completely.

3. For filling, combine sugar, flour and salt. Stir in milk until smooth. Cook and stir over medium-high heat until thickened and bubbly. Reduce heat; cook and stir 2 minutes more. Remove from the heat. Stir a small amount into eggs; return all to saucepan. Bring to a gentle boil. Cook and stir 2 minutes more. Stir in vanilla. Cool.

4. Fold in 1 cup of whipped cream. Pour into the crust. Top with remaining whipped cream. Chill for 2 hours. Garnish with chocolate sauce and/or raspberries if desired. **Yield:** 6-8 servings.

Frozen Mocha Marbled Loaf, p. 209

Apricot Peach Cobbler, p. 217

Chocolate Eclairs, p. 214

Strawberry Brownie Bombe, p. 213

Creamy Caramel Flan, p. 206

Just Desserts

Most folks agree that a meal just isn't complete without dessert. These luscious cheesecakes, fruit-filled cobblers, pleasing parfaits and more won't disappoint!

Raspberry Marshmallow Delight, p. 210

Peach Pizza Pie, p. 218

Creamy Caramel Flan

(Pictured on page 204)

Pat Forte, Miami, Florida

If you're unfamiliar with flan, think of it as a tasty variation on custard. One warning, though—it's very filling. A small slice of flan goes a long way!

3/4 cup sugar
1 package (8 ounces) cream cheese, softened
5 eggs
1 can (14 ounces) sweetened condensed milk
1 can (12 ounces) evaporated milk
1 teaspoon vanilla extract

1. In a heavy saucepan over medium-low heat, cook and stir sugar until melted and golden, about 15 minutes. Quickly pour into an ungreased 2-qt. round baking or souffle dish, tilting to coat the bottom; let stand for 10 minutes.

2. In a mixing bowl, beat the cream cheese until smooth. Beat in eggs, one at a time, until thoroughly combined. Add remaining ingredients; mix well. Pour over caramelized sugar.

3. Place the dish in a larger baking pan. Pour boiling water into larger pan to a depth of 1 in. Bake at 350° for 50-60 minutes or until center is just set (mixture will jiggle). Remove dish from larger pan to a wire rack; cool for 1 hour. Refrigerate overnight.

4. To unmold, run a knife around edges and invert onto a large rimmed serving platter. Cut into wedges or spoon onto dessert plates; spoon sauce over each serving. **Yield:** 8-10 servings.

True Love Truffles

Kim Weiesnbach, Claremore, Oklahoma

A few years ago, I began giving these smooth, minty truffles in tins as Christmas gifts. Now I can't go a year without sharing them. They also make a perfect Valentine's treat for someone dear.

1-1/2 cups sugar
3/4 cup butter
1 can (5 ounces) evaporated milk
2 packages (4.67 ounces *each*) mint Andes candies (56 pieces total)
1 jar (7 ounces) marshmallow creme
1 teaspoon vanilla extract
22 ounces white baking chocolate, *divided*
1/2 cup semisweet chocolate chips
Green food coloring, optional

1. In a heavy saucepan, combine sugar, butter and milk. Bring to a boil over medium heat, stirring constantly. Reduce heat; cook and stir until a candy thermometer reads 236° (soft-ball stage). Remove from the heat.

2. Stir in candies until melted and mixture is well blended. Stir in marshmallow creme and vanilla until smooth. Spread into a buttered 15-in. x 10-in. x 1-in. pan; cover and refrigerate for 1 hour.

3. Cut into 96 pieces; roll each into a ball (mixture will be soft). Place on a waxed paper-lined baking sheet.

4. In a heavy saucepan or microwave-safe bowl, melt 18 oz. of white chocolate and chocolate chips. Dip balls in melted chocolate; place on waxed paper to harden. Melt the remaining white chocolate; add food coloring if desired. Drizzle over truffles. Store in an airtight container. **Yield:** 8 dozen.

Almond Pear Tartlets

Marie Rizzio, Traverse City, Michigan

Although they're quick to fix, you'll want to savor these pretty pastries slowly. Delicately spiced pears are complemented by an almond sauce and a crispy crust.

- **1 egg, lightly beaten**
- **1/2 cup plus 6 tablespoons sugar, *divided***
- **3/4 cup heavy whipping cream**
- **2 tablespoons butter, melted**
- **1/2 teaspoon almond extract**
- **1 package (10 ounces) frozen puff pastry shells, thawed**
- **2 small ripe pears, peeled and thinly sliced**
- **1/2 teaspoon ground cinnamon**
- **1/8 teaspoon ground ginger**
- **1/2 cup slivered almonds, toasted, optional**

1. In a saucepan, combine the egg, 1/2 cup sugar, cream and butter. Cook and stir until the sauce is thickened and a thermometer reads 160°. Remove from the heat; stir in extract. Cover and refrigerate.

2. On an unfloured surface, roll each pastry into a 4-in. circle. Place in an ungreased 15-in. x 10-in. x 1-in. baking pan.

3. Top each with pear slices. Combine cinnamon, ginger and remaining sugar; sprinkle over pears. Bake at 400° for 20 minutes or until pastry is golden brown. Sprinkle with almonds if desired. Serve warm with the chilled cream sauce. **Yield:** 6 servings.

Raisin Bread Pudding

Sherry Niese, McComb, Ohio

My sister gave me the recipe for this delicious bread pudding that's dotted with raisins. A homemade vanilla sauce goes together quickly on the stovetop and is yummy drizzled over warm servings of this old-fashioned-tasting treat.

- **8 slices bread, cubed**
- **4 eggs**
- **2 cups milk**
- **1/4 cup sugar**
- **1/4 cup butter, melted**
- **1/4 cup raisins**
- **1/2 teaspoon ground cinnamon**

SAUCE:

- **2 tablespoons butter**
- **2 tablespoons all-purpose flour**
- **1 cup water**
- **3/4 cup sugar**
- **1 teaspoon vanilla extract**

1. Place bread cubes in a greased slow cooker. In a bowl, beat eggs and milk; stir in sugar, butter, raisins and cinnamon. Pour over bread; stir. Cover and cook on high for 1 hour. Reduce heat to low; cook for 3-4 hours or until a thermometer reads 160°.

2. Just before serving, melt butter in a saucepan. Stir in flour until smooth. Gradually add water, sugar and vanilla. Bring to a boil; cook and stir for 2 minutes or until thickened. Serve with warm bread pudding. **Yield:** 6 servings.

Cool Lime Cheesecake

Karen Donhauser, Frazer, Pennsylvania

I started baking this treat several years ago, and it immediately won raves. The mixture of tart lime and sweet, creamy cheesecake is absolutely scrumptious.

2-1/4 cups graham cracker crumbs (about 36 squares)
1/3 cup sugar
1/2 cup butter, melted
FILLING:
20 ounces cream cheese, softened
3/4 cup sugar
1 cup (8 ounces) sour cream
3 tablespoons all-purpose flour
3 eggs
2/3 cup lime juice
1 teaspoon vanilla extract
1 drop green food coloring, optional
Whipped cream and lime slices

1. In a bowl, combine crumbs and sugar; stir in butter. Press onto the bottom and 1 in. up the side of a greased 10-in. springform pan. Bake at 375° for 8 minutes. Cool.

2. In a mixing bowl, beat cream cheese and sugar until smooth. Add sour cream and flour; beat well. Beat in eggs on low speed just until combined. Stir in lime juice, vanilla and food coloring if desired just until mixed. Pour into crust. Bake at 325° for 50-55 minutes or until center is almost set.

3. Cool on a wire rack for 1 hour. Refrigerate overnight. Remove sides of pan. Garnish with whipped cream and lime. **Yield:** 12-14 servings.

Marshmallow Cream With Custard Sauce

Penny Klusman, Richmond, Indiana

This dessert has always been a favorite of my husband and children. The original recipe came from my great-grandmother and has been passed down through the generations.

2 egg whites
1/4 cup sugar
Pinch salt
1/4 teaspoon vanilla extract
CUSTARD SAUCE:
1-1/2 cups milk
2 egg yolks
1 egg
1/4 cup sugar
2 teaspoons vanilla extract
Fresh raspberries

1. In the top of a double boiler over simmering water, combine egg whites, sugar, salt and vanilla. Beat with a portable mixer on high speed until mixture reaches 160°. Beat until stiff peaks form, about 1 minute. Spoon into dessert glasses; refrigerate until chilled.

2. For the custard sauce, heat milk in a small saucepan over medium heat until small bubbles form around sides of pan. Remove from the heat. Combine egg yolks, egg and sugar in a bowl. Stir a small amount of hot milk into egg mixture; return all to the pan, stirring constantly. Cook and stir on low until mixture reaches 160° and coats a spoon, about 20 minutes.

3. Remove from the heat; stir in vanilla. Refrigerate for at least 1 hour. Serve custard over marshmallow cream; top with raspberries. **Yield:** 6 servings.

Chocolate and Fruit Trifle

Angie Dierikx, State Center, Iowa

This refreshing dessert layered with devil's food cake, a creamy pudding mixture, red berries and green kiwi is perfect for the holidays. I like making it in a clear glass trifle bowl to show off its festive colors.

- **1 package (18-1/4 ounces) devil's food cake mix**
- **1 can (14 ounces) sweetened condensed milk**
- **1 cup cold water**
- **1 package (3.4 ounces) instant vanilla pudding mix**
- **2 cups heavy whipping cream, whipped**
- **2 tablespoons orange juice**
- **2 cups fresh strawberries, chopped**
- **2 cups fresh raspberries**
- **2 kiwifruit, peeled and chopped**

1. Prepare cake batter according to package directions; pour into a greased 15-in. x 10-in. x 1-in. baking pan. Bake at 350° for 20 minutes or until a toothpick inserted near center comes out clean. Cool completely on a wire rack. Crumble enough cake to measure 8 cups; set aside. (Save remaining cake for another use.)

2. In a mixing bowl, combine milk and water until smooth. Add pudding mix; beat on low speed for 2 minutes or until slightly thickened. Fold in the whipped cream.

3. To assemble, spread 2-1/2 cups pudding mixture in a 4-qt. glass bowl. Top with half of the crumbled cake; sprinkle with 1 tablespoon orange juice. Arrange half of the berries and kiwi over cake. Repeat pudding and cake layers; sprinkle with remaining orange juice. Top with remaining pudding mixture. Spoon remaining fruit around edge of bowl. Cover and refrigerate until serving. **Yield:** 12-16 servings.

Frozen Mocha Marbled Loaf

(Pictured on page 204)

Cheryl Martinetto, Grand Rapids, Minnesota

This showstopping marbled dessert seems fancy, but it's really simple to prepare ahead of time and pop in the freezer. Frosty slices have a creamy blend of chocolate and coffee that's delightful any time of year.

- **2 cups finely crushed chocolate cream-filled sandwich cookies (about 22 cookies)**
- **3 tablespoons butter, melted**
- **1 package (8 ounces) cream cheese, softened**
- **1 can (14 ounces) sweetened condensed milk**
- **1 teaspoon vanilla extract**
- **2 cups heavy whipping cream, whipped**
- **2 tablespoons instant coffee granules**
- **1 tablespoon hot water**
- **1/2 cup chocolate syrup**

1. Line a 9-in. x 5-in. x 3-in. loaf pan with foil. In a bowl, combine the cookie crumbs and butter. Press firmly onto the bottom and 1-1/2 in. up the sides of prepared pan.

2. In a mixing bowl, beat cream cheese until light. Add milk and vanilla; mix well. Fold in whipped cream. Spoon half of the mixture into another bowl and set aside.

3. Dissolve coffee in hot water; fold into remaining cream cheese mixture. Fold in chocolate syrup. Spoon half of chocolate mixture over crust. Top with half of the reserved cream cheese mixture. Repeat layers. Cut through layers with a knife to swirl the chocolate (pan will be full).

4. Cover and freeze for 6 hours or overnight. To serve, lift out of the pan; remove foil. Cut into slices. **Yield:** 12 servings.

Raspberry Marshmallow Delight

(Pictured on page 205)

Gloria Iden, Kimmell, Indiana

This is one of our family's favorite desserts. It has a tangy, unique flavor. After a hard day of working on the farm, this fruity treat is most welcome.

1-1/4 cups graham cracker crumbs
1/4 cup butter, melted
50 large marshmallows
1 cup milk
1 carton (8 ounces) frozen whipped topping, thawed
2 packages (10 ounces *each*) frozen raspberries in syrup, thawed
1-1/4 cups water, *divided*
1/2 cup sugar
2 teaspoons lemon juice
6 tablespoons cornstarch
Whipped cream and fresh raspberries, optional

1. Combine crumbs and butter; press into the bottom of a greased 13-in. x 9-in. 2-in. baking pan. Bake at 350° for 10 minutes. Cool.

2. In a large saucepan over medium heat, stir marshmallows and milk until the marshmallows are melted. Cool to room temperature. Fold in whipped topping; spread over crust.

3. In a saucepan, bring raspberries, 1 cup water, sugar and lemon juice to a boil. Combine cornstarch and remaining water; stir into raspberry mixture. Boil for 2 minutes, stirring constantly. Cool to room temperature. Spread over marshmallow layer.

4. Chill until firm, about 4 hours. Garnish with whipped cream and raspberries if desired. **Yield:** 12-16 servings.

Valentine Berries and Cream

Tamera O'Sullivan, Apple Valley, Minnesota

Everyone was so impressed with this scrumptious filled chocolate heart served at a banquet held by our adult Sunday school class. I got the recipe, and now I enjoy rave reviews from family and friends when I serve it.

8 squares (1 ounce *each*) semisweet chocolate
1 tablespoon shortening
2 packages (3 ounces *each*) cream cheese, softened
1/4 cup butter, softened
1-1/2 cups confectioners' sugar
1/3 cup baking cocoa
2 tablespoons milk
1 teaspoon vanilla extract
2-1/2 cups heavy whipping cream, whipped, *divided*
1-1/2 cups fresh strawberries, halved

1. Line a 9-in. heart-shaped or square baking pan with foil; set aside. In a heavy saucepan over low heat, melt chocolate and shortening; stir until smooth. Pour into prepared pan, swirling to coat the bottom and 1-1/2 in. up the sides.

2. Refrigerate for 1 minute, then swirl the chocolate to reinforce sides of heart or square pan. Refrigerate for 30 minutes or until firm. Using foil, lift from pan; remove foil and place chocolate heart on a serving plate.

3. In a mixing bowl, beat the cream cheese and butter until smooth. Combine confectioners' sugar and cocoa; add to creamed mixture with milk and vanilla. Beat until smooth.

4. Gently fold two-thirds of the whipped cream into cream cheese mixture. Spoon into heart. Insert star tip #32 into a pastry or plastic bag; fill with the remaining whipped cream. Pipe around the edge of heart. Garnish with strawberries. **Yield:** 8-10 servings.

Caramel Fudge Cheesecake

Brenda Ruse, Truro, Nova Scotia

It's hard to resist this chocolaty cheesecake with its fudgy crust, crunchy pecans and gooey layer of caramel. I combined several recipes to create this version, which satisfies both the chocolate lovers and the cheesecake lovers in my family.

1 package fudge brownie mix (8-inch square pan size)
1 package (14 ounces) caramels
1/4 cup evaporated milk
1-1/4 cups coarsely chopped pecans
2 packages (8 ounces *each*) cream cheese, softened
1/2 cup sugar
2 eggs
2 squares (1 ounce *each*) semisweet chocolate, melted
2 squares (1 ounce *each*) unsweetened chocolate, melted

1. Prepare brownie batter according to the package directions. Spread into a greased 9-in. springform pan. Bake at 350° for 20 minutes. Cool for 10 minutes on a wire rack.

2. Meanwhile, in a microwave-safe bowl, melt caramels with milk. Pour over brownie crust; sprinkle with pecans.

3. In a mixing bowl, combine the cream cheese and sugar; mix well. Add eggs, beating on low speed just until combined. Stir in melted chocolate. Pour over pecans. Bake at 350° for 35-40 minutes or until the center is almost set.

4. Cool on a wire rack for 10 minutes. Run a knife around edge of pan to loosen; cool completely. Chill overnight. Remove sides of pan before serving. Store leftovers in the refrigerator. **Yield:** 12 servings.

Apple Strudel

Helen Lesh, Forsyth, Missouri

This is one of my favorite recipes during autumn. The aroma of this dessert baking on a cool, crisp day is absolutely wonderful.

1 cup cold butter
2 cups all-purpose flour
1 cup (8 ounces) sour cream
1/4 teaspoon salt
FILLING:
2 cups dry bread crumbs
1/4 cup butter, melted
4 medium baking apples, peeled and chopped
2 cups sugar
1 cup golden raisins
1/2 cup chopped pecans
2 teaspoons ground cinnamon
Confectioners' sugar, optional

1. In a medium bowl, cut butter into flour until mixture resembles coarse crumbs. Add the sour cream and salt; mix well. Shape into a ball; cover and refrigerate overnight.

2. For filling, combine the bread crumbs and butter. Add apples, sugar, raisins, pecans and cinnamon; mix well and set aside. Divide dough into thirds; turn onto a floured surface. Roll each into a 15-in. x 12-in. rectangle. Spoon filling evenly onto dough; spread to within 1 in. of edges. Roll up jelly-roll style, starting with a long side; pinch seams and ends to seal. Carefully place seam side down on an ungreased baking sheet.

3. Bake at 350° for 55-60 minutes or until light brown. Cool completely on wire racks. Dust with confectioners' sugar if desired. **Yield:** 3 loaves.

Minty Cocoa Mousse

Melissa Tarbox, Allen, Texas

Junior Mints give the refreshing mint taste to this scrumptious smooth-as-silk mousse. It's one of my best desserts because it's a snap to prepare, yet the flavor is beyond compare.

2 tablespoons baking cocoa
2 tablespoons milk
1 cup Junior Mints
2 tablespoons butter
1 carton (8 ounces) frozen whipped topping, thawed, *divided*
1/2 teaspoon vanilla extract
Fresh mint and additional whipped topping, optional

1. In a saucepan, combine cocoa and milk until smooth. Add mints and butter; cook and stir over low heat until smooth. Cool for 15 minutes.

2. Stir in 1 cup whipped topping and vanilla. Fold in the remaining whipped topping. Spoon into dessert dishes. Refrigerate until serving. Garnish with mint and whipped topping if desired. **Yield:** 4 servings.

Chocolate Almond Brittle

Pat Parsons, Bakersfield, California

Here in Kern County, there are thousands of acres of almond orchards. I like to experiment with recipes—always trying to come up with something new. This candy is the result of altering, adding and a lot of taste testing (somebody had to do it!). I think it turned out rather well.

1 cup sugar
1/2 cup light corn syrup
1/8 teaspoon salt
1 cup coarsely chopped almonds
1 tablespoon butter
1 teaspoon vanilla extract
1-1/2 teaspoons baking soda
3/4 pound dark *or* milk chocolate candy coating

1. In a 1-1/2-qt. microwave-safe bowl, combine sugar, corn syrup and salt; mix well. Microwave on high for 4 minutes. Stir in almonds; microwave on high for 4 minutes. Add the butter and vanilla; microwave on high for 1-1/2 minutes. Stir in baking soda.

2. As soon as the mixture foams, quickly pour onto a greased metal baking sheet. Cool completely. Break into 2-in. pieces. Melt chocolate coating in a double boiler or microwave. Dip one side of brittle in chocolate and place on waxed paper to harden. Store in an airtight container. **Yield:** about 1 pound.

Editor's Note: This recipe was tested using a 700-watt microwave.

Pretty Plum Parfaits

Norma Reynolds, York, Pennsylvania

With a plum tree in our backyard, I'm always eager to try new plum recipes. But none of them beat this wonderful dessert! Light, refreshing and easy to whip up, these fruity parfaits are an ideal summer treat.

9 to 12 medium ripe red *or* purple plums (about 2 pounds), sliced
1/2 cup currant jelly
1/2 cup packed brown sugar
1 orange peel strip (1 to 3 inches)
1 cinnamon stick (3 inches)
1 cup heavy whipping cream
1 tablespoon confectioners' sugar
1/2 teaspoon vanilla extract
Fancy cookies and additional whipped cream and plum slices, optional

1. In a heavy saucepan, combine plums, jelly, brown sugar, orange peel and cinnamon stick. Bring to a boil; reduce heat. Simmer, uncovered, for 10-15 minutes or until plums are tender, stirring occasionally. Remove from heat; cool slightly. Discard orange peel and cinnamon stick; coarsely mash plums. Cover; refrigerate.

2. Just before serving, beat cream, confectioners' sugar and vanilla in a mixing bowl until stiff peaks form. Place about 1/4 cup plum mixture each in four chilled parfait glasses; top with 1/4 cup whipped cream. Repeat layers. Top with remaining plum mixture. Garnish with a cookie, dollop of whipped cream and plum slice if desired. **Yield:** 4 servings.

Strawberry Brownie Bombe

(Pictured on page 204)

Joanne Watts, Kitchener, Ontario

A friend and I dreamed up this recipe. We use it when we entertain and serve it for special family dinners. For an extra touch, you can dip the strawberries in chocolate.

1 package (21-1/2 ounces) fudge brownie mix
1/2 cup chopped walnuts
1/2 cup strawberry preserves
1 quart strawberry ice cream, softened
2 cups heavy whipping cream
3 drops red food coloring, optional
1/4 cup confectioners' sugar
Fresh strawberries and mint, optional

1. Prepare brownie mix according to package directions for cake-like brownies. Stir in walnuts. Pour the batter into two greased and waxed paper-lined 8-in. round baking pans. Bake at 350° for 30 minutes or until a toothpick inserted near the center comes out clean. Cool completely in pans.

2. Line a 1-1/2-qt. metal bowl with foil. Cut and fit one brownie layer to evenly line the inside of the bowl (brownie may crack). Spread preserves over brownie layer. Freeze for 15 minutes. Fill brownie-lined bowl with ice cream; smooth top. Cover and freeze for 3 hours or until ice cream is firm.

3. Place remaining brownie layer on a serving plate. Remove bowl from freezer; uncover. Invert onto brownie layer; remove bowl and foil. Return to freezer.

4. In a mixing bowl, beat cream and food coloring until soft peaks form. Add sugar and beat until stiff peaks form; set aside 1-1/2 cups. Spread remaining whipped cream over top and sides of bombe.

5. Cut a small hole in the corner of a pastry or plastic bag and insert a #8b or #20 star tip. Fill with reserved whipped cream; pipe border at base of bombe. Holding the bag straight up and down, form stars on top. Garnish with strawberries and mint if desired. **Yield:** 16 servings.

Editor's Note: Unfrosted bombe may be frozen for up to 3 days.

Chocolate Eclairs

(Pictured on page 204)

Janet Davis, Murfreesboro, Tennessee

I won the grand prize with this recipe at a "chocolate lover's cook-off" contest in our town a number of years ago. This is one of my favorite desserts.

1/2 cup butter
1 cup water
1/4 teaspoon salt
1 cup all-purpose flour
4 eggs

FILLING:

1 package (5.1 ounces) instant vanilla pudding mix
2-1/2 cups cold milk
1 cup heavy whipping cream
1/4 cup confectioners' sugar
1 teaspoon vanilla extract

CHOCOLATE ICING:

2 squares (1 ounce *each*) semisweet chocolate
2 tablespoons butter
1 cup confectioners' sugar
2 to 3 tablespoons hot water

1. In a saucepan, bring butter, water and salt to a boil. Add flour all at once; stir until a smooth ball forms. Remove from heat; let stand 5 minutes. Add eggs, one at a time, beating well after each addition. Continue beating until mixture is smooth and shiny.

2. With a tablespoon or a pastry tube fitted with a No. 10 or larger tip, spoon or pipe dough into 4-in.-long x 1-1/2-in.-wide strips on a greased cookie sheet. Bake at 450° for 15 minutes. Reduce heat to 325°; bake 20 minutes longer. Cool on a wire rack.

3. For filling, combine pudding mix and milk; mix according to package directions. In another bowl, whip cream until soft peaks form. Beat in sugar and vanilla; fold into pudding. Fill cooled shells. (Chill remaining pudding for another use.)

4. For icing, melt chocolate and butter in a saucepan over low heat. Stir in sugar. Add hot water until icing is smooth and reaches desired consistency. Cool slightly. Spread over eclairs. Chill until serving. **Yield:** 8-9 servings.

German Chocolate Ice Cream

Peggy Key, Grant, Alabama

I found this recipe years ago and have been taking it to ice cream socials ever since. But you won't want to wait for a get-together to enjoy it. The cool combination of chocolate, coconut and pecans is delicious anytime.

1-1/2 cups sugar
1/4 cup all-purpose flour
1/4 teaspoon ground cinnamon
1/4 teaspoon salt
4 cups milk
3 eggs, beaten
1 quart half-and-half cream
2 packages (4 ounces *each*) German sweet chocolate, melted
1 cup flaked coconut
1 cup chopped pecans

1. In a large heavy saucepan, combine the sugar, flour, cinnamon and salt. Gradually add milk and eggs; stir until smooth. Cook and stir over medium-low heat until mixture is thick enough to coat a metal spoon and reaches 160°, about 15 minutes. Stir in the remaining ingredients. Refrigerate for several hours or overnight.

2. Fill ice cream freezer cylinder two-thirds full; freeze according to manufacturer's instructions. Refrigerate remaining mixture until ready to freeze. Remove ice cream from the freezer 10 minutes before serving. **Yield:** 1 gallon.

Butternut Apple Crisp

Michele Van Dewerker, Roseboom, New York

Over the years, I've collected lots of squash recipes. This one came from a friend, and it's been a hit everywhere.

3/4 cup packed brown sugar, *divided*
2 tablespoons lemon juice
1 teaspoon ground cinnamon
1/2 teaspoon salt
3 to 4 cups peeled sliced uncooked butternut squash (about 1-1/2 pounds)
1 can (21 ounces) apple pie filling
1/2 cup all-purpose flour
1/2 cup quick-cooking oats
6 tablespoons butter, softened

1. Combine 1/2 cup brown sugar, lemon juice, cinnamon, salt, squash and pie filling. Spoon into a greased 11-in. x 7-in. x 2-in. baking dish. Cover and bake at 375° for 30 minutes.

2. Combine flour, oats and remaining brown sugar; cut in butter until crumbly. Sprinkle over the squash mixture. Bake, uncovered, about 45 minutes longer or until squash is tender. Serve warm. **Yield:** 8 servings.

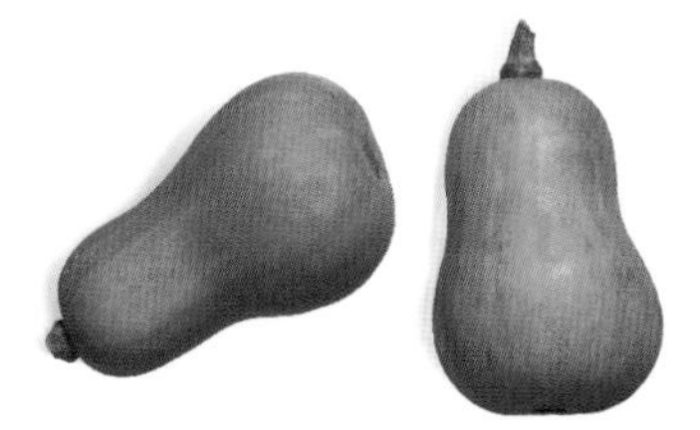

Cherry Cheesecake Tarts

Mary Lindell, Sanford, Michigan

When you don't have time to bake a cherry cheesecake, here's the next best thing! Keep all the ingredients on hand to make this easy dessert on short notice.

1 package (10 ounces) frozen puff pastry shells
2 packages (3 ounces *each*) cream cheese, softened
1/4 cup confectioners' sugar
1/2 teaspoon almond extract
1 can (21 ounces) cherry pie filling
Additional confectioners' sugar

1. Bake pastry shells according to package directions. Meanwhile, in a mixing bowl, beat cream cheese, sugar and extract.

2. With a fork, carefully remove the circular top of each baked shell and set aside. Remove any soft layers of pastry inside shells and discard. Divide the cheese filling between the shells; place on a baking sheet. Return to the oven for 5 minutes. Cool.

3. Just before serving, fill each shell with pie filling. Top with reserved pastry circles. Dust with confectioners' sugar. **Yield:** 6 servings.

Light Lemon Mousse

Joan Jay, Frisco, Texas

This smooth and refreshing dessert is popular at summer cookouts, but it makes a delicious light finish to hearty winter meals, too. For a pretty presentation, I serve it in individual glass dishes garnished with fresh sliced strawberries.

✓ Uses less fat, sugar or salt. Includes Nutritional Analysis and Diabetic Exchanges.

- **3/4 cup sugar**
- **1/2 cup cornstarch**
- **3 cups fat-free milk**
- **2/3 cup lemon juice**
- **1-1/2 teaspoons grated lemon peel**
- **1/4 teaspoon vanilla extract**
- **2 cups reduced-fat whipped topping**
- **3 drops yellow food coloring, optional**

1. In a saucepan, combine the sugar and cornstarch; gradually stir in milk until smooth. Bring to a boil over medium heat, stirring constantly. Cook and stir for 2 minutes or until thickened and bubbly. Remove from the heat. Stir in lemon juice, peel and vanilla.

2. Set saucepan in ice; stir until mixture reaches room temperature, about 5 minutes. Fold in whipped topping and food coloring if desired. Spoon into dessert dishes. Refrigerate for at least 1 hour before serving. **Yield:** 10 servings.

Nutritional Analysis: One 1/2-cup serving equals 145 calories, 39 mg sodium, 1 mg cholesterol, 29 g carbohydrate, 3 g protein, 2 g fat, trace fiber. **Diabetic Exchanges:** 1 starch, 1 fruit.

Pecan Pumpkin Dessert

Sue Williams, Mt. Holly, North Carolina

I always fix this recipe for Thanksgiving. It was given to me by a friend and I've shared it with many others.

- **2 cans (15 ounces *each*) solid-pack pumpkin**
- **1 can (12 ounces) evaporated milk**
- **1 cup sugar**
- **3 eggs**
- **1 teaspoon vanilla extract**
- **1 package (18-1/4 ounces) yellow cake mix**
- **1 cup butter, melted**
- **1-1/2 cups chopped pecans**

FROSTING:

- **1 package (8 ounces) cream cheese, softened**
- **1-1/2 cups confectioners' sugar**
- **1 teaspoon vanilla extract**
- **1 carton (12 ounces) frozen whipped topping, thawed**

1. Line a 13-in. x 9-in. x 2-in. baking pan with waxed paper and coat the paper with nonstick cooking spray; set aside. In a mixing bowl, combine pumpkin, milk and sugar. Beat in eggs and vanilla. Pour into prepared pan. Sprinkle with dry cake mix and drizzle with butter. Sprinkle with pecans. Bake at 350° for 1 hour or until golden brown. Cool completely in pan on a wire rack.

2. Invert onto a large serving platter; carefully remove waxed paper. In a mixing bowl, beat cream cheese, confectioners' sugar and vanilla until smooth. Fold in whipped topping. Frost dessert. Store in the refrigerator. **Yield:** 16 servings.

Poached Pear Surprise

Barbara Smith, Cannon Falls, Minnesota

Pears are my husband's favorite fruit, so he immediately declared this dessert "a keeper." It's elegant but easy, satisfying yet light. Plus, it's fun to watch the looks on the faces of our grandkids and great-grandkids when they discover the surprise filling inside.

4 medium ripe pears
1 cup water
1/2 cup sugar
1 teaspoon vanilla extract
1/3 cup finely chopped walnuts
2 tablespoons confectioners' sugar
1 teaspoon milk

CHOCOLATE SAUCE:
1/3 cup water
1/3 cup sugar
1/4 cup butter
1-1/3 cups semisweet chocolate chips
Fresh mint, optional

1. Core pears from bottom, leaving stems intact. Peel pears. Cut 1/4 in. from bottom to level if necessary. In a saucepan, bring water and sugar to a boil. Add pears; reduce heat. Cover and simmer for 10-15 minutes or until tender. Remove from the heat; stir vanilla into sugar syrup. Spoon over pears. Cover and refrigerate until chilled.

2. Meanwhile, combine walnuts, confectioners' sugar and milk; set aside. For chocolate sauce, combine water, sugar and butter in a small saucepan; bring to a boil. Remove from the heat; stir in chocolate chips until melted.

3. To serve, drain pears well; spoon nut mixture into cavities. Place on dessert plates; top with some of the chocolate sauce. Insert a mint leaf near stem if desired. Serve with the remaining chocolate sauce. **Yield:** 4 servings.

Apricot Peach Cobbler

(Pictured on page 204)

Tobi Breternitz, Bay Port, Michigan

Whenever I'm baking with apricots, I recall picking them fresh from my aunt's tree more than 25 years ago. They were so juicy and sweet! This comforting cobbler has a crumb topping that is super.

1 can (29 ounces) sliced peaches
1 can (15 ounces) apricot halves
1/2 cup sugar
2 tablespoons cornstarch
1/2 teaspoon ground cinnamon
1/4 teaspoon ground nutmeg
1 tablespoon butter

TOPPING:
1/2 cup all-purpose flour
1/2 cup sugar
3/4 teaspoon baking powder
1/4 teaspoon salt
1 egg
2 tablespoons butter, softened

HONEY CREAM:
1 cup heavy whipping cream
2 tablespoons honey
1/2 teaspoon ground cinnamon

1. Drain peaches, reserving 1/2 cup syrup. Drain apricots, reserving 1/2 cup syrup. Cut apricots in half; set fruit aside.

2. In a saucepan, combine sugar, cornstarch, cinnamon, nutmeg and reserved syrups until smooth. Bring to a boil; cook and stir for 2 minutes or until thickened. Remove from the heat; stir in butter until melted. Stir in peaches and apricots. Transfer to a greased 8-in. square baking dish.

3. For topping, combine the flour, sugar, baking powder and salt in a bowl. Add egg and butter; mix well. Spoon over fruit. Bake at 350° for 40-45 minutes or until golden brown.

4. In a mixing bowl, beat cream, honey and cinnamon until stiff peaks form. Serve with warm cobbler. **Yield:** 6-8 servings.

Peach Pizza Pie

(Pictured on page 205)

Ann Kidd, Lewes, Delaware

We have very good peach orchards in our state, so I'm always on the lookout for recipes with peaches in them. My family and friends have enjoyed this dessert for many years.

1/2 cup butter, softened
1/4 cup confectioners' sugar
1 cup all-purpose flour
4 to 5 cups sliced fresh peaches
GLAZE:
2 tablespoons sugar
1 tablespoon cornstarch
1/8 to 1/4 teaspoon ground mace, optional
1/2 cup orange juice
1/2 cup red currant jelly
Whipped cream, optional

1. In a mixing bowl, cream butter and confectioners' sugar. Add flour and mix well. Pat into a greased 12-in. pizza pan; prick with a fork. Bake at 350° for 10-15 minutes or until golden. Cool completely.

2. Arrange peach slices on crust. In a saucepan, mix sugar, cornstarch and mace if desired. Add orange juice and jelly; cook and stir over medium heat until smooth. Bring to a boil; boil for 2 minutes. Remove from the heat and cool slightly, about 5 minutes.

3. Spoon over peaches. Chill for 1 hour or until set. Garnish with whipped cream if desired and serve immediately. **Yield:** 12-15 servings.

Lemon Custard in Meringue Cups

Marie Frangipane, Eugene, Oregon

You may want to watch the weather before making this dessert. Preparing meringues on a day that is high in humidity may cause them to weep or bead with tiny droplets of water.

3 eggs, *separated*
1/2 teaspoon vinegar
1/4 teaspoon vanilla extract
1/4 teaspoon salt, *divided*
2 cups sugar, *divided*
1/3 cup cornstarch
1-1/2 cups water
6 tablespoons lemon juice
2 tablespoons butter
1 tablespoon grated lemon peel
Sweetened whipped cream

1. In a mixing bowl, combine egg whites, vinegar, vanilla and 1/8 teaspoon salt. Beat until soft peaks form. Gradually add 1 cup sugar, one tablespoon at a time; continue beating until stiff peaks form.

2. Cover baking sheet with plain brown wrapping paper, parchment paper or foil. Spoon meringue into eight mounds on paper. Using the back of a spoon, shape into 3-in. cups.

3. Bake at 300° for 35 minutes. Turn oven off and do not open door; let dry in oven 1 hour. Remove from the oven and cool on baking sheet. When cooled completely, remove meringues from paper and store in an airtight container at room temperature.

4. For custard, combine cornstarch and remaining salt and sugar in a saucepan. Add water; stir until smooth. Cook and stir until thick and bubbly, about 2 minutes. Beat egg yolks; add a small amount of hot mixture. Return all to pan. Cook and stir 2 minutes longer. Remove from the heat; blend in lemon juice, butter and lemon peel. Chill. Just before serving, fill meringue shells with custard and top with whipped cream. **Yield:** 8 servings.

Cream Puff Dessert

Lisa Nash, Blaine, Minnesota

I recently took this rich dessert to a fellowship meeting at our church. Everyone loved it! In fact, so many people asked for the recipe that the church secretary printed it in our monthly newsletter.

1 cup water
1/2 cup butter
1 cup all-purpose flour
4 eggs

FILLING:
1 package (8 ounces) cream cheese, softened
3-1/2 cups cold milk
2 packages (3.9 ounces *each*) instant chocolate pudding mix

TOPPING:
1 carton (8 ounces) frozen whipped topping, thawed
1/4 cup milk chocolate ice cream topping
1/4 cup caramel ice cream topping
1/3 cup chopped almonds

1. In a saucepan over medium heat, bring water and butter to a boil. Add flour all at once; stir until a smooth ball forms. Remove from the heat; let stand for 5 minutes. Add the eggs, one at a time, beating well after each addition. Beat until smooth.

2. Spread into a greased 13-in. x 9-in. x 2-in. baking dish. Bake at 400° for 30-35 minutes or until puffed and golden brown. Cool completely on a wire rack.

3. Meanwhile, in a mixing bowl, beat cream cheese, milk and pudding mix until smooth. Spread over puff; refrigerate for 20 minutes. Spread with whipped topping; refrigerate until serving. Drizzle with chocolate and caramel toppings; sprinkle with almonds. Store leftovers in the refrigerator. **Yield:** 12 servings.

Refreshing Lime Sherbet

Lorraine Searing, Colorado Springs, Colorado

One spoonful of this cool, fresh-tasting and delicious treat and you'll never eat store-bought lime sherbet again! It's terrific following a heavy meal, on a hot summer day or any time your taste buds are bored.

4-1/4 cups sugar
1-1/2 cups lime juice
3 tablespoons lemon juice
2 tablespoons grated lime peel
7-1/2 cups milk
1/2 cup buttermilk
1 drop green food coloring, optional

1. In a bowl, combine sugar, lime juice, lemon juice and lime peel until well blended. Gradually stir in milk, buttermilk and food coloring if desired; mix well.

2. Pour into the cylinder of an ice cream freezer and freeze according to manufacturer's directions. Remove from the freezer 10 minutes before serving. **Yield:** about 2-1/2 quarts.

Editor's Note: Recipe may need to be frozen in two batches.

Chocolate Peanut Delight

Karen Kutruff, New Berlin, Pennsylvania

Peanut lovers will appreciate this yummy dessert I dreamed up. A brownie-like crust is packed with nuts, topped with a fluffy peanut butter layer and covered with whipped topping and more nuts. It was so well received that I made it for a local restaurant where I used to work.

1 package (18-1/4 ounces) chocolate cake mix
1/2 cup butter, melted
1/4 cup milk
1 egg
1 cup chopped peanuts, *divided*
1 package (8 ounces) cream cheese, softened
1 cup peanut butter
1 cup confectioners' sugar
1 can (14 ounces) sweetened condensed milk
1-1/2 teaspoons vanilla extract
1 carton (16 ounces) frozen whipped topping, thawed, *divided*
1/2 cup semisweet chocolate chips
4-1/2 teaspoons butter
1/2 teaspoon vanilla extract

1. In a mixing bowl, combine the dry cake mix, butter, milk and egg. Add 3/4 cup of peanuts. Spread into a greased 13-in. x 9-in. x 2-in. baking pan. Bake at 350° for 30 minutes or until a toothpick inserted near the center comes out clean. Cool on a wire rack.

2. In a mixing bowl, beat the cream cheese, peanut butter, sugar, condensed milk and vanilla until smooth. Fold in 3 cups whipped topping. Spread over the crust; top with the remaining whipped topping and peanuts.

3. In a microwave-safe bowl, heat chocolate chips and butter on high for 1 minute or until melted. Stir in vanilla until smooth; drizzle over cake. Refrigerate for 2-3 hours before cutting. **Yield:** 12-15 servings.

Cookies 'n' Cream Fudge

Laura Lane, Richmond, Virginia

I invented this confection for a bake sale at our children's school. Boy, was it a hit! The crunchy chunks of sandwich cookie soften a bit as the mixture mellows. It's so sweet that one panful serves a crowd.

16 chocolate cream-filled sandwich cookies, broken into chunks, *divided*
1 can (14 ounces) sweetened condensed milk
2 tablespoons butter
2-2/3 cups vanilla *or* white chips
1 teaspoon vanilla extract

1. Line an 8-in. square baking pan with aluminum foil; coat with nonstick cooking spray. Place half of the broken cookies in pan.

2. In a heavy saucepan, combine milk, butter and chips; cook and stir over low heat until chips are melted. Remove from the heat; stir in vanilla. Pour over cookies in pan. Sprinkle with remaining cookies. Cover and refrigerate for at least 1 hour. Cut into squares. **Yield:** 3 dozen.

Heart's Delight Eclair

Lorene Milligan, Chemainus, British Columbia

This lovely and luscious treat is rumored to have been the favorite dessert of European royalty long ago. I know that it's won the hearts of everyone I've ever made it for.

- **1 package (17-1/4 ounces) frozen puff pastry, thawed**
- **3 cups cold milk**
- **1 package (5.1 ounces) instant vanilla pudding mix**
- **2 cups heavy whipping cream**
- **1 teaspoon vanilla extract, *divided***
- **1 cup confectioners' sugar**
- **1 tablespoon water**
- **1/4 teaspoon almond extract**
- **1/2 cup semisweet chocolate chips**
- **1 teaspoon shortening**

1. On a lightly floured surface, roll each puff pastry sheet into a 12-in. square. Using an 11-in. heart pattern, cut each pastry into a heart shape. Place on greased baking sheets. Bake at 400° for 12-15 minutes or until golden brown. Remove to wire racks to cool.

2. Meanwhile, combine milk and pudding mix until thickened. In a mixing bowl, beat cream and 1/2 teaspoon of vanilla until stiff peaks form. Carefully fold into pudding.

3. Split puff pastry hearts in half. Place one layer on a serving plate. Top with a third of the pudding mixture. Repeat twice. Top with remaining pastry.

4. In a bowl, combine confectioners' sugar, water, almond extract and the remaining vanilla until smooth. Spread over top. Melt chocolate chips and shortening; pipe in diagonal lines in one direction over frosting. Beginning 1 in. from side of heart, use a sharp knife to draw right angles across the piped lines. Refrigerate until set. **Yield:** 10-12 servings.

Northern Cherry Puffs

Barbara Hanmer, Benzonia, Michigan

Michigan is the top cherry-producing state in the country. This is one of my family's favorite cherry recipes.

- **1 cup fresh *or* frozen pitted dark sweet cherries, thawed and drained**
- **1 tablespoon lemon juice**
- **1-1/2 teaspoons almond extract, *divided***
- **1/4 teaspoon red food coloring, optional**
- **1/3 cup shortening**
- **2/3 cup sugar**
- **1 egg**
- **1 cup all-purpose flour**
- **1/2 teaspoon salt**
- **1/2 teaspoon baking powder**
- **1/3 cup milk**

SAUCE:

- **1/2 cup sugar**
- **4-1/2 teaspoons cornstarch**
- **1/4 cup water**
- **2 cups fresh *or* frozen pitted dark sweet cherries**
- **1/4 teaspoon red food coloring, optional**

Whipped cream *or* ice cream

1. In a bowl, combine cherries, lemon juice, 1/2 teaspoon extract and food coloring if desired; toss to coat. Spoon into four greased 10-oz. custard cups.

2. In a mixing bowl, cream shortening and sugar. Beat in egg and remaining extract. Combine flour, salt and baking powder; add to the creamed mixture alternately with milk. Spoon over cherry mixture. Bake at 375° for 20-25 minutes or until golden brown. Cool in cups for 10 minutes.

3. Meanwhile, in a saucepan, combine sugar and cornstarch. Stir in water, cherries and food coloring if desired until blended. Bring to a boil over medium heat; cook and stir for 2 minutes or until thickened. Invert puffs onto dessert plates; top with warm cherry sauce and whipped cream. **Yield:** 4 servings.

Maple Biscuit Dessert

Leslie Malter, Waterbury, Vermont

These biscuits have been made by the women in my family for a long time. We use the maple syrup we boil each sugaring season from the trees on our land.

2 cups all-purpose flour
1 tablespoon baking powder
1/2 teaspoon salt
1/4 cup shortening
3/4 cup milk
1-1/2 cups maple syrup

1. In a bowl, combine flour, baking powder and salt; cut in shortening until mixture resembles coarse crumbs. Add milk; stir just until moistened.

2. Turn onto a lightly floured surface; roll to 1/2-in. thickness. Cut with a 2-in. biscuit cutter. Pour syrup into an 11-in. x 7-in. x 2-in. baking dish. Place biscuits on top of syrup. Bake at 450° for 12-15 minutes or until biscuits are golden brown. **Yield:** 10-12 servings.

Brownie Baked Alaska

Carol Twardzik, Spy Hill, Saskatchewan

This cool and chocolaty dessert looks like I fussed, when really it's easy to put together. No one can resist the combination of brownies and two kinds of ice cream with a light meringue topping.

2 squares (1 ounce *each*) unsweetened chocolate
1/2 cup shortening
1 cup sugar
1 teaspoon vanilla extract
2 eggs
3/4 cup all-purpose flour
1/2 teaspoon baking powder
1/2 teaspoon salt
1 cup chopped walnuts, optional
1 quart strawberry ice cream, slightly softened
1 quart vanilla ice cream, slightly softened

MERINGUE:

5 egg whites
1/2 teaspoon cream of tartar
2/3 cup sugar

1. In a large saucepan, melt chocolate and shortening; remove from the heat. Stir in sugar and vanilla. Add eggs, one at a time, beating well after each addition. Combine flour, baking powder and salt; stir into chocolate mixture. Add nuts if desired. Spread into a greased 8-in. round baking pan. Bake at 350° for 25-30 minutes or until a toothpick inserted near the center comes out with moist crumbs (do not overbake). Cool for 10 minutes before removing from pan to a wire rack to cool completely.

2. Meanwhile, line an 8-in. round bowl (1-1/2 qts.) with foil. Quickly spread strawberry ice cream over bottom and up sides of bowl, leaving center hollow; cover and freeze for 30 minutes. Pack vanilla ice cream into center; cover and freeze.

3. To assemble, place the brownie base on a 10-in. ovenproof serving plate. Unmold ice cream onto brownie. Return to freezer while preparing meringue.

4. In a double boiler, beat eggs whites and cream of tartar with a portable mixer until soft peaks form. Beat in sugar, 1 tablespoon at a time, until stiff peaks form and meringue reaches 160°, about 5 minutes. Watch carefully. Quickly spread over ice cream and brownie. Return to freezer until ready to serve. Bake at 500° for 2-3 minutes or until meringue is lightly browned. Serve immediately. **Yield:** 12 servings.

Raspberry sauce is an appealing base for this fluffy white chocolate mousse. The treasured treat is surprisingly easy and a delightful change of pace from heavier cakes and pies.

- **1 package (10 ounces) sweetened frozen raspberries, thawed**
- **2 tablespoons sugar**
- **1 tablespoon orange juice concentrate**
- **2 cups heavy whipping cream**
- **6 ounces white baking chocolate**
- **1 teaspoon vanilla extract**
- **1/4 cup milk chocolate chips**
- **1 teaspoon vegetable oil**

1. In a blender, combine the raspberries, sugar and orange juice concentrate; cover and process until smooth. Press through a sieve; discard seeds. Refrigerate sauce.

2. In a saucepan over low heat, cook and stir cream and white chocolate until chocolate is melted. Stir in vanilla. Transfer to a mixing bowl. Cover and refrigerate for 6 hours or until thickened, stirring occasionally.

3. Beat cream mixture on high speed until light and fluffy, about 1-1/2 minutes (do not overbeat). Just before serving, melt chocolate chips and oil in a microwave or saucepan. Spoon 2 tablespoons of raspberry sauce on each plate. Pipe or spoon 1/2 cup chocolate mousse over sauce; drizzle with melted chocolate. Store leftovers in the refrigerator. **Yield:** 8 servings.

Raspberry White Chocolate Mousse

Mary Lou Wayman, Salt Lake City, Utah

Blackberry Dumplings

Liecha Collins, Oneonta, New York

As long as I can remember, my mother has been making Blackberry Dumplings. They finish cooking while you eat—and they really do make you hurry through Sunday dinner! It can be an everyday dessert, too.

- **1 quart fresh *or* frozen (loose-pack) blackberries**
- **1 cup plus 1 tablespoon sugar, *divided***
- **3/4 teaspoon salt, *divided***
- **1/2 teaspoon lemon extract**
- **1-1/2 cups all-purpose flour**
- **2 teaspoons baking powder**
- **1/4 teaspoon ground nutmeg**
- **2/3 cup milk**
- **Cream *or* whipped cream, optional**

1. In a Dutch oven, combine the blackberries, 1 cup sugar, 1/4 teaspoon salt and lemon extract. Bring to a boil; reduce heat and simmer for 5 minutes.

2. Meanwhile, in a mixing bowl, combine flour, baking powder, nutmeg and remaining sugar and salt. Add milk; stir just until mixed. (Dough will be very thick.)

3. Drop by tablespoonfuls into six mounds onto hot blackberry mixture; cover tightly and simmer for 15 minutes or until a toothpick inserted in a dumpling comes out clean (do not lift lid while simmering). Spoon into serving dishes. Serve with cream or whipped cream if desired. **Yield:** 6-8 servings.

Apple-of-Your-Eye Cheesecake

Debbie Wilson, Sellersburg, Indiana

My most-often-requested dessert, this exquisite cheesecake with apples, caramel and pecans wins me more compliments than anything else I make. My husband's co-workers say it's too pretty to cut...but agree it's well worth it to do so.

1 cup graham cracker crumbs
3 tablespoons sugar
1/2 teaspoon ground cinnamon
1/4 cup butter, melted
2 tablespoons finely chopped pecans

FILLING:
3 packages (8 ounces *each*) cream cheese, softened
3/4 cup sugar
3 eggs
3/4 teaspoon vanilla extract

TOPPING:
2-1/2 cups chopped peeled apples
1 tablespoon lemon juice
1/4 cup sugar
1/2 teaspoon ground cinnamon
6 tablespoons caramel ice cream topping, *divided*
Sweetened whipped cream
2 tablespoons chopped pecans

1. Combine the first five ingredients; press onto the bottom of a lightly greased 9-in. springform pan. Bake at 350° for 10 minutes; cool.

2. In a mixing bowl, beat cream cheese and sugar until smooth. Add eggs; beat on low just until combined. Stir in vanilla. Pour over crust. Toss apples with lemon juice, sugar and cinnamon; spoon over filling. Bake at 350° for 55-60 minutes or until center is almost set.

3. Cool on a wire rack for 10 minutes. Carefully run a knife around edge of pan to loosen. Drizzle with 4 tablespoons caramel topping. Cool for 1 hour. Chill overnight.

4. Remove sides of pan. Just before serving, garnish with whipped cream. Drizzle with remaining caramel; sprinkle with pecans. Store in the refrigerator. **Yield:** 12 servings.

Pear Sundae French Toast

Carol Schumacher, Menoken, North Dakota

Coming upon this creation in a potluck line, I left with a full plate and the recipe. Now my family oohs and aahs as soon as I bring out this fruit-topped favorite. It's great as a fancy finish to a meal.

- **1/4 cup plus 3 tablespoons packed brown sugar, *divided***
- **6 tablespoons butter, *divided***
- **1-1/4 teaspoons ground cinnamon, *divided***
- **3 medium ripe pears, peeled and sliced (about 2-1/2 cups)**
- **3 eggs, lightly beaten**
- **3/4 cup milk**
- **1 teaspoon vanilla extract**
- **1/4 teaspoon ground nutmeg**
- **6 slices French bread (1 inch thick)**

Ice cream

1. In a skillet, combine 1/4 cup brown sugar, 2 tablespoons butter and 1/4 teaspoon cinnamon; cook and stir until sugar is dissolved. Add pears; cook until tender.

2. In a bowl, combine the eggs, milk, vanilla, nutmeg, and remaining brown sugar and cinnamon. Dip bread in egg mixture to coat each side.

3. Melt remaining butter in a skillet. Fry bread over medium heat for 2 minutes on each side or until golden brown. Top with ice cream and pear mixture. **Yield:** 6 servings.

Chocolate Peanut Sweeties

Gina Kintigh, Connellsville, Pennsylvania

Inspired by my passion for peanut butter and chocolate, I combined a trusted recipe for peanut butter eggs with the salty crunch of pretzels. Now our kids have fun helping me make and eat these heavenly treats.

1 cup peanut butter
1/2 cup butter, softened
3 cups confectioners' sugar
5 dozen miniature pretzel twists (about 3 cups)
1-1/2 cups milk chocolate chips
1 tablespoon vegetable oil

1. In a mixing bowl, beat peanut butter and butter until smooth. Beat in confectioners' sugar until combined. Shape into 1-in. balls; press one on each pretzel. Place on waxed paper-lined baking sheets. Refrigerate until peanut butter mixture is firm, about 1 hour.

2. In a microwave-safe bowl or heavy saucepan, melt chocolate chips and oil. Dip the peanut butter ball into chocolate. Return to baking sheet, pretzel side down.

Refrigerate for at least 30 minutes before serving. Store in the refrigerator. **Yield:** 5 dozen.

Editor's Note: Reduced-fat or generic-brand peanut butter is not recommended for use in this recipe.

Peach Ice Cream

Lisa Tenbarge, Haubstadt, Indiana

Adding peaches to a mouth-watering vanilla ice cream recipe I got from my mother-in-law resulted in this fabulous flavor. My boys say it's the greatest and think it tastes best served outdoors under a shade tree!

1 cup sugar
1 cup milk
1 egg, beaten
3-1/3 cups heavy whipping cream
1/4 cup instant vanilla pudding mix
1-1/2 cups finely chopped fresh *or* frozen peaches, thawed
2 teaspoons vanilla extract

1. In a saucepan, combine sugar, milk and egg. Cook and stir over medium heat until the mixture reaches 160° or is thick enough to coat a metal spoon. Remove from the heat. Cover and refrigerate several hours or overnight.

2. When ready to freeze, stir in the cream, pudding mix, peaches and vanilla. Pour into the cylinder of an ice cream freezer. Freeze according to manufacturer's directions. Allow to ripen in ice cream freezer or firm up in refrigerator freezer for 2-4 hours before serving. **Yield:** 1-1/4 quarts.

Editor's Note: This recipe may need to be frozen in batches.

General Recipe Index

This handy index lists every recipe by food category, major ingredient and/or cooking method, so you can easily locate recipes to suit your needs.

✓ Recipe includes Nutritional Analysis and Diabetic Exchanges

COCONUT

COLESLAW

CONDIMENTS

COOKIES *(also see Bars & Brownies)*

CORN

CRANBERRIES

DEEP-FRYER RECIPES

DESSERTS *(also see specific kinds)*

EGGS

FISH & SEAFOOD

FISH & SEAFOOD *(continued)*

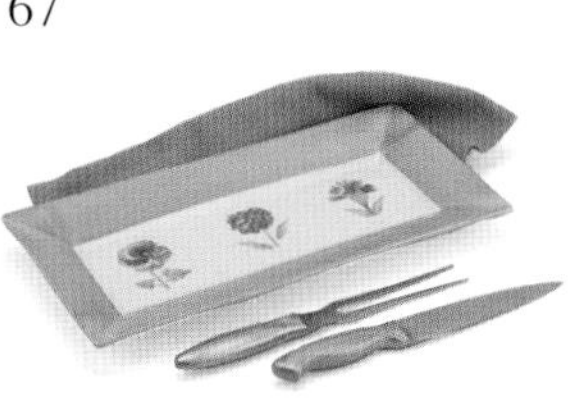

FRUIT *(also see specific kinds)*

GRILLED & BROILED

GROUND BEEF

HAM

ICE CREAM & SHERBET

LASAGNA

LEMON & LIME

PUDDING & MOUSSE

PUMPKIN

QUICK BREADS

RAISINS & DATES

RASPBERRIES

RHUBARB

RICE & BARLEY

ROLLS & BREADSTICKS

SALADS & DRESSINGS *(also see Coleslaw)*

SANDWICHES

Alphabetical Recipe Index

This handy index lists every recipe in alphabetical order, so you can easily find your favorite recipes.

✓ Recipe includes Nutritional Analysis and Diabetic Exchanges